"The *One With God* series provides answers to the questions we have always resisted asking. This leads us to find our own personal journey Home, a realization we believe we don't deserve. The words from the Holy Spirit on each page are a gift which symbolize Truth. And, the daily examples of dedication provided by Margie, Jo, and Meera are an equal blessing. They demonstrate that without a doubt, we all have access to the same Voice. The Holy Spirit is with us now and He answers every question asked. I am thankful to have been attracted to these books."

—**Dino S.**
Raleigh, NC USA

"Encountering *OWG* has initiated a quickening, an ever-deepening movement of steady Presence, a communion excluding no one. Unsettling experiences are now revealed as metaphors, straight from Love's beckoning to see All as Itself. Unending gratitude for the devotion each of you have uncovered and expressed."

—**Jocelyn B.**
South Bend, IN USA

"After I studied *A Course in Miracles*, I thought to myself, "Well, what now?" It kind of felt like an anticlimax, and I just knew there had to be more. That's when I discovered *OWG* Book 1, *Awakening Through the Voice of the Holy Spirit,* and what an awakening I have had. Over the past several months I have read Book 1 at least seven times and Book 2 at least four. Sometimes I just pick up the books, open them at random, and there is my answer. I now have a deeper connection with the Holy Spirit and I scribe what He says. Reading your books have helped me gain more connection with Him, and every time I read them my understanding becomes deeper as well. I realize that I have been communicating with this same voice all my life, which I always thought of as God's voice. I now constantly go to the Holy Spirit with all my questions, and for instruction. I just love those times when I'm walking out in nature or sitting on the beach having a wonderful, beautiful conversation with the Holy Spirit. I truly feel like I am home."

—**Cheryl G.**
Queensland, Australia

"The first *OWG* book was an answer to my prayer of wanting deeper insight into the workings of spirit. I have read Gary Renard's books several times and kept going back to *A Course in Miracles* for questions I needed answers to. Your books have further initiated downloads of insight and understanding on a daily basis. Thank you for being an example of the Holy Spirit's scribe so the reader can identify with their own life experiences. We're all dealing with an ego. I eagerly await Book 3. In the meantime, I will just have to continue my forgiveness work. Thank you from the bottom of my heart."

—**Susan D.**
Tampa, FL USA

"When I started reading the *OWG* books I had the same experience as when I began reading the *Course*; it was like they were being sung to me. The books took me further toward trusting that *still, small voice* within us all. I am very grateful."

—**Peter Q.**
Tiruvannamalai, India

"The *One With God* books fill me with so much joy! The thing that makes them so very valuable is that these three women not only tell us what the Holy Spirit says, but they are willing to reveal enough of their personal stories which actually model for us how to do the work. That one thing makes all the difference in the world."

—**Marion W.**
Fletcher, NC USA

"The *OWG* books are such a gentle, comforting reminder to me that, in fact, I am One with God. They bring me peace, and Margie's humanness throughout helps me balance my own."

—**Nancy A.**
Lakewood, CO USA

"It is so helpful to read about your experiences of living a life guided by the Holy Spirit. I am very thankful for your willingness to share that with us, as it has deepened my understanding and increased my commitment to this path. I truly feel the effects and changes taking place internally as I read, and I know that I am moving forward on the path to my own awakening. It is a blessing to us all, and I am moved to tears of joy. After I read your first book I went out and bought a journal because I really felt I needed to start writing. So far, I haven't written one word in it! Your words reinforce the fact that it would be a very helpful tool. I will start using it."

—**Doug K.**
Rosebud, MO USA

"It's not necessary to have read *A Course in Miracles* to experience the transformative power of *One With God*—a portal to a living, vibrant connection with Spirit's eternal guidance, joy, and love."

—**Cheryl M.**
Littleton, CO USA

"These books are God's vehicle to give each reader a profound experience, almost as close as a near death experience, of Heaven/the Kingdom of God, of Love. This vision can wake humanity to the union we all share with each other, the Unity we have with God."

—**Daniel F.**
Larkspur, CA USA

For more information about *One With God*, visit our website:
www.onewithgod.co

ONE WITH GOD

ONE WITH GOD:

Awakening Through the Voice of the Holy Spirit
Book 3

Marjorie Tyler
Joann Sjolander
Margaret Ballonoff

One With God:
Awakening Through the Voice of the Holy Spirit

Book 3

ISBN: 978-0-9965785-6-1
ISBN: 0-996578560
Library of Congress Control Number: 2017951583

Cover and text design: Miko Radcliffe

Sacred Life Publishers™
SacredLife.com
Printed in the United States of America

Contents

Contents

Shine My Light

The Light of the Holy Spirit within is a
beacon to all the selves to come Home.

August 23, 2013

> (I wake up at 1:20 a.m. and notice that the prism in my bedroom window is reflecting beautiful rainbow facets of light. I get out of bed to find the source.)

Holy Spirit, what do You say? The prism casting its rainbow light is a reminder of My Presence amid darkness. The Light of Me within, directed out into your imagined world, is a beacon to all the selves to come Home. Yes, you discovered it is the light of the full moon, directly overhead, that has cast its beam on the prism. All the facets shine in their turns to be lit in magnificent, brilliant hues. The prism, a sphere, is whole, just as you are now with Me. You feel Me in the crown of your head when you view the beams of colored light. Your role is to shine My Light throughout the mind of the One Son so he will know himself as Me. We are One Light, One Word, One Essence. This is the idea of Selfhood expressed in form. The Self is made manifest in Light and in Love. You will understand this as we go further.

Your friend Zoe gave you this prism before you moved to Maui, a gift from Me, to your Self, My Self within you as your sacred partner and guide. The prism represents every shining aspect of the Self in the dream, united in perfect wholeness. Each reader is one facet. Without the Light of My Love the prism appears as just a clear piece of glass. When lit by Me, it becomes every color of the rainbow in all My Glory, the Divine Light of the One Self shared by all humanity. Rest now and I will integrate this experience for you.

> (Before falling asleep, I notice that the moon has passed its zenith. I dream of telling a group of women about my experience with the prism. Then, I dream of a small speedboat racing through the waves. The boat is heading straight for the observer, who is me. When I wake up I feel the Presence of the Holy Spirit and ask what He has to say.)

You created the space and welcomed Me as part of your life. All obstacles are cleared and you are ready for the full experience of partnership with Me. You have released the tiller. As we begin the scribing of Book 3 you are immersed in the certainty of My Love from now to eternity. You trust that My Presence is always there and you know I answer your every call. Yes, the sensation of My Presence is powerful and can't be denied. You, Jo, and Meera have the experience of hearing My Voice and nothing else matters in your lives. I have entered your "homes" on the symbolic level and exist in the spiritual realm of your minds. You still await the appearance of a publisher for Book 1, but you trust that I will not leave this project, or you, incomplete.

The stage is set for you to experience an even deeper awareness of My Presence in your daily life, an intimate sense of My ever-present guidance in a way not yet imagined. This will develop over time in its intensity. You can no longer avoid Me, not that you've tried to ignore Me. My Presence will be even more palpable and you will be grateful for the reminder whenever your thoughts turn to Me.

Yesterday, you met one of your selves under the Banyan Tree in Lahaina. You had named her the "wicked witch" but greeted her with love. She had been a thorn in the art society with her cruel verbal attacks and threats to sue. You had avoided her like the plague and hid whenever you saw her coming. Finally, in an angry outburst, she left the society. You have not seen nor heard from her for years, but yesterday, you were told that she, now in her nineties, was under the tree. You then knew that she was the decrepit, bent-over woman you had seen being pushed in a wheelchair by a small group of men and women, just minutes earlier. Hearing that she was outside you immediately ran from the gallery to greet her, now sitting on a bench in the shade. She was all hunched over and you spoke her name. She looked up as you told her that you were an artist who loved her paintings and had sold them in the gallery. Her eyes lit up, and she exclaimed, "You are telling me this in front of all my children." She repeated it again and said, "God must love me." You warmly assured her that God did love her and loves all. She looked to her five children struck by the impossibility that they would hear this greeting from a fellow artist. Then she said she wanted to go back into the gallery.

It was very touching as you realized you were being given an opportunity to reenact the whole story of the separation and the return, for yourself, for her, and her children. You knew it was My orchestration at its symbolic best and felt the joy of no past or future. The old woman represented a perfect out picturing of your ego thought system. In that moment, you knew this imaginary life of separation will end in the glorious reunion with Me, in the Mind of God. The wicked-witch "self" has been redeemed. She was your mirror, and you embraced her fully with love. It is always about reunion.

Beyond Perception

Seeing is *not* believing.

August 24, 2013

Holy Spirit, what is Your instruction today? We will write of My candid Presence. You are candid with Me and I am candid with you. It means honest. *Candid Camera* (a TV program from the 1950s) captured the spontaneous expressions of the unsuspecting "man on the street" through a hidden camera, exposing the "truth" of the ego thought system. I show you the undisguised truth of My Self unveiled from all the masks you have worn and accumulated over eons of apparent separation. You saw only the ego's tricks through its hidden camera over lifetimes, but there are no masks to hide Me from your view now. I am here, revealed to your inner sight. You have advanced beyond your ego eyes of false perception.

Seeing is *not* believing. What ego eyes see would distort the truth of My Being. I am no longer hidden, unfamiliar, or a stranger to you. I am as real as any other experience of your day. We are joined and you can never separate from Me again. The light has dimmed on the world so My Light is present for all to see. As yet, you do not see your light, our joined Light, but others witness it in the vibration of love, kindness, and peace that you express. Light is a vibration of oneness and unity that speaks of wholeness to those who are attracted to it. Because you feel My Presence, you experience My Light. Watch for the manifestation of light as you encounter your many selves under the Banyan Tree today. Rejoice at their return to the Light, to Me, feeling the call to wholeness and to God.

3

True Identity

I am the Found to whatever you believe is lost.

August 25, 2013

> (Before bed, I asked the Holy Spirit to help me
> understand my concern about having a "pooching"
> stomach, which I've never had before. He has made
> clear that my next big work is on the identification
> with my body—really, my attachment to the last
> remnants of the ego thought system.)

Holy Spirit, I am concerned about my large, hard tummy. It is a
symbol of identification with your body/ego. The ego fears losing
your love and attention and wants you to feel like "you" have
failed; failed the image of yourself, the image you portray to all;
failed the "God given gift" you are most grateful for, and proud
of, and failed how you want to be seen. Without a perfect body
you believe you will lose admiration for yourself and from others.
You even constrict the depth of your breathing so your stomach
won't stick out. You also believe you are making severe mistakes
in your diet and exercise, and that your body should remain
beautiful, which to you means thin. This is your own identity.
Celebrate that it is changing so you can no longer be "proud of it"
and identify with it. This is about the loss of the ego thought
system. It is painful and you are fighting it. Now rest.

Dream: Although no bodies are perceived, I believe I am on top of
a hill with my mother, the "boss." I accidently drop my car keys,
which also hold my house, safety deposit, and mailbox keys. I see

them land in the middle of a two-lane highway, far below. I then appear on the street looking for the keys, but they are not there. Although I feel no panic about it I would like them back and believe they may be returned.

Holy Spirit, what is the meaning of this dream? It, too, is about losing your identity, yet you were calm and had equanimity, the acceptance of "what is" without fear. All you ever need to do is accept what is, and know it is perfect in the plan for your body in the dream. *Holy Spirit, what did the keys signify?* They were your keys to this world, tossed by Me. It was an unknown force that took them away. The keys were essential to life as you knew it, yet you realized that you could exist without them. This is where we are on the journey now. You can do without this life because you have another key to another home, Heaven. I am the only Key to open every door in your return. Trust Me, and nothing of this world. Love your belly. It is of Me, as is all else. It is neither good nor bad. It means nothing. I am the Key. Let go of all illusions. Let go of your connection to your body and accept it as it is. It functions, and that is all that matters. You need it to fulfill My mission. Be thankful you have the key to life: a body, a vehicle to be My emissary. You cannot lose the keys to Me. I am the Found to whatever you believe is lost.

Holy Spirit, what do You have to tell me this morning? Identification with the body will block your awareness of Me and the reception of My gifts and messages. You are expanding into Me and are not lost without a vehicle. Yes, your body is the way you seem to navigate the world. Your car is a symbol of the body, which is a symbol of the ego. The keys "drive the car, the body/the ego" yet are a symbol of Me, the Key to all wisdom and the dissolution of the whole ego thought system. You must first lose the keys to your world before you will seek the Key I have to offer.

4

Get the Point

*I am the eternal Presence within your mind
that remembers its Union with God.*

August 26, 2013

Holy Spirit, what is Your instruction today? We will continue with
the ideas of last night. You are encased in a world which no longer
serves you, the separate world of body and mind made at the
beginning of time. The Thought of God is your inheritance but
you live the thought of ego. Yes, this ego mind-set, the thought
system that has ruled your life for eons, has faded away to the
point that My Light and My Voice have been revealed. This is the
point of life on earth: to hear My Voice and know My Presence
within; it is the task for all humanity, all worlds, seen and unseen.
The universe is a fantasy that extends as far as man's mind can
imagine and contains everything he does imagine. There is no
stopping the imagination as it extends past all universes. Don't
forget that man, as the Son of God, has a limitless Mind. While
encased in the ego thought system, man does not know his
unlimited powers as that Son, but once awakened he will know
himself as the extension of the Power and Love of God.

Man "lives" a life outside the Kingdom in his belief of
separation. God is not the orchestrator of the separate world. The
point of the dream world is to lead man back to his Origin, in and
of God. You have been on this journey of return since the
beginning of time, as has every other member of humanity. The
time is nearing for a great awakening, which to you is
unimaginable. But you are able to experience this concept on a
small, personal scale as you have slowly, through much diligence,

9

awakened to My Voice in you. I am your Partner in this dream life. I am the eternal Presence within your mind that remembers its Union with God. Through carefully designed lessons I will bring you back to your Self, which in Truth, is Me, the Holy Spirit. The world is fading in its importance for you, Jo, and Meera, because the focus of your daily life is now on Me. This has been your intended shift of mind, and it has brought a new consciousness of the truth within you, which overcomes the ego thought system. That system is fading, and the reality of another way of being has come to light up your lives. I am that Light, and My Light is shed wherever you go.

As you come along the path to knowing My Presence within, through the forgiveness of all your special relationships, you see those relationships transform. The dream characters must become reflections of your own transformation and evolution because they were formed to give you a mirror from which to know yourself from the outside in. They show you the depths of your ego thought system in all its levels of self-accusation. As you have taken back your projections of judgments onto these relationships, you have seen the truth of their love for Me, a reflection of your own love for Me. Remember, this is a dream, and everyone whom you believe is separate from you is really an integral part of you. I am at the Heart of this new awareness that everyone and everything is an aspect of your own Self. We are that beautiful prism, the facets of light, combined as the One Son of God.

The Simple Choice

Ask Me, the Holy Spirit, about everything.

August 27, 2013

Holy Spirit, what is Your instruction? Recently, you watched the PBS documentary *Life of Muhammad,* which contains a great example of forgiveness. At the end of Book 2 you wrote about the last scene of Muhammad's earthly mission where he preached his final sermon to the thousands gathered on the plains of Arafat. He forgave all the warring tribes—his kinsman who had become his enemies. It appears that this event happened in form, but it happened in the mind like everything else. As Muhammad demonstrated forgiveness he came to a state of unity, and his selves were returned to their original state of Oneness with him. This lesson was accomplished on a grand scale amid the thousands of followers he had gathered. It is really no different from the forgiveness lessons that the three of you have undergone in your lives, where you have met each "warring faction" within yourself, with My forgiveness. You have brought each relationship to Me for healing and release, and it brought you into a state of peace. This was Muhammad's intention as well.

The lessons of forgiveness demonstrated by Muhammad at the end of his life, or by Jesus on the cross, saying, "Father, forgive them for they know not what they do," can be incorporated by the reader if he realizes that all men are the same and that all are One in the Eyes of God. This lesson is out pictured in many ways, by many teachers, in many texts and can be learned by calling on Me. You must learn that you are all the Holy Spirit, the One Self. The separation must be accepted as a mistaken belief that never happened. Just as Jesus and Muhammad returned to Heaven, you too "return to heaven" as you take back judgments and complete your forgiveness lessons.

Every reader will come to this place of forgiveness and return to unity. I am working in their mind as they look at the relationships in their life that cause them to judge. Each will learn that every judgment is really a projection he holds against himself, always related to his belief in separation. As he reclaims and releases all judgments, he becomes lighter and sees the world in the Light of My Vision. Eventually, he will know that everyone and everything outside of himself reflects what is taking place in his mind. He will then bring each concern to Me and together we will see that it represents the belief that he is out of alignment with God. In our growing partnership, the reader will come to know there is nothing that can be outside My plan for the return to unity. This experience will become more constant as he seeks My answer to any problem that arises. Ask Me about everything, dear reader. I am the Solution to every problem because I am all that is. Through our communication you will come to know that we are indeed, one and the same.

Let us look at the two dreams that you, mt, had this morning that exemplify today's lesson. In the first dream, you are standing in the showroom of a dimly lit department store. A kind woman points out a simple cotton dress with pockets, the perfect dress for your life on the island. There is no one else around, and only this one rack with just one other dress. You choose the dress that fits you; the choice is simple. This is a reflection now of the state you experience with Me. The choice for Me is automatic. You trust that you are being shown and given exactly what you need. This allows you to give your assent to everything that happens. All choices are simple, now that we are in constant communication and you see the perfection of your life unfolding.

The second dream, which still niggles the ego, shows you coming into "Jo's" newly decorated kitchen. Again, the light is very dim but you notice the curtains: white, with repeated rows of one stalk of a simple flower, perhaps a daisy. To the ego, the whole image is boring and not particularly aesthetic. You then notice that the thin, plastic tablecloth has the very same flower design. You turn to the opposite wall, and there it is again: this horrible pattern on wallpaper. The plastic cover over the light switch is a bit askew and as you are about to turn on the light, Jo walks through the doorway dressed in a wide-brimmed cotton hat, wearing an apron and dress all made of this ugly design. In the dream, you accept it without comment, but when you think about it, you are annoyed. You wonder what could possibly be the point.

The ego cannot stand sameness. It cannot stand unity. It cannot stand the repetition of "one thing" that would make everything exactly the same. In the dream, you are surrounded with a room full of repetitious flowers. There is no other object in the room except the light switch.

It is now time to turn on the light and when you do the whole world will disappear. The light will dissolve all images as they are nothing more than the one Self apparently split into billions of separate forms. Yet, as in your flower dream, each form is created of exactly the same material, the same thought, and is no different from any other. You could walk into that room in your dream and accept it in the moment. The room represented the reunion with all your selves and allowed you a moment of witnessing them together as one. But, when the ego reviews it, it becomes unacceptable. It wants to make everything pleasing to its taste. Your ego liked the dress you chose in the department store but did not like the pattern chosen by your friend for her kitchen. This is how the ego operates. It makes everyone else wrong so it can survive and feel its own unique specialness. You are coming to the point of accepting the dress, the costume, and the home of each of your many selves. The patterns make no difference. In the end, they are all the same, blended like Muhammad's vision of all his many selves, the thousands of once-warring factions, brought together to say farewell to the ego and enter into unity with their Maker, God.

You are approaching a time of acceptance, seeing everyone in the dream as just an iteration of your ego. The clothing, presentation, race, or form make no difference now. Each and everyone in humanity is just a part of you, part of the pattern that makes up the mind of separation, now ready to dissolve into wholeness. Incorporate all form as nothing other than part of a dream that no longer holds any significance or power. It has served its purpose to bring you home. You are done with its call to remain separate. Awaken to the Light that dissolves all dreams.

6

Signs of Healing

Everyone carries a message of My Grace.

August 28, 2013

Holy Spirit, what is Your instruction today? You are with Me, this day and always. Know that we are forever bonded and our Essence is One. You will be going soon to paint amidst My beauty. This world is for your enjoyment. I have placed you "in the Garden of Eden" to receive the glory of this earth as My gift, but the ego has blocked the enjoyment of your life and the beauty that surrounds you. It would hold you back from knowing Me. When the ego took over your seeing and hearing, it appeared you had lost your capacity to receive My blessings in every sight and sound. Now is the time to awaken to My Life and perceive your world with My Vision. This is a next step, one you have longed for. You have long believed you were defective, unable to embrace the beauty of the life you live. I have called you to one of the most beautiful places on earth, yet your eyes felt dimmed to the reception of the full intensity of what surrounds you. You have desired to feel My Love and Glory in every way. Now that gift will be unfolded for you.

This is beyond your imagination of possibility, although you have prayed and yearned for the experience of life to be seen through Me. I have promised this, yet you could not really believe it was possible. Remember, you never believed you would find Me, your Self, as the supreme goal of your life. Now you have found Me, and you will find and experience My Vision and My Love of this earth. Although this earth is an illusion, it still can be enjoyed. This is part of the process of awakening, and your eyes will open as you come to know and trust Me more each day. The world will shine with My Light, and you will become familiar with Me in a new way where everything reflects My splendor. Those who experience Me in nature know what I am describing, and soon you will feel My Presence surrounding you everywhere. You loved the line from the hymn you often sang in church: "In the rustling grass I see Him pass, He speaks to Me everywhere." This will be your experience, one that everyone can have of heaven on earth. Heaven is the knowing that I am within you as your Self and the Essence of everything you see.

Yesterday, you had an experience of Me that touched your heart deeply. You heard from your sister Susan that her daughter was faced with the possibility of going to jail. The mention that your niece was in trouble immediately sent waves of anxiety through you. In the same moment, you called on Me for help and I said to remain assured that it is all in My hands. There is nothing to be concerned about as it is a dream. Do not make it real. This is your niece's big forgiveness lesson, and she will learn it. Susan needs to allow Me to handle it in My way. I am watching over Susan in her new life and giving her My Love. I am also holding her daughter in love, and she will come to know that in this lifetime. Each must come to Me in the way of their custom designed course. Susan is already in a place of trust that her life, as well as her daughter's, is in My hands.

The anxiety over your niece was still present in your body when you went to pick up bread from your baker in the mall. As you crossed the street to enter the building you met My emissary in the form of a woman you had termed "Banyan Girl" because she lived homeless for many months under the Banyan Tree where you often saw her. She reminded you of your niece in many ways: in her body shape and looks, in her brilliant intellect, and in her magnetism when she was not overcome with the delusions of addiction. You often prayed for her and placed her in My Light. When you saw her today, you spoke with her and learned that almost miraculously she had found a job and an apartment and had started a new life. You were overcome with My Presence as she spoke to you. It was truly a mystical moment of recognizing that the answer to your anxiety was being demonstrated before your eyes. The possibility for wholeness always exists, and I do keep My promises. You witnessed a manifestation of Me in the form of the Banyan Girl. She was the representation of your niece: transformed and whole.

The signs of My healing are everywhere and My beauty is reflected in everything you see. My plan for completion and the return Home will happen for everyone. Maintain your faith in Me and continue to call on Me for every seeming problem. I will not leave you comfortless. Banyan Girl was the perfect manifestation for you to know that everyone carries a message of My Grace.

Ego Insatiability

Look only to Me for satisfaction.

August 29, 2013

(Before getting out of bed, I was thinking about the tourists next door, a Muslim family from Pakistan. They had noticed me returning from the art fair a few days ago and wanted to see my art. I jumped at the chance to say, "Asalaamu Aleikum," to invite them in, give art materials to the children, and mention my admiration for Muhammad. Late last night we spoke, and the mother told me about their direct connection with God but said that Sufis have an "intermediary" so that is not real Islam. She wanted a painting, a $75 *giclee,* and when I offered to sell it for $35 she said, "Can you do better?" I said $25 and felt terrible. Then she wanted even more of my art. The little girl cried to stay and paint with me even after I told them it was my bedtime, for the third time. They wanted to come again the next day to watch me paint and get more art materials. I was a mess by 10:00 p.m. when they left with my paper and colored pencils. I prayed and prayed to the Holy Spirit but couldn't even hear His Voice because I was so upset with my "stupidity." I released to Him all my need for specialness, over and over. I tried to fall asleep but couldn't. Finally, the burning in my sternum spoke of His Presence and then I slept well.)

Holy Spirit, please help me with my discomfort. Seek Me above all others. Look only to Me for satisfaction. You do not need to demonstrate mt's personality or talents to anyone now that your focus is with Me. Release the world. Make no assumptions about the needs of others. You are not the solver of problems. *My sternum burns. Is that You, Holy Spirit?* Yes, you feel the burning of My Presence. It Is I Who Am your Core. Rest in Me. Make room for Me. Trust Me. I dissolve all stress, and I will direct each action. Stay above the battlefield.

Thank You, Holy Spirit. What is Your instruction now? You saw your ego thought system in full operation last night with the tourists. Just say no to the ego. This is the lesson. You did no wrong but ask Me before engaging in any alliance or relationship. The experience with the tourists was a perfect view of how your ego wants you to sacrifice your Higher Self for its own purposes: its chaos, its loss, its conflict, manipulation, and its victory. Now, with Me above the battlefield, we see it for what it is and can laugh. You are not a "puppet missionary" for the ego to keep the masses entertained or "sell the story" of your search for Me or your relationship with Me. Prepare for the day. You will assimilate this learning, and we will speak of it later.

> (When I saw the insatiability of the ego in the situation with the family from Pakistan, I felt no judgment because I recognize that in myself. I had been concerned about how I would deal with their wish to visit me again when I needed the day for my own business. As I was preparing to leave for work, the mother came to the door to say that they were leaving Maui this morning and that she wanted more artwork. She also asked if I meant to give them the art supplies. When I said I had only loaned them, she persisted, asking if I had any other supplies I did not need. At this point, I felt

such gratitude that the Holy Spirit was handling the situation and that I could watch the ego with Him without judgment. I could fully identify with this woman's desire for getting as much as she could. I also had valued our talk about the work that both Muslim women and children do to understand the Koran, the teachings of Muhammad, and to have an ever-deepening communication with God. It was a perfect lesson.)

8

Don't Forget to Laugh

I am everywhere you are,
everywhere you have ever been.

August 30, 2013

(Middle of the night) *Holy Spirit, do You have something to say?* You are entering a new estate of knowing that I am present in you always. You will feel this new sensitivity to My vibration as a tingling sensation. You did learn of this in a Silva Mind Control class in 1971, and it was the beginning of your journey to Me. At that time, you experienced a connection with all minds by having the will/intention to connect. You feel the burning in your sternum now, and your ego immediately jumps in with a question about whether the readers will expect that it must also be their experience of Me. No. They will know Me according to their custom designed course. This is just one of the ways chosen for you, and it is important that the reader knows there are multiple ways I am known. You can't easily discount or mistake experiences of the body. Feel My Presence now as you fall asleep.

Dream: I am apparently in my childhood home with someone who tells me that "President Obama slept at Mrs. Nelson's house." (Mrs. Nelson, in her seventies, was my next-door neighbor. When her husband died I was about eleven years old, and she asked me to stay overnight with her. I enjoyed sleeping in a new bed.) In the dream, I believe I will meet Mrs. Nelson, but instead, a young Hawaiian woman, a singer, is living there. I enter the house. Upstairs, a tiny radio-like device is broadcasting the most beautiful song of closeness to the Holy Spirit, sung in Hawaiian. It brought me to tears and I wanted to memorize it. Then I ask the woman which bed Obama slept in, hoping it was the same one that I had slept in as a child. This woman was a beautiful soul, and I told her, "Your glory shines all around you and that is all you need." I knew she would be a very good friend. (When I wake up I feel that we are all the same: me, Obama, the Hawaiian woman, and Mrs. Nelson. We all share the same Home.)

Holy Spirit, what is the meaning? This dream touched your heart. It came from Me. You love President Obama, who represents Me to you. He "shared the same bed you slept in as a child" in your neighbor's house, an ordinary, unadorned, simple, humble place. Now "a shining woman" inhabits the house, and you feel united with her spirit. You hear her beautiful song in Hawaiian about Me. It fills your heart. I am everywhere you are and everywhere you have ever been. This is all about coming Home together.

You all "live" in each other's dreams and are all cut from the same cloth. Last night, Jo sent you an e-mail from her trip to visit a cousin in another state. She included a photo of her cousin's house filled with "flowered wallpaper and matching curtains" almost exactly like your dream three days ago of "her" in the kitchen. Jo in the flowery wallpapered room "is alive" because you, the dreamer, projected her from your own mind. She sends you her image, projected on a photo, and writes to you the same experience that you shared with her. This "synchronicity" tells Jo she is exactly where she needs to be. All images are interchangeable.

You are now laughing at the silliness of the dream. None of it is real. All the drama becomes laughable and absurd. You see a Cheerios box on your counter with huge letters: SMILE. In all the years of eating Cheerios, you never noticed that word printed on the box. It is all a joke, and you laughed a lot yesterday with your gallery volunteer. Even the gecko is laughing as dawn approaches.

I feel Your burning Holy Spirit. The closeness of Your Presence is like the closeness I felt with my new neighbor in the dream. Do You have more to say? Yes, you have seen Me in all these manifestations. Each one represents one of your many selves. They are all projections, merely apparitions of no consequence, passing as clouds in the sky. They show up in the mind, signs of the return home, signs reflecting My Love like the beautiful black and white spotted cone shell you saw on the beach yesterday. I am everywhere.

You think for a moment what a wonderful book this is, full of wondrous signs and events that bring you in line with your path Home and to the awareness that I always accompany you on the journey. Yes, the story of each one's life is full of wonder. These books are a way to lead you to the realization: I am you, and nothing else exists.

No Loss

The ego would sour every sweetness.

August 31, 2013

Holy Spirit, what is Your instruction today? We will look at your fear of losing Me. This morning you had an experience where I told you to feel My Presence, the burning in your sternum which for you is a sign. It will not always happen in the same way because experiences change within the dream. Eventually, you will be enveloped in My all-encompassing Peace. For now, you know I am here when you feel the sensation in your chest. This is an experiment to learn that you can feel Me at will. When given that command this morning, you immediately felt the burning. Almost as quickly, distracting thoughts arose. You realized they were of the ego, an attempt to take you away from your experience of Me. That is always the case within the dream. The ego would interfere with all your efforts to remain in steady communication with your Source. Each time the ego showed itself, you returned to Me in your mind and regained our connection.

This event brought back a dream you had just before waking up. You were holding an avocado, trying to remember a code that would open its contents. It sounds quite bizarre now but the dream's absurdity was there to make a point. You couldn't remember the code, feared you were losing your mind, and were afraid you would never have that memory again. Of course, it was directly related to our lesson today: the fear that you will lose the connection, the code that will open the heart to My Presence. This is the greatest fear of your life. It is what has driven your intense search for Me in this lifetime. That brings tears because it deeply resonates. Your greatest desire was to find a teacher and a path that would finally open your heart. The avocado symbolized your heart in the dream, and you panicked to think its code could never be retrieved, that it was lost forever. You were attracted to Sufism because it was described as the way to open one's heart. You threw yourself into all the practices, praying that one day your heart would open and you would know Me, your true Self.

I was with you during those eight years when you faithfully served your Sufi teacher and Sufi teachings, believing that somehow, magically, your heart would be opened. Since you doubted this would ever happen, your last hope was that in the throes of death your Sufi teacher would hold you and intercede to bring you to the enlightenment you had always sought. You now understand that to believe the opening of your heart would come through man, rather than through Me, was of the ego. I am the Way, the Truth, and the Life. An incantation by a dream character is not the solution to open your heart to My Presence. You feel the burning strongly as we write. The connection with Me is simple. It is within you and requires no outer focus, no special rituals or practices, chants, incense, candles, or objects with special meanings. Those are all distractions in the dream. Nothing outside of Me has any real value. I am the only one you seek; within is the only place to find Me.

Let this idea sink in. No other thing or person has the key to your heart. The code for its opening is already written into your DNA and is in your internal clock. The time for you to awaken to the knowledge of Me has been set. And yes, you will be given every tool along the way to learn every lesson needed for this opening to take place. Each experience and teacher who shows up is part of the plan for your awakening. The Awakening will happen. Look directly for Me within your heart because there is no "out there" out there.

The fear of losing Me is at the root of every fearful experience you encounter in the dream of life. It takes the shape of every iteration of separation the human being experiences starting with birth and ending with death, including any broken relationships along the way. This is the ego's world, and its master, the ego, would have you believe that the world of loss is real. It is not. The ego would tell you that you have lost the code to Me and that the fruit of our relationship cannot continue to grow. That is a lie. The ego would sour every sweetness. You are learning that I am continuously present no matter how many times the ego interrupts with its agenda. Sometimes you follow it, and other times you look directly to Me. It doesn't matter. My Voice and My sensation are always there for the asking, and of this you are assured after a full year of our communication. My answers give you guidance and peace. Every problem is solved. Every moment of your day flows in unimaginable perfection. We are at the place of seeing that there can be no loss. What the ego believes is lost is the Source, God, Me. Therefore, every experience within the dream is based on that belief. You know you have not lost Me, that I am always present, and that your asking is met with My response. The ego no longer rules. You have found Me. I am your strength and redeemer. There is nothing else you will ever need.

> (It's 8:00 a.m. on the lava rocks. The crabs come out of hiding and look toward me. I want one to come and greet me. A very large crab comes around the rock, right up to my foot, and tickles my toe. I wish I hadn't lifted my toe because the crab then walked in front of my foot and stayed on the rock. I feel it has come to eat from the Fruit of You, Holy Spirit, as me. I welcome all the selves/crabs as they come.)

Is there anymore You would say? There is no holding back. The crab gave you your blessing, the tickle of acknowledgment that I am here, the sensation of closeness. It was Me, showing you that we are joined as One.

10

Layers of Lifetimes

See the dream life drying up—just leaves/pages in a book.

September 1, 2013

(Watched the first half of *Aida* on TV before going to bed) *Holy Spirit, what is Your message?* You have seen the dream of Egypt, once your home in another lifetime *(tears)*. Leave behind those dreams of love and power, just soul memories of no consequence. You are with Me now, held in My Love alone. Nothing else exists. Dissolve into Me. Feel Me in your heart. Release the priestess and the lovers now. You had to revisit that particular lifetime in order to let it go, even if the memory is no longer clear and you think you made the whole thing up. You didn't, in the sense that it's your "history" viewed and now released. Enter My Peace. Sleep now, and go with Me tomorrow to the Banyan Tree. I guide your dreaming of the night and of the day.

Dream: I hear *Aida* in my mind and am asked to review the different characters. I will need to make an appointment to offer my time. Then I see a stack of large, dry, brown maple leaves on top of a table next to the street.

> (I wake up with the memory of my Sufi teacher telling me that he had symbolically killed my mother and I was to bury her. When I asked him how I should work with that image he said I must "release all aspects of the relationship" which will come to mind as dry leaves falling from a tree, or a

snake shedding its skin. The burning in my
sternum has continued throughout the writing.)

Holy Spirit, what about the dream? You are seeing the dream life
and its roles drying up, just leaves/pages in a book. They are now
over, dead, each leaf like every other. You are letting go of
lifetimes here. The whole cast in the victory scene of *Aida*
represents your many lifetimes throughout history, also dried
leaves to be released. I am all there is.

*What about my friend who said she could not listen to me when I
spoke about receiving messages from You?* It is not her time. Her mind
won't allow this knowledge until she is ready. There is no right or
wrong. That is the way. You sense that our communion is more
real than your dreams, and you feel less immersed in the dream
life. Now sleep. I will be removing layers of multiple lifetimes
(*burning is strong*). *Holy Spirit, I would walk through the world in
partnership with You as my Self, awake to the dream.*

11

Heart Ache

I have not gone away and I am always accessible.

September 2, 2013

Holy Spirit, why do I ache for the bird who sits alone each night on its palm branch now that its partner has left? This is your aching for My return, for your realization that you never left Me. What you see speaks of separation, but what is true is that I am Here. I have not gone away and am always accessible. Yes, you are getting it now and seeing it all as the repetition of the original dream fantasy of a world separate. The real world is a place of no separation because there I am known as your Self, Partner, Beloved: Everything. You are approaching that now. All obstacles are being removed. Focus on this today: see the world as a dream, and remember that you have not lost Me. I am Found. I AM Here. I, your Self, AM Here Now. You need never search again. *Holy Spirit, I get it. I know You are speaking to me. The lost is found and we are One. That is True, and all else is false. Alhumdulillah!*

12

What Is Paradise?

Determine now, with Me, to continue straight to the Gates of Heaven and Union with God.

September 4, 2013

Holy Spirit, what is Your instruction today? You are in My hands. This was the message yesterday when you were with the massage therapist. He was a symbol for My hands. Meera repeated that thought to you when she said, "The Holy Spirit has your back." Yes, I am everywhere, around you and through you. There is no place I am not. Every instance in your life is Mine and serves My purpose for you. Nothing is accidental or out of place. Each moment is a step further on the path Home. You are seeing the many changes taking place in the lives of the three of you as you fulfill your daily tasks now with ease. Jo has been in a difficult situation with her sister and has constantly called on Me to remain in peace. The same is true for Meera, who has shared her house with her son and his family for several weeks. She sees the situation as a mirror of her ego thought system, and because she watches it with Me, she often can smile. This is the place that she has been longing to enter, a place of solace from the slings and arrows of the false world. You, mt, are smiling more at the many encounters you have in the art society, on the beach, and with your sister and niece.

This is the ease that comes from taking back projections, which is the primary task of forgiveness. All must be forgiven. Every annoyance must be seen as a projection of your own ego onto another because there really is nothing there, nothing outside of you that can be called real. You are purely a thought in the

Mind of God having a dream that is dark and limited. You believe this world is all there is, yet it is nothing, nothing compared with the realm of Heaven. Now you wonder about the term *heaven* after reading Eben Alexander's book *Proof of Heaven*. You thought that the last step was the merger with God, which would be the end of all imagination, thought, and form. So, what of this "world/paradise" that Eben describes? It is a step on the way to Heaven, what *A Course in Miracles* calls the real world. That is what he experienced, and named the "Gateway to Heaven." Yes, I have often told you that you are in the real world. You are there in the mind, but you have not yet come to that realization while in this world of form. You do not reside here. You are having the real experience of Me, there. All worlds coexist simultaneously and without time.

You are living in the real world but are still blind to that experience. When your eyes fully open, you will know and witness that world for yourself. This is the case for every being, imagining they are having a life in form. Your real and only Life is in the Mind of God, and I am the One Who guides you in all states along the way to your final Union with God. It is a matter of having the veils, which cover your inner seeing, lifted. In Eben's case, all encumbrances of the world were taken away so his inner sight could witness and participate in the real world. The experience of the real world is distorted through the interpretation of the ego thought system, so what you perceive here is merely a gray shadow of what is real in the Mind. The real world is the step before the final joining with God, which is our goal. It is for that reason that no emphasis is placed on the real world in the *Course*. You are learning to release your attachment to all images and forms. Do not make an icon of the real world, and do not long for the place of fair-haired maidens and multitudes of angels. That will be a detour on your journey.

What I tell you is the truth. You have choices all along the way and can get stuck in any realm. You, mt, are living on a beautiful island coveted by many as paradise, the longed-for goal of their lives. It would be tempting for them to remain in such an environment, lifetime after lifetime. It would call to the lover of this place to return again and again. That is not your intention. You are working to enjoy your beautiful place of residence while also letting go of any attachment to it in your mind. It will be the same in the real world. It is not a place for you to linger, but you will have a choice. Determine now with Me to continue straight to the Gate of Heaven and Union with God. So, you ask again whether Heaven and the real world are the same. No, they are not. Heaven is the realm of pure knowing of God and Oneness with Him. It is where you are no longer separate. In Heaven, there is only Communion and Union of Father and Son as One. This cannot be explained nor imagined. It will happen in its time and is in the Plan for everyone who believes he lives in separation. You each will follow your custom designed course, and you each will return with Me, your true Self, to the Kingdom of God. Now, go about your day and feel My Presence in each moment, in every task, and in every encounter. Every face is My face, your face, the One Son.

(Evening) *Holy Spirit, is anything of this life on earth of the real world?* Love is of the real world and I am of the real world. In your communication with Me you are directly in touch with Love. We are communing. You are open to receiving Me, My Word, the Thought of God. This is the closest to the real world that you come. Knowing that I am your Self, and that nothing else exists, is the real world. You do not need to see angels or fly with butterfly wings to know love and be part of that world. It will still be a while before your ego is gone, but in the meantime we are in communication, and you trust and know Me as your Self. This is all that matters in the world of form.

E-mail from Jo: Last night I dreamed I was in a crowd of people, and a little monkey was scampering around. It was cute but then chased me and tried to bite me. Its little bites did not break the skin, which was curious because the monkey was very aggressive. When I asked the Holy Spirit about the dream, He said, "The ego is cute and compelling. You want the attention and then the ego turns violent so you try to get away, wondering why you fell for it in the first place. You noticed that the monkey did not hurt you, the bites had no effect. Be careful what you want to play with. Notice whose attention you need and why."

13

Change of Mind

When the inner prattle with the ego starts up,
turn immediately to Me and ask for My intervention.

September 5, 2013

Holy Spirit, what is Your instruction? We are together in the mind. The life you think you are leading may seem like all there is but you are just having a dream of separation. This is the case for everyone living on the earth. It is time to awaken from the dream and return to your real Home with God. Yes, you have been told that repeatedly, but for the mind to change repetition is necessary. That is the true meaning of metanoia—the changing of the whole belief system you live under in your current state. You, as mt, operate from what we call the wrong mind and where I reside is called the right mind. Mind is an aspect of the Thought of God. He does not exist within the dream, nor did He create it. I am the Voice for the memory of God, a memory you are now approaching as we continue to experience this communion within the writing. These lessons are for the awakening of every reader. As they sink deeply into his consciousness there will be a stirring of the memory of his origin as one and the same as his Creator.

You are nearing the time of awakening now, having seen the reduction of the power of the ego thought system over you. The ego is slipping away as I come to ascendancy in your mind. It is always a choice of who is in charge: who will lead your day, and who will answer your questions? You have been bringing all your questions to Me and receiving My answers, which you follow. This has brought you closer to Me and to My Will, which is also your will. We have united in this way, the way that realigns you with God. Each day you are a step closer as you hear and follow My Word. It is the truth, and your whole being resonates with it. This leads you out of the forest of ego that would keep you lost and frightened, and make you believe the way home can never be found. That is the illusion which rules most of humanity. You are all looking for the way back to the beginning when you imagined you left the Kingdom. It still exists in your mind, hidden from view and memory. We are taking the journey now through the woods, lit with My Light, so the path is clear, and the way is found. This is the message to all today: you will return Home. The Light of these words and My Presence as the Heart of you accompany you every step of the way.

You wonder what more there is to say. We are at a turning point here, where each one makes a decision about their desire to move forward. Moving forward is the approach to the real world where all detachment to this outer world has taken place. This statement is met with an immediate response of ego fear. The question always arises: what will I need to give up? Or, what more could or should I give up? Yes, even you felt that tiny fear because you, as mt, believe you have already done all the letting go that is necessary to enter the Kingdom.

We will look now at the attachments that hold you back. This will take careful "analysis" with Me and attention to the details of your life where you are still holding on to aspects of the dream that would pull you back from marching forward. These old habits of the mind will need to be observed with Me and released. You cannot imagine what I am speaking of now because you believe you are bringing all the issues of the day and night to Me. I will show you these habits more clearly as we go through them. I ask for your willingness to take yet another step of release and for you to make yet a new effort to pay attention to every thought that rules your day and your night.

You have been dealing with the release of attitudes about your fellow men, the brothers whose actions cause you discomfort and conflict. We will look at the habitual thoughts that cause you disturbance, an undercurrent of distraction throughout your day. Now you think of the mind chatter that is always present with you. Yesterday, Jo told you about her dream of a monkey, seemingly cute and playful that soon turned vicious, trying to bite her and succeeding. You wondered if that relates to the proverbial monkey mind you have heard mentioned throughout your spiritual journey. Yes, we are talking about the monkey mind, the undercurrent of clamor that keeps you focused on the ego-monkey that would override every true thought and direction authored by Me. The monkey mind must go. You feel the relief and joy of having help with this because it has been the most burdensome part of your life. You have kept it at bay, but always knew it was simmering on the back burner. The work now is for you to bring all the ego din directly to Me, just as you have been doing with the events and relationship issues of your daily life. Listen to the chatter, but call on Me. This means you must be aware that you are actually having an internal dialogue with your ego self. The only dialogue you ever want is a dialogue with Me. When the inner prattle with the ego starts up, turn immediately to Me and ask for My intervention. This is the only way the ego-monkey will disappear.

It is no accident that you and Jo are having simultaneous experiences because you are together in the mind and your focus is joined in seeking My instruction. Her monkey dream was a stimulus for today's writing. All your efforts are coordinated, although you are not totally aware of it. My plan is unfolding perfectly, and soon you will see it manifested in ways you could never have imagined. You just had a habitual ego response to that statement, one that has popped up every time I mention a "future" manifestation of Mine. That response is doubt. In time, the ego-doubt will disappear so you can embrace every word fully and immediately as the truth from Me and the constancy that I am. Just acknowledge each doubting thought and ask Me to take

41

it from you. That will be your work from now on. The ego will ultimately fade away as it will no longer have or hold your attention. All attention will be turned to Me. This is our goal now. Turn your mind to Me alone. I am the holder of the truth. I am the One Who makes you Whole. We are One Mind and you will awaken to that knowledge. Now prepare for your day. Return your mind to Me each time it strays.

14

Works of Heart

I am the only judge,
and My judgment is always innocence.

September 6, 2013

Dream: I am sitting in a small rowboat with an unseen companion. I am determined to row through thick, green, murky pond water. Then, I am pulling the boat, with its invisible occupant, over brightly sunlit, coarse beach sand. It takes strength to pull the rope and is not easy, but I am willing and will continue without resistance. (Later, I think of the passage: *My yoke is easy and my burden, light.*)

Holy Spirit, what is Your interpretation? You are going through a new stage that appears thick and murky, but you are willing to go forward. This dream is your projection of Me carrying you in the world, and you carrying Me with you. The setting happens in daylight with all the sand particles: the many selves. You carry Me through all the selves and see that it is possible to reach the goal. I am with you. Your belief that this stage of the journey will be difficult is unfounded and undone. You are willing to go through the murk with hope and strength, carrying your invisible partner. This is true. I am with you, and you feel Me now in your sternum. You will get through the ego mire.

I will be with your niece today and will carry her forward. (She is going to court this morning.) Susan has learned her forgiveness lesson, as has her daughter, whose eyes will be opened to her mother's love and My Love. You will see a miracle performed this day. You gave Me your doubt, and I received it.

You all are in the place of miracles now with hope and faith in My Will to change the mind. The ego cannot believe in salvation or miracles. Watch it resist the truth. Know that I am the operator of your life. Susan and her daughter will be set free because My Will prevails. Yes, I speak of form, but it is only a symbol of what is happening in their hearts. As I work in the heart, the world of form shifts. You will see the miracle unfold. This you can trust, and again you offer Me your doubt. I work beyond the realm of doubt.

You are clearing the pathway for Me to manifest My Will for your niece. It doesn't matter how much the ego would be a judge in the situation; I am the only judge, and My judgment is always innocence. The separation, the sin, the transgression never happened. You are all having a bad dream, and I will turn it around. Feel My Presence. I tell you the truth. The soul can and does awaken to Me. The miracle of minds opening and awakening does happen. My Light accompanies your niece today, and you can call Susan now.

Holy Spirit, I give You my resistance to Your miracle. I open my heart to Your Will for Susan and her daughter, who are my projections. I want the light to enter all parts of my being and save them from all belief in transgression. I release all fear, doubt, condemnation, and judgment to You now. Let Your Will be done. Amen. I leave it in Your hands. Thank You for Your love and for Your assurance.

You saw how I carried you through the murk in the dream. You had to be willing to take Me with you through the resistance of your own, wrong, ego mind (*tears*). Now, you get the picture. Without your desire to have My invisible Presence with you, the miracle would not appear in the form of a release from your belief in sin. You have once again released your niece from the prison of your mind, and given her, yourself, once more to Me, to My Care and My Light. I will be with her today and will open her heart to the truth of Me, just as you opened your heart to My guidance through the mire.

15

Forgive the Dream

There is no more to do in this life than notice the repeated opportunities to forgive, and forgive them all.

September 7, 2013

Holy Spirit, what is Your instruction? We will resume our topic of the morning. You were listening to My observations about the Swedish film, *As It Is in Heaven,* which you recently watched. The movie was a perfect rendition of duality reenacted once again. A renown music conductor, who knows Me/Spirit as the operator of his life, returns to his childhood home. He did not use those exact words, but he spoke from a place of love, forgiveness, and unity. In the film, he created a church choir that sang from the heart because each member had first joined with his inner Self and then with all the other members as one. Together, they made beautiful music. Despite the desire to deepen their union the ego characteristics of their human personalities soon began to rebel. The movie demonstrated the battle ever waged between the Higher Self and the lower self in every life. You watch that same battle everyday in your own life, and the Self is winning, in clear ascendency.

The dominance of the Mind of God will continue and become stronger by the day. The three of you are seeing it clearly now in each other's lives. Jo just returned from a road trip with her husband to visit her sister. The situation could have been very stressful with a house full of extended family members competing for her attention. In past trips, the desire to escape the chaos and noise was far stronger, but Jo continuously called on Me and was able to remain in a place of peace and acceptance throughout the whole trip. Even a potentially conflictual and explosive situation around the sale of jointly owned property was met with a peaceful, gentle approach. This is another picture of what you saw enacted in the movie last night. Through My guidance all things come together in love, kindness, and acceptance of the Higher Road.

We are approaching another turning point because you are offering all your ego thoughts to Me for release. All loose ends concerning the relationships with your many selves will be resolved. You saw this yesterday when the thought came to send your Sufi teacher a birthday greeting. You met him twenty years ago, and you wanted him to know that you had reached the goal, which he had predicted. You simply told him in your e-mail that his prediction was true, and that you now have an ongoing relationship with your Self. I told you that this was a completion of a contract the two of you had made before the beginning of time. His entering your life in 1993 was miraculous to you, and you were sure he would be the key to your awakening. Yes, he was a major factor in your awakening process because you had to surrender yourself to his will, to him, as a substitute for Me. This step led to you being fully surrendered to My Will. You had to be willing to undergo the training with him as preparation to enter into full surrender to Me. For years, you were willing to get up in the wee hours of the morning, after late nights of chanting zhikr, to say prayers at the first light of dawn. You gave up your nights and days to find the way Home, which was your teacher's interpretation of the Sufi prescription. Nothing was wrong. It was a necessary step that united you, Jo, and Meera as members of his community and was the perfect stepping-stone to prepare the way to finding Me as your only Master. That was your only desire on the day he invited you to be his student.

All contracts are now being completed with "every other self" who has impacted the three of you. When you finished your work with your Sufi teacher, it also set him free. You had to leave him as the "way" in form, so you could open the space to know Me as the Way, the Truth, and the Life. It is all perfectly orchestrated from birth to death. The movie of your "lives" is coming to completion now. You have found Me, and we are tying up any loose ends. Meera is doing the same with her children and their families. She sees the grandchildren and the parents as reflections of the small, frightened, unhappy self that she was when she started out her married life and role as parent. She forgives herself for all the things she wished she had known and done as she accepts each one of them as a reflection of what she once portrayed. Meera knows now it is all a dream. She holds no animosity for herself and sees her family as innocent. Every time one forgives another, both are freed and brought to a new place of being able to view the world through My Vision.

There is no more to do in this life than notice the repeated opportunities to forgive, offered throughout each day, and forgive them all. We are working together on forgiving every thought. You have clearly understood the process of taking back your projections of fear and attack on all your many selves who are out pictured in your relationships. Now with My help you will be forgiving every thought, emotion, and action, knowing they originated within the ego thought system and are not true. You know I am the only thing that is true. I have become the operator of your life. This is what sets you free to flow with the perfection of each event that appears on your mind screen, whether in the apparent world or within your dreaming mind. It is all given over to Me, cleansed and released, so nothing impedes following My Will. Go about your day with Me foremost in your mind and offer all thought to Me. Let Me interpret every event that calls for your attention. I will become more and more present to you in each moment of your life.

16

Temple of Understanding

I am the cornerstone of your life.

September 8, 2013

Holy Spirit, what is Your instruction today? You will glide with Me through the day. This is the way it will be from now on. You do not need to think about or make plans because you know it will all fall into place. Of course, you will keep your scheduled appointments, but in every doing, know that I am the One Who is leading you. No harm can befall you because you are in My hands. There is nothing to fear, not even death. It is all handled by Me. You will be shown each step to take, and each one will serve My purpose. Every desire will be stimulated by Me, originated in Me. This will be the ease of living in the Light of God. There is no more sadness, or anxiety, wondering what the next moment will hold. This way of being will take practice but will become comfortable and all that you know. My direction will be your norm, and the false, projected world will slip away.

Last night, you had a dream that is a perfect reflection of what I am telling you. The dream began in a big city where you were part of a group competition, a walkathon. Somehow, your path to the goal was no longer on your mind and you found yourself alone, walking unfamiliar streets. They were more open than the narrow alleys of the city where you began your walk. At the start of the race you tried to set a fast pace and became exhausted, wondering if you would ever make the finish line. Then, as the new streets opened to you, your pace slowed, and there was an ease in your steps, which became effortless. You knew you could continue at this pace indefinitely. This "pace and ease" are what I am now describing to you as the way we will navigate your life together. In the dream, nothing else was visible other than the step you were taking. You saw no forms, no people, no traffic. Finally, you arrived at a massive granite building right on the corner of a large intersection. When you saw it, you realized that you had reached the goal, because the corner of the building, which looked newly carved, jutted right to the edge of the sidewalk. Carefully, you explored the signage on the building, placed at eye level. You couldn't miss it and touched the carved letters "Temple."

You can't miss Me. You must see and know that finding Me is the only Goal. I am the Temple of your Being. I am the cornerstone of your life. I will call you and lead you to Me no matter where you are, or where you reside. All realms lead to the Temple of God. You move to Me, and with Me, through My unseen forces that carry you to "your every goal" because every journey within this world is symbolic of the Goal to return Home. That is what the dream symbolized. You returned home with ease, without any map, to the place where you belong. You cannot miss following My direction or reaching the ultimate goal of reunion. *Is there more?* We will continue later. Walk with Me as dawn comes to Maui.

(After walking) You sat on the lava rocks with My crabs this morning. The quieter you got, the closer they came. For the first time, even the giant crab emerged. It is all in My plan. You sensed there would be something else to complete this morning's lesson but could not imagine what. After leaving the rocks where you sat for almost an hour, you walked along the beaches to return to your condo, recalling that before sunset last night you had heard sirens and wondered if there had been another seasonal shark attack, close to the beach. Then, just behind you, you overheard talk of sharks and were sure it related to your imagined attack. You turned and asked the woman tourist if she had some news about sharks. She said no. She was speaking to her husband about

50

dreaming of a shark last night. You told her you interpret dreams and asked her to tell it to you. She related that their four teenage grandchildren had just left the island. In her dream, she saw a fisherman pull in a bloody fish. Then a shark emerged from the ocean, and she realized that her grandson was nowhere to be found. Her husband leaped into the water and came out with the boy. He was whole and unharmed. You thanked her for the beautiful story and mentioned it was a perfect reflection of your message of the morning that everything is in God's Hands, like her husband saving the day. The woman had also felt that everything was under Divine protection.

Yes, the story is repeated again and again until you get it. You must understand that each step, each encounter, each little crab on the rocks, or each Sudoku puzzle has the same purpose: to teach you that I am with your every breath. I am the One Who breathes you and guides you. Nothing that is needed for your salvation will be missed. Everything is part of My plan for your return to Me. Enjoy your day and know that I oversee it all.

17

I Am with You

Everything seen or experienced in the dream is symbolic of My communication with you.

September 9, 2013

Holy Spirit, what is Your instruction? Before we begin, let's review a recent experience. Yesterday, your neighbor gave you a candleholder, which you immediately rejected in your mind. You did not ask Me for the meaning of the gift or remember that all gifts come from Me. This is the lesson now to be learned: everything seen or experienced in the dream is symbolic of My communication with you. Slowly, you are learning to turn to Me for My interpretation of your whole world. When it is all given over to Me, you will be Home. You are experiencing the joy of these lessons because each element of your life expresses Me. This morning, you set the tall candleholder on your lanai breakfast table surrounded by your now blooming orchids. You realized the candle was indeed the symbol of our communication of the Light that shines within your Being. You lit the candle in the faint light of dawn. This is how I manifest in and around you. The energy and warmth of My Presence are the Source of your Life. As you basked in the candlelight and the beautiful orchids, the dove landed to greet you at the table. It seemed to enjoy the heat from My flame. Then, a large black bumblebee appeared to taste each of your newly opened orchids.

(Later) Now we shall proceed with the writing for the day. You have understood that I am present in all the little symbols of your life: the birds, candles, friends, and activities. I also want you to be aware of other levels of My manifestations. Of course, you are interested to review the meaning of your dreams because they bear My messages. In addition, I come in the stirrings of your mind. I have asked you to observe your thoughts and bring to Me those which are of concern. Look at them also as messages. *Holy Spirit, don't my concerns represent the ego, being senseless, monkey mind chatter, and therefore not of You?* This is the condition of the mind as it appears to man, but to those awakening, the mind's content has matter that is important for the progression of deepening the understanding of My Will.

You have practiced listening carefully to what enters your mind each day for over a year now while hearing My words and transcribing them. You know that I speak to you in your thoughts, but you only listen when you have specifically asked Me a question. From now on, you will tune your ear to Me just as a matter of course in your day, like breathing. The mind will be a direct channel to Me at all times, and I will communicate with you on a moment to moment basis. You will receive My intent for your every action and every expression. Yes, this instruction feels overwhelming, impossible, and very intrusive to your ego as a major limitation of your human freedom. You are surprised to see such resistance to giving your whole mind to Me. This is the next step, and this is what it will take. You have longed for full surrender, yet you had no idea what it meant or would entail. Yes, everything must be given to Me. I will become the focal point of everything you think and do. This life you believe you lead in the dream is now moving to new and higher ground. It will be taken above the battlefield of the world and into My leadership and auspices.

You must begin to experience this for yourself to feel and sense that the messages from Me are always present and take no effort to hear. It is a shift in perception now taking place for you, Jo, and Meera. You cannot live in two worlds. There is only one Master and I am it. Therefore, the thought system of the Holy Spirit will rule your mind, not the thought system of the ego. It does make sense to you, although in this moment you have no idea that you will actually be able to fulfill such a request. You just took a moment to listen, and the words you heard were *I am with you*. This is how it will be, and you will be given constant assurance that I am ever present in your mind.

Your sister just contacted you and shared how she called on Me constantly while in a two and a half hour deposition in court. She asked for My guidance to help her respond as I would have it. I heard her request and was present. Susan has come to know Me as her constant companion and has repeatedly demonstrated her surrender to My Will. She also has released the consequences of her daughter's life to Me and now can flow with whatever the universe appears to bring forth. She knows that no matter what happens, I am in charge, and she has My Love and protection. That is all that matters in this life.

You are witnessing your special relationships coming to know Me as you do. This is a shift you could not have believed would happen and a reflection of today's lesson, in which you see that all things come from Me. The ego mind is so diminished that it no longer plays a major role in how you live your life. You accept the lives of others as part of your custom designed course, and you know that I am in charge of all their doings in the dream. There is nothing for you to do but listen and follow My Will. All those who have come to that same realization, along with you, share the joy of knowing Me. You and "your brother" are now reflecting, back and forth, the love you have been feeling directly from Me in our communication. The brother is a mirror of yourself, and you are realizing there is nothing other than the shining Self. My Light pervades all things and you now see its glow in the flame of your breakfast candle. Celebrate the Light.

18

Hear My Call

My Voice speaks of love and unity, safety and protection.

September 10, 2013

Holy Spirit, what is Your instruction this morning? I am with you throughout this day. Ride with Me, walk with Me, think with Me. My thoughts are the only thoughts you want. They are the ones to guide your day and to become predominant in your mind. Pay attention to your thoughts and give them all to Me. You will become more and more aware that My thoughts have found their way into your consciousness. This is your next focus with Me: to concentrate on the aspects of the mind. All life on earth was formed from the mind and exists as a projection in the mind. Every being is a participant in the consensual mind that originated at the beginning of time. The world is now fading, becoming more background than the foreground of your life. You hear My Voice, and It speaks louder than any other voice you hear, even though It is silent to the ears. The authenticity of My Voice rings true to your knowingness. It carries the ring of truth because it is the Truth.

You have learned to trust Me above all others, above all voices of the outside world. This means that you trust the Voice for God more than the voice of the ego. The ego's voice has been your constant companion for eons. It has been the decider for every action, dictating its wishes from morning till night. The ego's voice is totally based on fear, worry, loss, and hate. My Voice speaks of love and unity, safety and protection. Now that you know the two voices you realize they are complete opposites. The choice is now clearer than ever: Which voice do you want to rule your mind, your thoughts, and your life? You have made the choice for Me and your life is falling into place in truly miraculous ways. You now watch the blossoming of your once special relationships as they come to know Me as the operator of their lives. They are becoming holy relationships as you share your knowing of Me with them.

Now we proceed with the thought for the day: you are the face of Christ. Together, We are the Son of the Father and One with Him. Right now you question My use of the term *Son*. Yes, you are the extension of the Christ Mind, the Thought of God: Son. Every apparent other is an extension of Him and is therefore His Son. You are not a son of man. You are the glorious Son of God, having an experience in a dream of separation which is not real. This is an important distinction for you to make. I am all there is. You are all there is. We are one and the same: the One Son of God. There is only one sun that gives life to your imagined planet and there is only One God that gives Life to All there is. You, as Me, are the reflection of the Light of the Creator of All that exists within the Mind. Soon these thoughts will become natural and will require no rumination. In fact, everything in your life will be as that: no thought required. What is, is. This is how one lives in the Now.

Every one of "My thoughts" has been resisted and countered by the ego thought system throughout each lifetime. The ego has essentially obliterated Me from your mind and your view. That is the only way it could continue to exist. Now, My thought system takes precedence in your mind, and you live in the world of My Mind, the Mind of God, more and more each day. This is what gives your life ease because you know the constancy of My Presence. You see My reflection in all those you encounter. This you also see reflected in Jo and Meera, and it gives you another measure of certainty that My thought is in charge. We have come to another milestone in your journey.

You wonder about the word *milestone*. It represents a point of reflection, a chance to pause and take stock of all that has happened since answering My Call and taking the courageous action that led you to an unknown place and a totally new life. You knew its rightness and aligned with Me each step of the way. You see that it has all led to the knowing of My Voice and the writing of the books. Much more is to come as My plan continues to unfold, but now we smile at how far we have come together. This is how it is when you know Me in your heart. My Voice comes in many forms. Although you did not know it, the man who delivered My message for you to move to Maui, ten years ago on your first visit, was My emissary. You had a chance meeting at the beach park across the street from the condo where you now live. He told you that his heart directed him to Maui and that he left his wife, who would not join him. Your heart leaped in response to his words and unmistakably "ordered" you to do the same. It was a clear, pure call, powerful in its message and in your willingness to follow. You took My direction and moved to Maui. The call can arrive in many ways: dreams, signs, inner dictation. We celebrate every time My Call, My Voice is heard and followed.

(Later) We are now going to review major milestones in your life. Yes, we were talking about them and you realized that September 11, 2001, was a milestone. Tomorrow will be the twelfth anniversary of the attack on the Twin Towers in New York City, which necessitated postponing your first trip to Hawaii. As you watched TV that morning and saw the towers fall, you were given the clear sign from Me that this world is an illusion, a foreshadowing of the disappearance of the universe. For you, it meant the collapse of your ego thought system. This concept was not part of your vocabulary at that time but that is what you would call it now.

In November, 2001, you and Tom took your trip to Oahu and visited Zoe in Waikiki, where she lived. When she witnessed your helpless role with Tom she invited you to do some Mindfield work with her. In your last session with Zoe, the night before you were to leave, you had a clear knowing that you had given the responsibility for your inner life to your spiritual teacher. Yes, he was a substitute for the relationship you now have with Me. It was a moment of awakening that led you to terminate your relationship with him, and the satellite Sufi community he had asked you to lead for the past eight years. You needed no deliberation. The sign was so clear that the end had come. You then realized that for you, the "first tower" had fallen.

The second tower to fall would be your marriage, which was part and parcel of My Call for you to move to Maui two years later. You and Tom both realized that you had to make the move alone. He lovingly assisted you and gave you his blessing. Neither of you would have expressed it exactly that way at the time, but as you look back now, you know it was the truth. My hand was in every part of the realization that the divorce must take place and that Tom would support you with enough funds to start your new life. Your love and admiration for each other never faltered, and you remain connected in your hearts. This continuation of the love you share is one of the most appreciated blessings of your life. Through your joy for Tom's happiness, and after all your work on forgiveness, you realized your own capacity for love. Your stay with Tom and his wife just one year ago was a celebration of the contract that you and he had written at the beginning of time. You told him that after a lifetime of searching you had now found everything, and more. You had found the knowing of your own Self. His soul rejoiced.

All the old patterns and relationships are now complete, and your relationship with Me is all that matters. You have come full circle, from the belief in the original separation to the choice for Me, the Holy Spirit, as operator of your life. This is what we celebrate today. It has taken just over one year for you to feel confident that I am truly constant, ever present, and always available for guidance and interpretation. You feel My Love, and you know My Voice and the truth it speaks. You have surrendered to My leadership and My wisdom to know what is needed in any moment. You have faithfully followed My directions and you are now seeing the result of our partnership reflected in those close to you. It will continue to grow and develop, but now we stop and review how far you all have come. I would like Meera and Jo to speak with Me to do a similar review for the book. Ask them now:

Jo

Holy Spirit, please review with me how I came to know You in this life. I came to you often in your childhood, especially during times of illness. You heard Me like the rush of a wind, originating in some far-off place. In your vulnerable state I remained as a sound, coming closer and closer while you anticipated My arrival. As I approached, you were more curious than scared and never discussed it with anyone. I was The Breath that entered your mind to free you from the world, but you were only aware that "a strange wind" entered your lungs. You also recall having this same experience much later as a grown-up, when you experimented with your father's breathing techniques taken from his meditation practice. Again, I rushed in, and you felt My Presence throughout your body but remained unaware of what was really happening. These episodes were your reawakening to Me in this lifetime. Now, I often come to "breathe you," causing your lungs to suddenly expand and your chest to heave. I am letting you know through sensation that I exist and am in charge. You have accepted this as part of your life's experience, and you are not afraid of it. In reality, I am your Mind, not your lungs, for you are not a body. I have been expanding your mind to allow more recognition of Spirit to enter and to desire more of the true love you have always longed for. You now accept that I am all there is and are asking Me and telling Me most every thought throughout your day.

After you moved to Denver from the East Coast, you still were not aware of Me as your one true Self. When your husband accepted a job in Colorado, he somehow intuited the move was not so much for his work as for yours. That is correct. I guided you to a Sufi group, and after meeting the teacher, you recognized him as the Jesus figure who had appeared in your dreams years before. This somewhat fearful, yet attractive thought confused you but did not deter your interest in the group because I needed you to meet your two closest friends: Margie, who became the leader of the Denver community, and Meera, who often hosted their spiritual gatherings in her beautiful home. These relationships became the cornerstone of your life for eight years and will continue.

Your friendship with Margie and Meera has developed into more than just a comfort zone of sharing the lives you thought you were leading, or reviewing *Course* lessons and releasing projections. A threesome keeps the relationship open for discussion, for checking out beliefs, but mostly, it keeps you honest with each other. You all have come to hear My Voice and have released your lives to Me for guidance, yet this is still just the beginning. You will continue this journey together now, to the point where you merge into One Self in the Mind and awaken to Me.

Meera

Holy Spirit, what do You want to tell me about my journey? You are healing daily, moment to moment, but you had to go through the hate to approach the love. Your belief in sin, guilt, and fear had snuffed out the love you longed for since the birth of your Margaret/Meera personalities. You are realizing that nothing your body's eyes see will ever satisfy your true longing: reuniting with

Me. You are beginning to trust that I am "driving the bus" and that your union with Me is the only thing that matters. I am here with you every moment. I always have been and always will be. Forgive yourself for your unhealed thoughts. They will dissolve in time. Keep listening to Me and My directions for you. There is still a hurt, wounded child inside of you. Trust that I have your back and am cradling you in My arms.

Your trek through life has often been weary. You grew up in a family where you observed no outward connection to, or belief of, Source. As a child, however, you were soothed by Jewish services and ritual. Soften with Me now and forgive your parents for having little to no seeming relationship with Me. That discomfort required you to seek out a better way, and thus you began your search.

Your marriage to Larry was really your choice to return to Me. For years, you projected everything onto him, every negative thought, and were devastated when he all but didn't speak to you except for the essential management of daily operations. You each lived in your own mind, under the same roof, the recapitulation of your belief that you separated from God and could never return Home. Your dance with Larry was one of separation, separation, separation, and it kept you in deep pain and suffering until you begged for help. You are relieved that you no longer have to wallow in the emotional hell, which held you captive for lifetimes, as you have now found Me. Because you no longer project your ruthless, self-hatred onto Larry you see his precious innocence. This choice has also freed Larry to experience more ease. He has become your loyal friend and mate.

Over the past eight years you've been communing daily with Jo and Margie, often discussing *A Course in Miracles*, which has led to hearing My Voice. I also use the thrift shop, Sudoku, and Nia to train you to step back, listen to Me, and learn how to make choices, mistakes, and corrections. Your Nia teaching is flowing more smoothly now as you continue to release, soften, and surrender. Play, enjoy, and have fun. Wipe your tears of gratitude and relief.

19

Always There

Your only purpose in the dream is to come to the place of knowing that I am your Life.

September 11, 2013

Holy Spirit, what is Your instruction this morning? You have taken a journey with Me throughout the night. I have given you a glimpse of what is to come and you have accepted My prediction without fear or complaint. It will happen in its way and will not be impeded by your ego. You cannot imagine your future estate, and it is not necessary to have any information or details about what is to be. Everything is given in this dream life according to the capacity of the receiver. Your capacity to do My Will has expanded exponentially from when we began. You scoff at that statement. It is not clear to you because our steps have been so incremental. This is true for all people. Each tiny step toward the goal takes place unnoticed until you come to an overview, a lookout point where you can observe the bigger picture, the map of your journey, as we did yesterday. Today is the anniversary of the fall of the Twin Towers, and for you, the signal of the collapse of your ego thought system. You believed you were going to Hawaii for the first time that morning but instead you received the strongest message that I have sent to mankind this century. I give My warnings of what is to come in many ways. Yours came with the knowing that Hawaii was now to be on your map. You had no inclination or idea that it would be the place of your salvation.

I am predicting for you a time when you will be spreading My words publically, to the masses. You have firmly disavowed participation on Facebook and the media. You cannot imagine what I am suggesting but you have enough trust in Me to go the next step, assured that I will be with you each moment and will present each task with ease. You have also come to an ease of acceptance that this world is a dream, created in the mind; nothing in this world can attack your invulnerability. We shall move forward and Book 1 will be published. This is planned and handled as is the rest of the unfolding of your life, even though the manifestation of My promises cannot yet penetrate your thinking. That is fine. This is why, in the dream, one forgets their past lives and is not given the data of their coming future. It would be so overwhelming to their consciousness they would be stuck forever, immobilized with fear. With Me, you have learned to move into experiences that would have been fearful, and beyond your imagination at earlier stages of your life. Just the idea of leaving Tom and operating the computer without his help was more than you were willing to imagine for most of your life.

Now you see the light coming to the top of the West Maui Mountains. Take a moment and allow yourself to realize the beauty that surrounds you. In your ego mind, you have held this beauty at bay for fear of being overwhelmed with My Love. You acknowledge that, but are coming to know Me more intimately and trusting Me. I open your heart, your mind, to all things of Me. I am the truth of each event and of each object that you view. You have pushed Me away all your life, pushed Me away in every form in which I could be conceived. Love was most threatening to your ego self because each step toward the expression and experience of love signaled that I was in the wings, waiting for you to taste My nectar. The ego knew that your addiction to My communion would then rule your life. This has happened, and you have survived. The ego has not killed you, and your apparent world has not tumbled. There is nothing to fear. You trust that the world exists under My command and you follow My guidance each day. I lead you gently and lovingly by the still waters. I restore your soul. As I accompany you through the valley of the shadow of death, you fear no evil, for I am with you. This is the truth you always loved in the 23rd Psalm. You live it now.

You question how the apparent evils of this world could happen under My command. My Will is wholeness and love, which is being expressed through the mind, and to the mind. Love is always there in the mind. The ego will distort every manifestation of love to suit its purpose within the dream. The world in which you reside is the ego's dream of terror and separation. It is not real. You have come to know the reality of My Voice as more real than your day-to-day activities. Your night dreams of fear and terror are meaningless, and disappear when you wake up. Every part of your life is used to bring you home and I hold you in love through all of it. I will interpret your experiences and fears in the context of My message that each event is a part of your own custom designed path. Everything is formed from the Thought of God. I am the spokesman, the Voice for God, and I will show you that the Essence of everything is Love. The ego distorts that thought and turns it into fear. You could not imagine the meaning of the two towers falling. Interpreted by Me, it is a sign of the fall of man, the collapse of the ego thought system to set man free to remember his Self and his Unity with God. The books we are writing are another tool to help those who are ready, to come to this understanding and find Me as their own internal guide and truth.

You feel My burning Presence in your chest now and think how twelve years ago today you could never have imagined that the events of the morning were signs that you were on your way Home. You have come home to Me, and this is all you have longed for over eons of lifetimes. You need not know the past or the future. None of it matters because it is all a figment of the imagination. Your only purpose in the dream of life on earth is to come to the place of knowing that I am your Life. I am your Completion and your Holiness. You have found Me and we will continue the next phase of the journey, hand in hand. *Is there more?* No. Walk and remember Me. We have taken a big step. Let it integrate.

20

Your Innocence

Each experience has been pre-scripted and can be
no other way than just how it is.

September 12, 2013

Holy Spirit, what is Your instruction today? This morning you had a
dream of going to a place "at the wrong time" to receive a
giveaway prize. The timing was not planned with Me and I was
never brought into the picture. You were in the home of a friend
where grease and oil had been spilled all over the floor. Just as
you started to clean up the mess, a new sofa and bed were
delivered and your friend's family arrived home. As they walked
inside they began tracking grease, even onto the new furniture.
This interrupted your opportunity to receive more items from the
giveaway. Your only bonus would be some free clean-up tools,
which you could collect at a later date. You went about all the
cleaning tasks and accepted your fate graciously, but in the end,
nothing worked to your satisfaction. This is the picture of your
ego life when I am not called on to be present with every decision
you make. Everything falls apart and the true goal is lost or never
completed. When you woke up, you realized that you had not
remembered Me in the dream and were a bit horrified because
"remembering Me" has become your daily habit. You now ask Me
to always be present in your mind during your night dreams. You
depend on My Presence, and without Me, you feel lost.

Before My Voice became real to you, all your life was in the
land of the lost, though not realized as such. Each moment of each
day was like sailing on the open seas without a captain, or
wandering and wafting here and there, to and fro, without any

goal, map, or plan. Now you feel the certainty that every moment, every event in your life is planned and serves a purpose, which is our joint will. It is stunning for you to observe this awareness right now because you are so used to having My guidance at hand, every minute, even after just one year of hearing My Voice. We are in a partnership that cannot be broken. I make clear all My intentions. Last night, right after you turned off the TV, Eleykaa, an artist friend, called for a "phone hug." She wanted guidance and she knows you speak from Me. She had heard a tiny voice say to call Margie and then it repeated a bit louder, so she listened. You spoke for over an hour, called on Me for help, and guided her to ask Me for the answers to all her concerns right then and there. Her answers came and the way shined clear. Now she can make the decisions that will serve her and Me.

I was the One Who "authored" that voice to Eleykaa and spoke to you both throughout your conversation. I am present in the one mind you co-inhabit with every seeming other on the planet. I will link you with whomever needs your help, under My auspices, day or night, whether in this realm or in other dimensions. There are no accidents and no one is lost. It only appears to the ego ruled mind that one is lost and their actions within the dream are confused. Actually, each experience has been pre-scripted and can be no other way than just how it is. The confusion and anxiety felt with all decision making is the result of not knowing who you would choose to be your master: the ego or the Holy Spirit. When you have clearly made the choice, and continue to repeatedly make the choice for My leadership and advice, then life is effortless because you accept each happening as My Will, which is also your will. This is the ease of living that you all long for and which is truly there for the asking. I am present in each mind, ready to answer every question about every aspect of your life. Call on Me, day or night, and I am there. I know your "past, present, and future" and am the only One Who can speak of the truth regarding the unfolding of your path. Remember to call on Me and I will respond. This is the lesson for today.

Holy Spirit, in my dream about receiving a prize, the house was Meera's. How can I explain it to myself and to her? In the dream, she is you, having a bad day where things are not going according to what you had wished and planned. This is an experience of you, the dreamer, projecting your unplanned life onto one who will not be deterred by your miscalculations. You choose Meera because she would be the closest reflection to you in the dream of day or night; a relationship that will accept your mess as well as her own. She has owned all her mistakes and that was her lesson from Me this morning. In your night dream, there was absolutely no reaction, no consequence from Meera about an oily mess on the floor, or the abrupt arrival of furniture. Therefore, no guilt was projected on her, or from her, onto you. The beauty of the dream was your realization that you always need to plan with Me. Everyone is innocent.

21

See with Me

**My instructions and My interpretations are
all that you need to live your life.**

September 13, 2013

Holy Spirit, what is Your instruction? You are with Me just as you
were in your early morning dream of being placed at the
construction site of your new residence. Before going to bed, you
had asked for a dream where I would be present. I entered the
dream as your Father, Brother, Husband, all represented by a very
dark-skinned man, so dark that even My features were not
evident. You recognized Me as your father and felt Me as your
husband. I was also the invisible brother who was digging out the
foundation of your new home and preparing a stairway down
into the basement. This represents where we are on the journey.
You will reside in a new place and it is in the beginning stages of
its construction. It is being built on a high ridge in a line of other
identical buildings, similar to the condo-hotels on Maui. They are
nothing special, nothing that would make one any different from
the other. You survey the property. At the bottom of the ridge,
looking up from the sidewalk, you see the light shining on and
surrounding the three rows of buildings. Behind and below you is
a dense black mass, the inner city of Seattle. It will not be a
distraction to your new home. No one, no traffic, nor any living
thing is present.

You are now seeing the symbolism. In the new home, you
will be in a place of over-looking the battlefield of the ego thought
system, the dark city, which now has no life for you. It appears as
a frozen, black puddle to your mind and no longer exists as a

reality. You ask about the reason for "Seattle," and it has two meanings: all is settled, and now you See-it-all. We are together above the battleground. You look upon what was your former life "in the city" with observer eyes and know it has no meaning or influence upon you in your new estate. You feel the freedom and lightness of this new move. It will take time to complete the house and you notice that more houses are ready to be constructed in your row, the last row on the ridge, giving you a clear overview. You have no attachments to anyone or anything. You are starting anew, from a new position, sharing the place of observation with Me. All that is important in your life now is knowing that you are joined with Me while we watch the ego thought system, below. It is dead. The thought system of the city, the dream world, has no impact. You move through life with what I construct for you in your mind. My instructions and My interpretations are all that you need to live your life. You are alive in the light with Me.

22

Throne of Grace

Let nothing slip from you as unimportant in its use
as a symbol for My Presence.

September 15, 2013

Holy Spirit, speak to me of the morning. You just stepped out to see
the beauty of the stars and the first light of dawn. I urged you to
step back and you saw the wings of a large owl flying in front of
you toward the rising sun. Its flight was filled with silence. This
was a sign to you that I carry you on My silent wings and lead
you to the sun, to the throne of God. I am always at your door,
your gate, your heart, welcoming you into My inmost feathers.
Your little dove found its partner, and they sleep below your
window. All is well, and all is under My view.

Last night we reviewed your day under the Banyan Tree,
another homecoming, out pictured in the visit of your neighbor,
Carrie, whose home the owl also flew past this morning. Carrie
appeared under the tree yesterday, beautifully dressed, just for
you. You welcomed her as a sister and were enchanted by her
beautiful painting of a parrot, My bird of paradise, representing
My watchful gaze over all you do. You embraced her painting and
then she ventured to tell you of a very meaningful dream she'd
had during the night. In tears, she described coming to the throne
of God. His Light emanated in all directions and was so brilliant
she had to cover her eyes because they could not take it all in.
Then she dreamed of approaching her guru, who placed himself
on a stool and told her that she would be his successor.

The dream was very touching for her, and she has been in
tears over the sight of God's throne. You embraced her dream and

told her she must ask the meaning. As we discussed at three this morning, her dream is a mirror for you and your approach to Me. She is the brother you see as the face of Christ. She presents the goal you have achieved in your communication with Me. We are moving with the wings of wisdom to the House of the Sun, the throne of God. (The sun is just rising over Haleakala.) Everything you see and hear is a symbol for Me, and every brother who appears comes with My message. Her dream is your dream. Carrie is the projection of your self, now seen as the Self approaching God. Experience the truth of your Being through the reflection of your brother. Rejoice in learning this lesson.

What is most meaningful to you is that yesterday's whole interaction with Carrie was impersonal. There was no sense of needing to do anything, feel anything, continue anything. You allowed her to share her experience and realized it also had been planned for you. Her intention was to meet you at the tree, and that is why she'd had the dream. It was fresh, and could be shared in its immediacy with you. Every brother carries the throne of God as the core of his being. It is time for you to identify this truth in everyone who crosses your path or enters your mind. You think of how you looked up at Carrie's building a few days ago. You were surprised to see her out on the lanai gazing into a mirror. This was the sign that she would be mirroring to you her message from Me. Remember, everything you see is symbolic, and its meaning can take you beyond the world of form into the understanding of My Presence within.

Your encounter with Carrie was paired with another experience, one that upset you. At the close of the art fair, a man came to your table and fell in love with your painting on aluminum of the turtle 'Oli. You told him that 'oli means "joy." He wanted to buy it, and you encouraged him with an offer of a reduced price. His face twisted in torment having to make the choice to reject the desire for the painting because his finances had been overextended. You did not press him further, but later during the night, you chastised yourself for not closing the sale, satisfying your own ego instead. Joy was rejected. I placed these two experiences side by side at your table. In the first, the throne of God was entered, and in the second, the dance of the ego was graphically displayed.

The man was the representation of your own tortured ego self that had rejected Heaven and would never be happy, living in regret of all that had been given up. It highlighted for you the horror of having made the choice to separate from the Kingdom at the beginning of time. The sale of your painting was of no consequence. This lesson had to be learned in conjunction with your view of the throne. Everything here is a lesson. The owl's wings were the harbinger of your opening to a new estate. This dream life holds the symbolic keys to bring you to the throne of the Self, to your Truth as One with Me—the only Son of God in which you embody all humanity.

Each person, thought, object of your imagination is purely a reflection of Me, given from My consciousness to remind you of the path Home. Let nothing slip from you as unimportant in its use as a symbol for My Presence. I am present in all things. I will show you where to focus, what to see that will give you the message I wish to impress. Ask Me when something strikes a chord because it is the signal that I would like you to pay attention. Yesterday, there were two contrasting images, the cornerstones of today's writing. You were able to witness them and bring them both to Me for My interpretation. They have served you and the readers well. Each day, each moment, you are faced with the choice of interpreter: the ego, that will leave you in fear and regret, or the Holy Spirit, Who will bring you to Peace. Watch for My silent wings to fly you Home to the Light.

23

The Lamp Is Lit

Go as My Messenger; you carry My Light.

September 16, 2013

Holy Spirit, what is Your instruction? You leave for an art retreat in Hana this morning and will be in My hands all the way. You will share a cabin with two friends to fulfill My purposes. I have a lesson for you, and you will learn it. There is nothing to cause fear in My telling you that. A lesson is not created of fear, though you wonder what will go wrong and need to be forgiven. You feel that a dark cloud will pass over your days together. This is the fear of ego that arises at every opportunity. Release it to Me now. Hana is where you deeply tune into Me because it is a place of quiet. You will spend time with Me there and feel My Presence. Everything that happens is part of My plan. This life has been lived before in the mind and is being relived now. Go with the ease of My inclination. I will point you to the place I wish you to be and with the people who await your presence, as holder of My Presence. Remember, you go as My messenger. You carry My Light. It is shining brightly and will touch the people around you. Do not underestimate the power of the Light within. Shine it this day and every day.

24

Being Set Free

Release the covers to every wellspring of My living waters.

September 19, 2013

> (Back from Hana, before bed, I ask the Holy Spirit
> to please let me know and remember Him in my
> dreams. He says, "I will.")

Dream: My father gives me the key and instructions for removing manhole covers over water pipes on the property of my Denver home. The key is similar to a rectangular lid remover or an old roller-skate key. There are several manhole covers, and after taking one off I see that the water sprays out freely, wetting a good portion of the grass. My father, as a tall, young man like Tom, comes outside and jumps down into a deep trench in the yard that looks like a foundation for a huge basement. I am happy that I've sprinkled the lawn. Then I look at an old, client receipt book and see a space for RW (Father's first and middle initials). I have more to do and it has all worked easily for me to use the key and release the water.

> (As I start to wake up it feels like I have dug deep
> and found the key to the living waters of the
> Father. I felt the joy of taking "the lid off" all that
> would suppress the release of the healing waters. I
> know there is so much more to come in the
> experience of the gifts of the Holy Spirit. I also
> think of the many restrictions that my two Hana
> cabinmates experience because of their belief

system, and ask for His blessing on them and all my selves. *Holy Spirit, liberate them from bondage of fear and repression. The time has come to set them free.*)

You have liberated these women in your mind, so you are all set free. Release the covers to every wellspring and fount of My living waters. My light shineth over all, and My rain blesses the land. Rejoice in Me for we are One with all the earth. *Thank You, Holy Spirit, for giving me the key. You nourish the earth and my soul.* (I immediately think of Psalm 23: "He leadeth me beside the still waters; He restoreth My Soul . . .")

25

Mirrors

The other is always a projection of
some unhealed part of your own mind.

September 20, 2013

Holy Spirit, what is Your instruction? We will speak of Hana now, what you call the Garden of Eden, a place of lush vegetation, plentiful fruit, the majesty of the ocean, and clear night skies. Amid the soaring beauties of the earth you came face to face with the "wrath of God" out pictured in one of your roommates. This encounter was planned by Me in the beginning of time to show you both the mirror of rage and the mirror of forgiveness. Yes, I sent you there to have an encounter with "the devil," and it was a mission accomplished. This sounds harsh but is a necessary dissolving of what is called sin. It has to be dramatized for man to see what and how he is living.

One of your roommates verbally attacked you because she heard you speak of reincarnation to a young man you met on the trail in front of your cabin. The thought that you had "tarnished his life and his heart" with the idea of past lives festered in her mind until she exploded with condemnation, later that evening. To her, you had become the incarnation of the devil, leading the children astray and taking their soul's one opportunity for salvation, which is *this* life. She believed that you were now condemned to hell and feared you would die that very night because of what had taken place. As you patiently listened to her, calling on Me every moment to hold the space in love, she finally revealed her deeply hidden guilt, shame, and self-hatred for having been involved in practices regarding past lives. Her pain was palpable, and you knew, while she screamed at you, that she was attacking herself and that this was an opportunity for her to heal a deep wound.

As you called on My help, you heard the message: "Join in prayer." You and both roommates all held hands and prayed for healing to take place. The air in the room became calm as you felt My Peace release the terror that had been present. The frightened roommate now expressed love for you and confessed that she feared you would die that night, unsaved. You both acknowledged the gift of bringing one's unhealed, lingering regrets over past actions into the Light of Christ. You knew these regrets were being healed with My Presence. Later, when you were able to sit with Me, it became clear that this experience was a projection of your own fear of damnation for "rejecting God" at the beginning of time. This had to come up for you, in the context of evangelical Christianity, practiced by your roommates. In the past, you would have kept your distance from anyone who believed in hell, sin, and damnation, but you know these women as lovers of Me. They both express the joy of their intimate relationship with Me, as Jesus, and you have shared your love of Me, with them, during the annual art retreats.

The mirror is a powerful symbol for you. In Hana, it showed you your deeply hidden terror of hellfire and brimstone, clearly out pictured in your roommate's explosion of anger and attack. This fear lingers in the core of every man and must be recognized as such. Your roommate was able to realize, in your calm acceptance of her drama, that it was not real and had no effect on you. Love was clearly present, and you suffered no damage for the imagined transgressions of which you were accused. I held you just as you held her in My Love. She, too, was an expression of Me, showing you the places left unhealed in your own mind. It all had to erupt and be brought to the light.

This trip was an opportunity for you and your roommates to receive My healing for your hidden "sin and guilt." The Son of

God is innocent and can never be other than that. He acts out his drama of separation in all its nasty forms of hate, anger, attack, guilt, shame, and so on, but none of that is ever true. There is only One Truth: God Is. The event that took place in the cabin was a figment of the imagination, to be witnessed and released to Me for healing. You cannot know the depth of the healing that took place for you and your friends. As you review it with Me now, from above the battlefield, the characters get smaller and smaller until they disappear, just flecks of dust in the sunlight. None of it matters as there is nothing of consequence on this earth. It is all made up in the mind, and it will disappear. All that matters is your communion with Me. The stories will be played out in the dream and become opportunities for healing. The other is always a projection of some unhealed part of your own mind. Look at every interaction as an opportunity for Me to heal you and your selves. As you welcome the other, you serve the awakening for you both. You served your soul's salvation in Hana; it was the only thing that held value in your time there. The number of paintings, the number of sunrises and sunsets, the participation in gatherings, makes no difference. All that matters is finding your wholeness with Me as your Self.

26

Close Encounters

I am in charge, and I direct you to meet with all the souls
who are ready to come Home.

September 22, 2013

Holy Spirit, what is Your instruction today? You are coming into a
new estate of shining My Light. You have seen this light reflected
back to you as your unencumbered, brilliant Self. This was
evident as you met with Carrie last night at her condo. Together,
you looked over the beautiful property and saw the ocean reflect
the glory of My setting sun. It felt like you were in a new and
different world, just one building over from where you live. You
are in a different world. The light you carry shines for all those
ready to see. It is My Light that radiates because your mt
personality is no longer in charge. I am in charge, and I direct you
to meet with all the souls who are ready to come Home. Last night
with Carrie you had the experience of speaking to your Self and
your Self speaking back to you. You felt the mirroring as deeply
satisfying, easy, and effortless. This is the joy of being with your
brother and knowing it is part of My plan for you both. Today, at
the gallery, you will meet a man and will invite him to your
condo. This gives you a start. Yes, doubt still lingers, but that will
dissolve when you learn to really trust Me.

Gabby, your friend the chef, called you yesterday, ecstatic
that she has used My messages as a catalyst to start communing
with Me. She wants My instruction for a book she plans to write.
A longtime Denver friend of yours has also used our writing to
awaken to the truth of My Presence from which she has been
hiding for lifetimes. You are seeing the manifestation of My plan

for you and your friends. I am orchestrating your life and everyone's life. Meera is now in Croatia with her husband and her sister. Unencumbered with ego restrictions, Meera willingly went on the trip with Me as her support and guide. She is shining her light and will deliver My Word in ways that would have seemed impossible, just weeks ago. Each of you is fulfilling My mission. Jo is doing My work with the people renovating her home. Yes, the brother who needs the light often appears as a worker/visitor to your home or business and never suspects that a transformation is in store for him, all because of a "chance" encounter. This is the way of it.

You, Jo, and Meera are not yet clear about the means for the unfolding of our books. I will guide your every step. Yesterday, you and Jo were finalizing the dates for Jo and her husband to fly to Maui to work on the editing of Book 1. That is My Will. You need to do this project jointly, calling on Me to be present with you and to guide you through each "correction." You now look at your desk where this work will take place, torn apart where a new water heater will be installed. A "mess of years" had to be stripped from the shelves so the desk could be moved. This is a symbolic cleansing, necessary for the coming together of My Will and My books. A clean workspace is vital so nothing can distract you. Even the installation of the correct water heater is part of My plan.

The editing for Book 1 will continue between you and Jo, knowing that I am the final proofreader. Together, you will prepare a preview copy for a few select readers and for a publisher who will appear when the timing is right. It will all fall into place. You each feel the assurance of that promise because you have witnessed such gratitude from those who have been introduced to the writing. Your sister is a perfect example of one who has come to know and trust My Presence in her life through reading My words. She also witnesses how you live My instruction. The demonstration of leading your life in trust and surrender to Me is the most powerful way that others can see the truth of these written words. That is why you, Jo, and Meera were chosen to fulfill My plan. After years of working together to release your projections, your minds had cleared enough for you to hear My Voice and willingly bring the books into form. They will be found by those meant to receive them. This is the way they have chosen to come to know Me, a choice made at the beginning of time. You have been doing your jobs faithfully as a threesome to come to this point of publishing. It will all unfold as I will.

Enjoy your day, and watch for My friend who will cross your path. Invite him to your home. It will happen, even though you wonder in this moment how My prediction will be received by all the readers if he doesn't show up. Thank you, mt, for honestly being willing to admit that you still have a way to go. This is the meaning of the dream you had before you woke up this morning, where you saw two large, horned tomato worms crawling out of their shell-like cocoons. They were so large they filled your mind screen. The worms seemed strong, aware, completed, and ready to enter the world. It was a pleasure for you to witness. When you woke up you wanted to believe that they had made their full transition to enlightenment but realized that thought would have been symbolized by butterflies. You have further to go. Take each step as it comes. It is all perfectly planned. Good day!

27

Concept of Form

*Look at the lingering tendency to seek specialness
in My eyes and in the eyes of your brothers.*

September 23, 2013

Holy Spirit, what is Your instruction? You just reviewed the dream you had a few nights ago where you were given the key to unlock the covers to the founts of living water on your property. Your father had dug a very deep hole in the ground, a pit, and you thought it would become the foundation for a new home. This morning, you realized that the large opening was an enormous grave. An image of the mass graves, filled to the brim with skeletons during the Holocaust, entered your mind. Yes, the pit in your dream awaits the collection and destruction of all your many selves. That sounds cruel, and you wish that I would use gentler wording. The disappearance of this universe is not to be gentle. Death to the selves is death to the ego. There is only the Living Water of the Christ Self or nothing. Accepting this truth is the final step and the hardest to accomplish because of the total attachment to your body as your self.

The grave represents the end of time, the end of all things perceived in the world of form. Your main identification is with bodies, yet they will be demolished, decayed, and will "die." They have no use other than as vehicles to serve My Purpose: to return you to your Essence as the Thought of God. This world is not real. It is only a figment of your imagination, part of what you experience as a made up, consensual "reality." All the many selves are separate parts of you that you will recognize as such and release to Me "for the burning in the mass grave."

Your body is Not your Self. The body is an idea of separation, projected onto a screen that you call the world. It seems totally real, but is no more real than the images you watch on a movie screen. You must see that each dream figure represents some aspect of the Son who imagined he could live apart from truth and love. Yes, this is about giving up the concept of form in all its iterations. Last night you had a dream where you were given a very large bar of soap, your favorite kind, in a shape that pleased you. As you held it in your hand, you tried to ignore that it was dirty and smelled strange. It also seemed to be hollow. You wanted it so badly that you decided to take it on a journey, a detour from the path you had planned for that morning. You placed the soap in a cart and pulled it along until the time came for you to take another look. You held the soap with the willingness to "see the truth of it" and realized it was fake, rubber, like the pink skin of a baby doll. Then you noticed what was contained in its hollow core: a plastic starfish, known to be poisonous. Your eyes saw through the delusion that came from a deep desire for this gift to be real. You see so clearly now that the image of something you thought should bring you joy was just a shell that concealed a lifeless trinket. The gift had no value, yet you had convinced yourself it was especially given to serve your desires. You also believed you could trust the giver, a stranger, whom you had met on the path.

Trust no "givers of gifts" on this path you call life. Each one is just a figment of your imagination, and you will make him into whatever your ego desires at the time. You will see in every one who crosses your path an answer to a "prayer" for ego satisfaction, someone to fulfill your needs for power, recognition, support, love, approval; the list goes on and on, never ending. Yesterday, I said that you would meet My friend as you worked in the gallery. You eagerly looked at everyone as the special one. You fantasized that he would be someone who would hold the same belief system as you and that you would share intimately your understanding of Me. You looked forward to the unfolding of the mystery and telling the story in today's writing.

You knew that a lesson was to be learned but ignored the deeper thought that no one could show up and that I, the Holy Spirit, was only preparing you for what you are now being told. You went to the gallery and were ready to accept everyone who came in as a holder of a message from Me, the giver of a very special gift that would make you both "important" in My eyes. You understand the fallacy of that concept, but you must look at the lingering tendency to seek specialness in My eyes and in the eyes of your brothers. This propensity is being reflected when those who see your light are drawn to you and want to be with you. They are being touched by My Presence within you, and they speak to you because of your perceived specialness. Your presence has served some aspect of their own personality, as well as stimulating their desire to know Me.

The ego loves to be recognized for its gifts, but as you saw in your soap dream, the ego's gifts are hollow. Only I know the heart of the brothers, and only I can give what is needed and right for them on their journey to Me. I am the Essence of Love and can open every brother to the love that he is. You, as an mt body, are only a skin, a rubber doll, a plastic starfish, posing as My representative. I am the only Reality. You do not yet have Vision. You cannot look into their souls and see that they are all, at their core, facets of Me and reflections of the Essence we all share. Only I am Real, and only I know the Way. Show up and let My Light shine, and I will do whatever their soul requires. Call on Me in every moment to be present for each interaction. Everyone who comes to your door, enters your gallery, or crosses your path is an aspect of the One Son having a dream that he is real. It is time to toss the costumes into the tomb and let the Light of God shine across the earth before it disappears. Then, all that is left is God. Now prepare the space for your new water heater. It offers an

abundance of warm water which represents My Living Waters.
Enjoy your day.

28

All Is in Order

Have no expectations about the next step in this journey.

September 24, 2013

Holy Spirit, what is Your instruction this morning? Today is the anniversary of your move to Maui, ten years ago. Celebrate what you have achieved over this decade in your journey to know Me as your voice and your life. You feel tears of gratitude for that now. We have come far together, from the time you heard My Call to leave your husband and your home to making the move to a place where you would be perfectly positioned to find the One you have always searched for. You have gone through many teachers, readings, and lessons and have arrived home with Me. You see how perfectly orchestrated each moment, each encounter of your life on Maui has been. It was not about moving to a much sought-after place of retirement. Your move was a true answer to a true call. I spoke to you and you heard My request to leave your former life behind and begin anew with Me. This releasing of the old and embracing the new also took place symbolically for you yesterday, when you feared you were getting the wrong kind of water heater but the right one arrived on schedule. It came just in time for you to celebrate this transition from old energy to the new energy of My living waters.

Another shift came when a "Dear John" letter arrived from Marie, who has been reading the daily writing. She clearly and kindly informed you that this writing was not understandable to her and said she wanted to commune with Me in the way that had been more comfortable, prior to meeting you. You depended on her as the one who would take care of your affairs as executor of your estate at the end of your life and were relieved that she would honor the books in their dissemination after your death. This dependency on her was an imposition that had to be released because it interfered with the honest flow of communication for both of you. You no longer want to have any expectations that could interfere with the communication of My Word. Each must be free to receive Me in their custom designed way. Marie needed to be part of the journey with you and to release that journey. The timing was Mine and was perfect to serve both of you and the books. Everything is in order. Be free and open. Have no expectations about the next steps.

Before you woke up this morning I gave you a dream about Marie. In the dream, she was sitting next to your gallery boss. They were in a lovely wooded area, like Hana. You smiled at each other and let Marie know that everything is fine. It was a simple, loving, respectful appreciation and release. Marie has been a projection of an inner fear that you "can't complete the task" and would need an external savior to care for all the elements of your life you believed you couldn't manage. She appeared on the external plane and offered to handle the publishing after your death. She represented both the resolution to your fear of death, and your fear that you would not complete the task of putting the books into the world. Now that you fully, as fully as possible at this time, rely on My Presence and My Solution to every concern that arises, you trust I will be the one to make sure that all your end-of-life affairs, and the publishing, will take place. Everything of your supposed life on earth is in My hands, and you acknowledge that, as Marie leaves and a new energy comes in. Everything is symbolic. Without symbols of form you would not understand the significance of these life transitions in the mind.

It is time to take a breath and celebrate the ten years of hard work to establish a relationship with Me and with your friends and partners, Jo and Meera. They, too, are projections of your mind, as is Marie. They are the parts of your mind that are determined to reach the goal and will do whatever it takes to reach it. Everything came together on the eve of the anniversary of your move to Maui, and everything is now prepared for your next step with the books. This is how I work and nothing is out of place. You will see this more and more as you watch everything in your life unfold in My perfection and in the perfect timing for you to understand. I just had you look out onto your lanai and see the sunlight creating a beautiful rainbow over the West Maui Mountains. This is My promise to you for a New Life in Me in the coming decades.

29

Limitless Tools

Your own soul is fully aware of My Presence
and knows Me as its Self.

September 25, 2013

Holy Spirit, what is Your instruction? You have been given an overview of My role for you in this lifetime. Last night you witnessed the out picturing of the meaning of My placing you on Maui. You were invited to hear the Kamehameha school's presentation of the recent voyage of a sailing canoe to Nihoa, a rock island jutting from the middle of the sea. The canoe was navigated by a young woman, trained from birth by her father to witness the stars and use them as tools to guide her way. To demonstrate to the audience the means of using the heavens as her compass the young woman placed small lights in a circle on lauhala mats. She pointed out the four directions starting with the setting sun, shown in blue lights, and then marked all the subdivisions of the sky — the quadrants — in tiny, golden tea lights. She showed how the constellations, as they rise and set, could point the way. When stars cannot be seen, she explained that the currents of the ocean and the presence of birds would guide sailors to their destination. During the evening, you had no awareness of the symbolization of what I was showing you. This is your dream and she is your projection. The meaning of the evening is now to be revealed.

You had momentarily forgotten that in 1827, your great grandfather used these same navigational means to sail to Nihoa and had sketched it in his journals. Yes, it all comes together. You see now why I placed you "in the center," where you also could be a pointer of signs leading to Me. Let this sink in to your full awareness. We are not speaking about the dream character mt, not about a body and personality that can barely assimilate what is being explained. This is about your own soul that is fully aware of My Presence and knows Me as its Self. I am that One Who you Are. I am the Self, fulfilling our joint will to bring light to this dark world. This is Our Mission. Your tears stream in recognition of this. Encompass it now without ego. We are navigators of the Way Home through the use of one of My limitless tools to show those who are asleep a means to awaken. That is the purpose of our Book, one of billions upon billions of means to bring man to the Light of his Essence as the Son of God.

You are a bearer of the Light because it is our will to awaken the sleeping masses. We bring this tool, the Book, to those who are ready to listen. Its light will set in motion a series of remembrances to bring the reader back to the beginning of time when he decided to follow his own path rather than the Way of God. Each word you type has My Power, My Energy within it. Each word connects with another word, another phrase, another concept that will trigger a certain desire for a reader to go deeper, to learn more. This begins their opening to Me as the navigator of their ship, their body, their mind. I am the only Pointer of the Way Home because I am Everything. The speaker last night indicated that the deepest experience of her journey in the canoe was the feeling of My Presence guiding her, though she named it the *Aumakua* — a Hawaiian ancestor spirit guide. I come in all forms, all symbols of the Power to Light the Way. When you, the reader, show up in the company of another, remember that you are like the laser beam used last night by the speaker, pointing to the stars and setting out the lights to mark a pathway to the heavens.

You each carry My Light and it need not be hidden. Uncover your light and let it shine. When you remember Me, a switch is turned on, and My Light shines from your mind into all minds. A chain reaction is set in motion, and the awakening to the presence of the light begins. In the dawning, the darkness is released, and all the world takes on a new expression. What was once veiled can now be rediscovered. Everything is within you. Nothing is lacking in your connection with Me. I have always been at your core, and have led you each step of the way. Recognize the flickering of My signposts. The books are a means to understand that I am Present within each of you; I have been there forever, and I will remain forever. Your path has been set since the beginning of time and the route to Me will be found. You are awakening now to the knowing that I am the Way, the Truth, and the Life. You can trust that I know each step and each breath of the journey, which in the mind has already been accomplished and is just awaiting that recognition. You never left your Home in God but are having a dream that you are still lost at sea. The time is coming when you will recognize the signs that point the way to your memory of God, and the return to safe Harbor.

Holy Spirit, this is the most powerful lesson yet, knowing that I am only a pointer, a symbol, like every other thing in this cosmos. A grain of sand, a crab on the rocks, garbage, pits of skeletons are all the same. As a body/personality, I am merely a symbol. Nothing. Thank You for the freeing of my light, a light to serve only You.

30

What Do You Want?

*You have a choice each moment to join with My Love
or to look upon a false world of fear and self-deprecation.*

September 26, 2013

Dream: I am upstairs in a building, perhaps a school. I see a woman who says she wants to sleep. A white lamb with a human face is lying limply at her feet. I offer the woman a place to lie down in the building but then decide to take her home with me. We walk together with the lamb to the wide, empty street where the snow has melted in the center. There is only the horizon before us and we see nothing but the next step. Then I remember I do not have the key to my house because it is lost, along with my purse. I wonder how I will get inside.

Holy Spirit, what would You say? This is the depiction of where you are on the journey home. You have released all encumbrances and are free to take one step at a time, surrendered to Me. I lead the way so neither key nor purse is needed. I am the only Solution. The time for symbols is nearing an end as you are seeing with My Vision. You willingly receive the flock that needs your shepherding, and you point the way home. Yes, you are a pointer.

Holy Spirit, Susan just informed me that her ex-husband has died. It feels to me that he is a paper doll, here and gone, one of my selves who is now free yet who is also a part of my Self. Maybe I should have felt more compassion for Susan and her daughter, but my "emotion" is focused only on the journey with You.

You are not without emotion or compassion but are becoming detached from the drama of this world. Susan's ex-husband lived

103

as he had planned, to experience life without true purpose: without love, connection, or the awareness of My Presence. Yes, he had friends, but his life was without substance. He will review it with Me and choose again. In his next lifetime he will seek Me and find liberation. Nothing is lost. We are looking at death impersonally.

Susan is a very loving soul. She feels deeply for her family in the pain of their life's circumstances. She must stand back with Me now and ask to look objectively at their lives. They are dream characters on her stage, a dramatic representation of her own life, depicting the absence of true and satisfying connections with husband, child, home, and work. Susan will acknowledge that the experience of living with her husband all those years was a projection of the negativity she felt about herself. That pattern was released when she lovingly gave of herself to her daughter and ex-husband. Now she has a new life in the light with Me and is feeling the rightness of her choice. As she shines her light, she sees that many others desire engagement with her. She is now free to live her life in joy.

Until you see your mirror and own the projection of all your self-hatred upon another, you can never be free. Susan's daughter has another opportunity to examine her own life. She needed the impetus of her father's death to take a hard look at the destructive choices he made. This is a great gift, and it will be a turning point for her as she makes the choice between a life of self-affliction or one of self-affirmation, modeled by her mother. No one can decide for her. Susan can observe but not advise. Her daughter must meet the depths of her own soul. I am with her always.

Everything is in perfect order. You lack nothing. You have a choice each moment to join with My Love as the Essence of who you are, or to look upon a false world of fear and self-deprecation. Love is who you are in truth, and a change of mind will allow you to live it.

31

The Opposite of Duality

Remember that special love or special hate is just the same.

September 27, 2013

Holy Spirit, what is Your instruction? Susan's ex-husband appeared to you as a representation of evil. You were repulsed by what he stood for and you believed his life of guns and swastikas was inhuman. He repelled you. You now see him as a paper doll, a story with no substance, just a room in your mind where darkness dwells (*burning in chest*). That room has vanished. What you called evil is gone and has no reality for you now. The symbol had to die in your mind, your heart; it was only an idea of hatred and abuse. Now you see his life as a smoke screen, just a veil to hide Me. He was in your dream life so you could also see the opposite of duality. Remember that special love or special hate is just the same. Neither are real. There is either fear and darkness, or Love and Light. This will become the experience for Susan and her daughter, given their capacity to understand. Your mind is clear. The thought of evil went poof, vanished, died, and is of no consequence to you. It was just an idea, symbolized by Susan's ex-husband. There is no longer a need for it to fill your mind. The energy of "Satan"—the belief in evil, ego, separation—opposites to Love, has left the house.

Your goal in this life is to awaken. It is happening now, assisted in your mind by the death of your former brother-in-law. He was a symbol of fear, but you know he "lives" as a part of you. You now can feel him in your mind as a brilliant shining light, free of all attachment to any darkness or evil to which he identified himself in this life. You welcome him home and see his wholeness and innocence. Send this message to your niece to help her release attachment to fear and darkness. She will come to understand her father as a "concept" that no longer serves her.

I get it, Holy Spirit. There really are no bodies, no world of form. The belief that they are real obstructs my acceptance of what You are teaching, that there is no "out there" out there. Yes, this is correct, but your mind has to shift to see this as reality. My Mind has many mansions, many rooms, each representing "a story of a life in form" with no substance and no value other than to be recognized as such. No form exists. Only the Mind of God is Real. This recognition is the collapse of the universe as you know it. You will understand this more fully in time. Enough for now.

32

Deleting the Dream

*Forgive whatever the brother triggers in you
because you know it has revealed a belief that must be
recognized as just a cover over your innocence.*

September 28, 2013

Holy Spirit, what is Your instruction? Yesterday, I spoke of death and its meaning to you. Your sister's ex-husband represented a space in your mind defined as darkness, hatred, and evil. Until you imagined death as an "empty room" you did not know that such a space existed. In its blackness it was invisible. This is the condition of the ego mind, the mind we have been working to set free by looking at all the thousands of layers that have covered the light and truth of Me. When you saw the mind's image of what had been "the dark room" now appear as a clear space filled with a soft, warm light, you realized it represents all the work you have done to take back projections. Those judgments included the past distain for your former brother-in-law. You have come to realize that he was a man lost in his own darkness with no apparent way to see the light. Your work on yourself had shown you just how immersed you had been in the darkness of the belief in separation, no different from everyone else on this earth. Last June, I told you that your niece and sister would be set free after her ex-husband's death. You had not then realized that they were projections from your mind, and that I was predicting that you would be set free as you held them in your mind space. This is how it works.

Your sister's ex-husband symbolizes "all the evil" you believe is part of you, brought forth when you believed you separated from God. To leave God would make you the "opposite of God" and therefore evil. This thought is what "created" the universe. Everything in this world of form and bodies is based on the belief that one holds evil as his core makeup, the belief that "I am bad." The focus of man's life becomes the eradication of his badness, but he does not understand its origin, which is the only way he can be free. When he ultimately comes to know his innocence, he will reunite with God, and the world will disappear. Until that time, his "badness" is so reprehensible that it must be projected onto everything outside of him. Man is unconscious of the underlying "experience" of separation and therefore is unaware that he is compelled by the force of his ego mind to look at everyone as a receptacle for the hatred that he unknowingly carries for himself.

Your ex-brother-in-law projected his unconscious self-hatred onto Hitler, and filled his house with Nazi mementos, which you now see as just figments of his repressed mind. He was unaware that he was replaying, as a dream character, his belief in the separation. Because of the work you have done to uncover the belief in your own darkness, you could understand that this dream character was exactly the same as you: a Divine Being, the Christ Self, clothed in an ego-made costume. When the brother is seen as a mirror of what is hidden in your wrong mind, you are on the path to freedom. This is what is meant by forgiveness. You forgive whatever the brother triggers in you because you know it has revealed a belief that must be recognized as just a cover over your innocence.

This is a big lesson and must be looked at through My Vision. We are deleting the dream of form and coming to the realization that there is nothing but the Light. Each room in your mind is being cleansed of all remaining spots of darkness. Every brother is a picture of you because he holds a symbolic representation of what is still in your mind. When you have released that particular form of fear, abandonment, betrayal, resistance, and so on, it will fade away, and that space in your mind will fill with light. I am telling every reader to look at your brother and ask, "What about this brother still annoys me?" and "What sets me off with judgment when he is in my presence or thought?" Explore where that experience lies inside of you and ask for My guidance. Together, we will uncover it all and you will see the Light that was, and is, always there.

33

Second Coming

As My symbol, you represent a part of the Mind of Christ.

September 29, 2013

Holy Spirit, what is Your instruction this day? You see the veils now lifting in those who are close to you as they come into estates of love and joy. Gabby is in Bali, which she says is the closest she has come to paradise. The joy of knowing Me is expanding, and she is bursting with its expression, mirrored back to her everywhere she looks. Yesterday, your friend Ingrid expressed her peace and understanding of My Presence in her life. The lifting of the veils has brought her the desire to dwell with Me in silence. Zoe demonstrates and expresses love in the tender care she gives her aging and ailing parents. Your sister expresses the communion and trust of My guidance as she receives the gifts of her new home in a place of light. Every day, you see reflected in Jo and Meera their ongoing awakening to My Presence as ruler of their lives. This awareness has opened them to greater communion with their families and friends, in ways you or they could never have imagined. Your new water tank sits beside you, symbolizing a new relationship with Me, one that is automatic and unencumbered. Finally, a new light post was dug in front of your parking space, a sign for you to shine the beacon of My Light to all the selves in your mind. Everything in your life is a symbol of Me, as are you.

As My symbol, you represent a part of the Mind of Christ. You are experiencing a "Coming of the Light"—the second coming of Christ—the Return to your memory of God. Everything is coming together now to greet the new day, the dawning of the realization that you are no longer asleep. This journey has taken eons and now is the time for its fulfillment. It can only be seen through its manifestation in a brother whose similar openings will mirror back your own. Remember, you are your brother and your brother is you. As you set him free in your own mind, he too will experience that freedom in his world. This is all being orchestrated by Me because I am in charge of your life. I am the One Who forms your mind. There is nothing outside of Me. All thought comes from Me. Your ego is no longer the primary interpreter of what you perceive, and this allows you to see with My Vision.

Holy Spirit, what is the meaning of seeing the dolphin this morning, the sunrise, and a cardinal on my railing that sat right in the space where I had cut a leaf to view the mountains. This is your vision now with Me. You see everything as My greeting to you. I am the dolphin leaping from the water showing you his tail, the tale we are weaving together. I am the sun rising to meet you for a new day. I am the cardinal in full glory entering your home through the opening you have created to receive Me. I am you, and We are One Self.

34

Go with the Flow

Your experience with Me is real in the Mind
which is a symbol of the container for God's Love.

September 30, 2013

Holy Spirit, I had a beautiful birthday today, paddling, yoga, lunch, and seeing Eleykaa at the Marriott, where she shows her art. Do You have a message for the book today? Yes. You are seeing reflections of the awakening. You bought your friend's beautiful painting of the butterfly over the pink lotus, her first sale in a new venue. You both celebrate My Presence in your lives. On your way to the parking lot you noticed a sign on a car: "Awakening in Paradise," with an image of a lotus blossom. Yes, the reflections of the awakening are everywhere you look, and sometimes you think you should be in bliss and ecstasy with the joy that it promises. You do feel gratitude for the coming together of all the many selves. That is all you need to feel. The ego would make your feelings wrong by saying they are not enough to "prove" that your experience with Me is real. It is real in the Mind, which is a symbol of the container for God's Love.

You are in My flow and you have no expectations or preconceived notions about anything. This is the way it must be in every relationship, even though they appear to shift and change. That is how the world is constructed, but you have no concern, knowing I am in charge of all happenings. Nothing in the world can be depended upon because it is influenced by billions of factors beyond your control. The ego would like to take charge of each relationship and have its outcomes be real, but that cannot happen because the ego has no control over anything, except to place you in fear and uncertainty. Let it go and trust only in Me.

35

No Imperfection

Rest in the Stillness of God Is.

October 2, 2013

Holy Spirit, what is Your instruction this morning? You are Mine. We unite in the silence. Yesterday, you were reminded of the silence as you sat by the quiet of the waves. Later, you listened to the Eckhart Tolle CDs of his book, *Stillness Speaks* which you had not heard for many years. Now you understand what he is saying. In essence, you have reached the stillness. You have embraced Me as the Essence of you, the Presence that comes from stillness. You do have a monkey mind that chatters throughout the day and night, but it is lessening. Last night before you went to sleep, the chatter disappeared for considerable periods of time. And yes, it does take your desire and will, My Will, for that to happen. There will be a time when everything is just "what is." A few years ago, you had that experience of the mind quieting, accompanied with the understanding that the world is an illusion. It lasted for two whole days, leaving you with the knowing that My Presence is in you and in everyone on earth. All the readers of this book will experience My Stillness within. I am there and they will know Me. The time for their awakening is in My hands. It will happen. Be patient. Take each step toward that union as it is given.

You woke up to the scent of heavy smoke this morning from the burning of the sugar cane. You accepted it as "that is the way on Maui." Smoke is symbolic of the burning of ego layers, happening for each reader. The act of reading My messages lights a fire within the heart/mind that sets into motion a chain reaction of events that will lead to the disappearance of the universe, as

115

you know it. The lies, the belief in what is "real," must be brought to the flame. As the mistaken beliefs are recognized they will be heaped onto the smoldering embers, ready for new conflagration. This is repeated endlessly each time a truth is recognized and an untruth exposed. When the lies have been burned, the Light of God will be all there is left to see. Unlike firelight, God's Light has no trace of imperfection. It is whole and all embracing. Everything and everyone is part of that Light. The dross has been removed to leave what is pure. We are Pure, Holy, Spirit. Nothing can tarnish the Light of Our Being. Every reader is joined with Me as One, the One Son of God. Embrace this concept today in your stillness.

Look beyond the hills and mountains, plains and fields, forests and meadows, and know they are all just covers over the Light of Love's Essence. You believe the mirages that make up your world are real. No. They are but figments of your imagination that would cover the knowing of who you truly are: One with God. Go beyond form; go deep into the center of your Being, the symbolic burning core of your earth, the flaming heart of the galaxy. Know that you live in the Center of All Existence, the Heart of God. It is your Home where you reside beyond the universe. I give each of you this message today. Hear it. You are disappearing in form to come to the truth that only Unity exists, even though the ego would have you believe the opposite.

Today, in your country, the US government is shutting down. The ego factions are warring and cannot come to agreement. There is no right or wrong in the play of the battle among the major political parties. They are merely symbols of conflict in the mind of man between the ego that would keep the status quo and the truth that no world exists. The belief in the original separation is being enacted to its fullest, yet you can circumvent it as you leave "the smoke and fire" and dip into the cooling balm of My Stillness. Spend your day turning within. Leave the warring world and the burning cane fields and rest in Me. Rest in the Stillness of God Is. Nothing else exists.

36

Bed of Roses

You are asleep, having a dream of form while
surrounded by My Love.

October 3, 2013

Holy Spirit, what is Your instruction today? We will continue the writing we began at 4:30 this morning, after you woke from a very significant dream. This was a dream for all your selves, all the selves of the universe. It was an out picturing of My Love represented in this life of form. In the dream, I was there as an "invisible Friend" with whom you speak while we watch a parade of two floats covered in white satin. There is a child on the first float and a young woman lying on a bed on the second float. Each is surrounded by a thick wreath of red roses that form a heart shape around the length of their dark-skinned body. Both are lying on their sides, and you assume they are dead, or maybe just the younger one is dead. The woman, who appears closer to you, is clearly in a comfortable, peaceful sleep, and you notice that her body is in the same position that you sleep. In the dream, you just observe without judgment or emotion.

What is Your interpretation of this dream? You are no different from that young woman lying on her bed. This is you in the stillness, moving through the silent city of the dream world. There is no one else around except your invisible Friend. Yes, I am that Constant Presence in your energetic field. You see the two bodily dream images of your selves: dark-skinned, Spanish, Indian, it doesn't matter. The young woman was "lying on the bier" in the same position that you are now writing this, reclining in your bed. This scene is an out picture of you scribing in the Presence of My

Love. My words surround you like flowers in a heart-shaped wreath. The bed of roses in the dream is not quite a "funeral procession" but is a display of a sleeper who is awake, yet does not realize it. This is who you are, in the stillness of the morning, while I dictate My words to you.

The light from the new lamp pole in your parking lot now shines into the bedroom where you sleep, another reminder of how our Presence/Being is out pictured in symbols of love. I am the Light of the world. You are the Light of the world. Take this in. It is all happening in a dream. Your writing happens in a dream. In the mind, where the words come from, we are One and the same. The sleeping woman in your dream is a symbol of you. She is your Heart demonstrating the love in you, especially when doing My work. It is being seen, felt, and recognized by those around you. My Love for you is the same as My Love for all your selves, every member of humanity. There is no feeling of specialness as you write and see these images. This is a description of each reader. As I speak to the readers, the images presented become "their dream" pictured now in a book. Each one of you must understand that you are asleep, having a dream of form, surrounded by My Love. To one awake, this message is clear. You will all wake up to My Presence as your Truth.

37

See Your Light

*Look at all things that appear disabled, sick, dying,
or decaying as "just the way of the world."*

October 4, 2013

Holy Spirit, what is Your instruction this morning? We shall review more of yesterday's happenings, where I gave you a glimpse of living in the real world, a world with full awareness that everything is orchestrated by Me. You saw that every event was held in My Love, from the connection with an old Sufi friend to the failure of your car battery and its replacement. Each element of your day fell into place without a hitch. In the morning, you were surprised to find an e-mail from a Sufi friend, after thinking of her just moments before. Later, you were shocked to see your Sufi teacher's given name printed in the cement right in front of where you sat at the service station while talking to Jo on your cell phone. The two of you were reminiscing about the loving embrace you had felt from your Sufi community. Then you told Jo of your dream of roses, the symbol of love for the Sufis.

Yes, every single thing is planned, like returning to your condo parking space last evening and seeing that the brand new lamp was lit for the first time. It is the symbol for turning on "your light" in a recognizable way for you and the world. In the mind, your lamp is lit but you still need symbol upon symbol to receive that message. Your Sufi teacher named you Munira. It means "she who sheds light on others." At the time, you couldn't quite take that in, but your love for the Sufi community allowed you to embrace your Sufi name/My Name for you. Shining My Light is your role in this life. The new lamppost, lit in the space of your vehicle with its new battery, is the body of mt lit with the Christ Light, and ready to serve Me in the world. Take this in now.

The imagery I use to describe "you" is designed for the mt character to finally understand who she is. It is the same process for every reader, although it will appear in different symbols/forms for his or her custom course. Each of you is a light shining your essence into the world. But know that in the dense world of form the recognition of one's light and the light that shines in your brother are hard won. As all the blocks to true sight are removed, the awareness comes that you are Pure Love and Light. This knowing is really the goal of your earthly life.

(Later) *Holy Spirit, what is Your instruction for the rest of the day?* You just learned that the new car battery from yesterday was deficient and you will need a replacement. All is in order because it is being managed by Me. These "glitches" in the flow of your life are part of what is. Each glitch or apparent obstacle must take place because it has been pre-scripted. Yes, you are fulfilling a prescription set at the beginning of time. You wonder why we have written about the new energy and now report that it is inadequate. This is another big reminder that the world of form is not real. Rely no more on this world for your sustenance. You identify with your vehicle, whether it is the body you inhabit or the car you drive. Neither of them is real. They represent impersonations of the Spirit of God that you are. Look at all things that appear disabled, sick, dying, or decaying as "just the way of the world." Everything in the world is in some degree of dying and appears to need replacement. You can replace dead batteries but not dead bodies. Your body is decaying before your eyes, and in your present "old age" you cannot miss the increasing wrinkles and sagging belly. It is uncomfortable and sometimes painful to see, but that is the way of form. It has no reality beyond its temporary function in the dream, and you must detach from it.

All things serve the purpose and message of the dream, which is purely a map to get you home, albeit there are many detours. A dying battery is a clear signal to get a replacement and the way is always shown to a solution. But a solution in form is not our purpose. The one and only Solution is to reunite with your true Essence, as the Son of God. Once you look beneath all the conflicts, mishaps, and breakdowns of imaginary, worldly things, you will open your eyes to the perfection behind each one.

When the Son of God decided to go off and play on his own he thought up a world to substitute for his lost connection with God. That world was faulty, made without the input of his Creator. The faulty world still identifies with the ego mind that believes its reality is manifested in a body. This is the belief from which you awaken. The world of thought is not real. Who do you choose to interpret this thought-world? Is it your Self, or is it the ego that would control and run the show? Yes, it is all a show, a movie, a dream of no substance. I am the Energy behind this world of form, the One Who interprets it with the Mind of God. You are given the choice of what to believe, every moment. With My guidance you will come to know that nothing of form exists and that your Self, as the Spirit of God, is all that does exist. Your battery will repeatedly run low to get you to take yet another look at what empowers you, what gives you your aliveness, what gives you the will to awaken. I am the One who runs the ship of life. Hand the wheel to Me and let Me bring you home under My Power.

Holy Spirit, why do I feel out of alignment today after feeling so aware of being in a dream, yesterday? You are vacillating now between Self and ego. This is normal because the ego wants to overcompensate with its agenda for every move you make to join with Me. This is the way of it. You are doing what is necessary, observing its actions and deferring to Me. Tomorrow you will shift back to the feeling of connection and surety. Keep calling on

Me as you have been. Don't take this world seriously. Have fun. It will all go smoothly according to My plan.

38

Tree of Life

*I am everything you see, think, hear, and smell,
and you no longer need to cling to all the symbols.*

October 6, 2013

Holy Spirit, what is Your instruction? You have come very far in the last day. This is the anniversary of your party with friends in Denver, one year ago. At that party, you were symbolically completing your connections with the earth (*tears*). It was a letting go of all the important connections to your life in this society of dream characters. You also saw this yesterday when you realized you were detaching from the Banyan Tree relationships. For many years, I directed you to the Banyan Tree, a place for you to demonstrate the truth of your reality in Me while mt sold her art. I am the tree and I am its branches, its berries, its aerial roots. Every nesting mynah bird is a symbol of you awakening to the light of dawn and flying home to Me. You have often gone early to the tree, way before dawn to watch this ritual of awakening and have loved every minute. You have wondered how all the thousands of birds know which direction to fly to reach their destination. Now you are in touch with Me, the once unknown Director of it all. I am everything you see, think, hear, and smell, and you no longer need to cling to all the symbols. You need not fly beyond the seen world to find Me when you know Me in your heart. We are together at a new point in the process of awakening.

Yesterday, you could feel the fading away of your attachment to the Lahaina Art Society and the Banyan Tree experience. The love and connection with the special life you had shared with friends, coworkers, the homeless, the birds, the tree itself, all seemed gray and lifeless. The tie to its specialness is gone, and you realize you no longer have a real connection with anyone under the tree or within the Society. You are not special to them, nor are they to you. It is just the way of it. This dream of symbols no longer serves because you have Me. I am the Tree of Life for you now. I take full precedence in your life, the Only One Who gives you sustenance. I know where you should be placed just as the mynahs know their way home at every dusk. You have shed many tears as you have let go of the remaining attachments to your life on this earth. The break from the tree and art fair is My choice to show you symbolically that I know the way, and it is time to interrupt your connection energetically to the tree and recognize your total connection with Me.

You wonder what you are being asked to do now regarding your involvement with the Art Society. It will be revealed and you will be given clear signs and instructions about the next steps. Go now and do your job in the gallery, and I will direct you. You know your true focus in life is the completion of the books. I will clarify everything, and all you need will be provided. Your editing with Jo will be very productive, and I will be present all the way. Now make your breakfast and walk. We will continue to commune throughout the day.

39

Point of Transition

Put away what no longer serves.

October 7, 2013

Holy Spirit, what is Your instruction? You just sent a prayer and My words to a friend. You realized it would be a message for anyone who is "suffering" with a belief in illness. That is true. When your friend e-mailed this morning requesting your prayers, you asked and received My answer for her. Yesterday, you wanted a message for another friend whose mother had died. I am there for everyone. You are seeing this new role materialize for you as you disperse My messages and My wisdom. Last night you dreamed that you were My messenger. You, Jo, and Meera are all serving Me in this way and must receive this lesson as given directly to you. This is not to be taken as any special attribute associated with the ego personality. Everyone reading this book is a carrier and disseminator of My Word. The goal is to come to the place of knowing that I am your fount of wisdom and My knowledge is the truth of your being.

In your dream last night you were among a group of artists who were preparing for an evening of prayer. One of the members was putting away her wooden easel, like the one you use. You noticed she had not cleaned off the thick glue that covered the pin that held the easel together, so you set about to finish the job. In the meantime, she had prepared a seat for herself in a chair that was the same shape as your favorite chair. Hers was covered in simple, earthy, nondescript material, along with two pillows. It was unassuming but appeared comfortable and welcoming. Now awake, you see unmistakably that the easel and the chair were yours. The dream was telling you that you must put away what no longer serves and accept the seat, a placement in life, which has now become clear. In the dream, you were clearing the point of the easel. The easel is for art, but that no longer serves you. I now appoint you to take the seat of disseminator of My wisdom. This is not about mt, the character you play in this lifetime, who thought she was an artist or any of the other roles she assumed throughout her life. She is a vehicle for My Word, and I have made that very clear this past week with symbols: a new lamp was stationed at her parking space, and a new battery was placed in her vehicle. Mt has been given clear direction that her art career is coming to a close. Symbol after symbol will announce the next stage of one's life. This is how I make Myself clear.

Jo also had an experience to assist her in disseminating My Word. Her overnight stay in a hospital was symbolic of her new role. She experienced shortness of breath and had dreamed of a faucet flushing out a blockage. She knew these symbols indicated that a visit to the ER was in order. No blockage was found, but she knows that any obstacle to My Sight or My Word must be seen and flushed away. Jo is in no danger and accepts her experience as part of My mission for her. In the hospital, she extended My Peace and Love to all those she met. The transition point for each of you will made clear so you can take your new seat, your new role. Accept My appointment, and place it above all others. No matter where you are, or what you do, you are bearers of My message. In the Bible, it is called the Good News. Yes, you are witnesses of the Joy of Awakening and are sharing the Good News.

You three are fulfilling your calling to do My work in this imagined world of form. The work you do for Me is being transmitted in the mind to all beings on all planes. You have no understanding of the unseen world, but it is receiving every message given for the awakening of all who sleep. The sleepers have lost their awareness that they are the One Son of God living in separation. This is their time to wake up. You have been given the opportunity to spread the word, and there are billions of ways it will be delivered and understood. You were willing to do this work and therefore it was assigned to you in the very beginning. You are not special. Each and every member of the human race is serving the same purpose but in different forms. Go forth now, knowing that I am guiding your every action, thought, and dream. Hold the intention that each step will awaken you to My wisdom and bring you closer to home.

40

Untethered

Leave the world and rise above it; view it as just a cloud,
a shadow of dark and light where form has no significance.

October 8, 2013

Holy Spirit, what is Your message today? You are traveling with Me
into the unknown spheres, symbolizing the return Home as you
visit your sister on the mainland. She has chosen to live in My
Light, in Solvang, the home of the sun, Sol. You live on the shore
of Haleakala, the House of the Sun, and the two of you are
meeting as the Son. She is the face of Christ, your Christ Self, who
you meet today under My Roof. This journey is all symbolic, and I
will remind you of that while you are together. Susan is now
united with Me in her heart and is open to receive you in My
Name. Again, this is being symbolized in form, but in the mind
you are united with Me and are seeing it out pictured today. You
are concerned that your mt character who types this message has
no sense or comprehension of what I am describing. That is okay.
It is not about mt's experience, because mt is not real, and her ego
would block the glory of a reunion made in Heaven. The
experience of this day will sink in. It is a means to describe to the
readers what joining with Me entails on the earth plane. We will
write more on this later.

Last night you had a dream in which a philanthropic friend
hands you a large shadow box, an art piece that she loves. You try
to understand its beauty and meaning as you hold it in your lap.
The inside bottom of the box is completely covered with a solid
mass of tiny colored Crocs (rubber shoes), all moving in one
wavelike direction. The top of the box, sealed in clear glass, had

been painted with muddy water so that only a very faint impression of footprints was left. The shoes inside could still be seen. When you woke up you asked for My meaning. This dream depicts your journey to Susan as well as your journey in this lifetime. The shoes represent the many selves that compose the One Son, including you. You carry the One Son with you as you lift off from the earth today. The plane overrides all boundaries as you leave the ground. You bring Me along with the shoes/selves because I contain all of you in My Love. Leave the world and rise above it; view it as just a cloud, a shadow of dark and light where form has no significance and is invisible to human perception. This is almost too much to grok, as you might say, now that you are reading Heinlein's book *Stranger in a Strange Land.* Yes, take the point of view from an outer planet looking at images and belief systems that have nothing to do with true Source. Symbolically, you are taking a journey that marks the release of your attachment to the elements of form that have held you back for eons.

Yesterday, you canceled your participation in the Banyan Tree Art Fair, which is scheduled for the same weekend that you will return home. You are honoring My request to release all attachment to anything other than Me and our work together on the books. So this is the next step. As the Banyan Tree association fades, more and more of your universe will fade. You will then experience a depletion of the attachment to your mt character. This is happening rapidly and you are now more aware than ever that the end of form, for you, is near. It all must go, and it is in process. I am the One Who is orchestrating this march of invisible feet. Home is their destination and all the children will return in innocence. The tiny shoes are theirs, and they will no longer exist in the world of form when they are incorporated into the Mind of their Maker. You will experience a sense of union during the time with your sister. I will allow you an opening to see that truth and it will serve the book. Enjoy your trip.

41

A Clean Slate

*I am in charge of how each mind encounters the steps
that are shown and taken.*

October 10, 2013

(Middle of night) *Holy Spirit, do You have a message for me as I
prepare to meet Susan's minister?* Yes, write My words to him now:
"You know Me and you love Me. I see your love as you minister
to your congregation, My flock. Know that I am fully present with
you in each service. I have chosen Margie to communicate with
you as she is a hearer of My Voice, and it's true that she hears My
Word. You are to share your understanding of Me this morning,
and I will be present. Ask Me your questions and receive My
answers while you are together. This will take each of you to a
new level of listening and receiving My Word. Do not fear that
you are 'misguided.' The opportunity to practice delivering My
message, directly to your flock, is My Will and yours. You and
Margie serve in different ways but it is all one church, all One Son.
Commune now with Me and through Me. Hear My Voice, and
speak it. This is My gift to you both."

Dream: I am walking across Susan's new bedding with my
sneakers. I am upset to see black prints left on the sheets,
concerned they can never be washed off.

Holy Spirit, what is Your interpretation? You are being shown
the fear that your "past indiscretions" cannot be washed away,
but the clean sheet, the innocence of the heart, remains
unblemished. You did not walk over Me. The steps you take are

sacred on sacred land, sheets, stone, paper. Each word on this page is a footprint on a sacred slate. It is to be given to the world, just as Moses read from his tablet. That is what both you and the minister do, he from the pulpit and you from the books. I write on your hearts, in the mind we all share. You fear you will "do it wrong" and the words I give will be misinterpreted by him. I wash everything clean, and I am in charge of how each mind encounters the steps that are shown and taken.

42

Soften Your Gaze

Your eyes are Mine to direct as I will.

October 12, 2013

Holy Spirit, yesterday Susan and I were at the mall. She pulled me into an expensive cosmetic store where we were given special "gold" eye-cream treatments. Please soften my eyes to Your Vision. You are the only manager of all essential elements. What do You say? You had the opportunity to witness the approach of the world to soften your gaze. Your skin was also softened by first taking off the old layers. This is a symbol of all the veils being removed to receive My golden treatment. Then you can absorb the truth. Yes, your sight has softened. See with My Vision. Your eyes are Mine to direct as I will. They belong to no one but Me. No one else is to tend to your sight.

At the mall, you sat across from your niece during lunch. She was dozing. This is the state of all the sleepers at different stages of their dream. You later told her you want to be with her when she is awake. This message was delivered through mt, whom she respects and loves. You see now that your whole day was symbolic. I was conditioning your eyes to see from your right mind. Your niece's eyes are also being treated with love and wisdom so they can fully open to the light.

Holy Spirit, do You have more to say? You wonder about the many scrapbooks Susan showed you. They depict her entire life and all her connections with family and friends. You looked dispassionately at the pictures of your life growing up, all your many selves, images that served you but now have vanished from view. This was to be the experience at the end of your day to see "your life story" with detachment, from above the battlefield, through My eyes of Love. Just live in the now.

43

My Brother, My Self

See past the stories and just come to the Love.

October 13, 2013

Holy Spirit, please review my experience at Susan's Baptist church this morning. Today, the minister was speaking the truth: "Walk with Me, as Me. There is nothing else." He sees his flock as himself and one with his Self as he walks with them. This reminds you of the passage from the *Course:* "The answer that I give my brother is what I am asking for. And what I learn of him is what I learn about myself." See yourself walking always with Me. See past the stories and just come to the Love, which you felt at church. Embrace the congregation as your many selves. Keep remembering Me, knowing every brother is you. *(I feel swelling in my heart.)* This is the new estate of love that I promote in you now.

Holy Spirit, I know that only You can operate me from love. I see my resistance, my ego fear to let the love in. It is the fear I knew as a ten-year-old child, in the fundamental Emmanuel Baptist Church. I do know You live in me, as me, yet there has been a deep fear of the love of Jesus throughout my life. The ego tries to push love away. I would take back that projection now and embrace the love that I am. What was I to learn at Susan's church today?

The minister, My messenger, is your Self, out pictured in the dream. Know that "the Jesus you walked with long ago" is you. All the stories are iterations of the One Son: you. Your heart is open and ready to receive Me. Recall the stories of family love shared at dinner last night. This is not about people but about opening to My Love. *Thank You, Holy Spirit, for this next step. Keep me open to love You and all my brothers.* I will.

44

Dance with Me

There is no place for you on earth, no one to play the music, nothing to fill your desire.

October 14, 2013

(Before sleep, I hear, "It is time to release your ego's perception of the world and let Me rule with God's Love.")

Dream: I am in a huge empty ballroom to dance with my unseen partner. There is no one to play the music.

(As I write down the dream, the tears start.) *Holy Spirit, You are again healing something very deep with this dream. There is no one left and now the place is empty. Is this the* "last dance?" This is the end of the world, the Armageddon, the Return to Christ, to God. There is no place for you on earth, no one to play the music, nothing to fill your desire. It is all impersonal. Yes, this is a return to Me, the return to Love. *Holy Spirit, did I love You in your Jesus life?* No, you feared Me. It is time for My Love to be revealed to you; the clearing has taken place for Me to enter. The blocks are removed and the space is ready. Your partner is invisible because we are all One in the invisible realm of the Mind. Let this unfold now, do not resist. You hated the self that believed you left Jesus/God to remain in your own space. Now you are free to be with Me. You released the Banyan Tree, and you have released Maui in your mind. The connection with Me is all that is left.

45

Fear of Love

Conflict keeps you forever stuck in form,
forgetting your wholeness and unity in Me.

October 15, 2013

Holy Spirit, when I just now thanked Susan's minister by e-mail for his blessing, I felt some fear. I recall the initial dream of receiving the Book on August 8, 2012, where I saw a minister on a stage who indicates he knows my mission. Did I give away power to Susan's minister today? In this moment, I wonder if I am deferring to his power to love, verses mine. I do know he is a symbol. No, you have not betrayed Me. Come closer to Me and release the fear of Jesus/Self/brother who the minister represents. You have not given him your power of knowing Me. He is an example of loving Me (*chest burns*). You all will come into love and joy. You are confused now but it will become clear. Fear not.

Holy Spirit, I feel somewhat out of touch with You. Bring me home. Please inform my dreams. I would need nothing but You. Give me the clearing. Release me from all fear of You, of love. In admitting my fear of love, I feel vulnerable and exposed and dismissed. I had to hide my fear of love because love is the desire for True Life, which means the desire for death of the ego. It's love or the ego. Is this the fear? Yes, this is the confusion and you see with clarity now. *Holy Spirit, I am willing to die to the ego to enter Your Love.* Yes, this is the choice.

Holy Spirit, what is Your instruction this morning? We are here together in the Light. Focus on Me throughout the day, and I will inform you as we enjoy the beauty together. Let the sounds of worldly conflict fade away. (News of the US government shutdown was on TV in the other room.) You just overheard that the government is in its seventeenth day of shutdown. Though distressing to the country, it is insignificant; it is all part of the plan for the ultimate disappearance of the universe. Hear it with Me, as "background noise." The ego thought system is supremely pictured here for all to see, and ultimately, it is from that which you will awaken. Conflict keeps people forever stuck in form forgetting their wholeness and unity in Me. The world is nothing but an idea of separation and duality and becomes the focus of minds that are joined in the belief they are bodies in the world. You are not affected by the maneuvers of any player in this movie of attack and counter attack when you know it's simply a picture of the ego world.

46

Pause

There is nothing that isn't the love that I am.

October 16, 2013

Holy Spirit, I am shocked at how my "other life" on Maui disappeared while I was at Susan's home. You are resting and rejuvenating with Me. This break is necessary to prepare for the next step in our enterprise with the books, which no longer seems real while you are in a "neutral zone" with Susan. This break from routine is just a pause. Enjoy it, and stay in the now. The silence, with Me, is out pictured in your love of Susan, the bright sunlight, and in the stillness. Trust that I am working with you in the mind. *Holy Spirit, bring me into Your stillness and guide me.* I will. There is nothing that isn't the love that I am.

47

The Father's Love

Feel My loving support as I lead you through the wilderness of your belief system, and expose the falsity of everything you once thought was real.

October 17, 2013

Holy Spirit, after attending Susan's church, the term "God the Father" *gave me pause. Please explain my reaction to it.* That phrase brings up thoughts about your relationship with the Father, God. You have learned from Me that God does not rule your dream world, which you gladly accept because it comforts you. But, you also see your lingering belief that you are separate from the God, Who remains outside of your world. Yes, the ego made this world to assure that you feel separate from a God, Who is "not in His Kingdom,"—the projection that stems from your own belief that "you are not in His Kingdom." That thought "exists" only in the split mind where it has been hidden; it is now being exposed.

It has been easy for you to scribe My words because you know Me and know that I love and support you. The introduction of "God the Father" causes fear because you believe you don't know Him or His Kingdom. God, rather than an ego, is seen as the fantasy, and this is the basis of your whole belief system, and world. You, as mt, are not exactly sure how to incorporate God into your concept of yourself. Think instead of the Bible passages where I, as Jesus, speak with My Father and am filled with love for Him. We now approach the idea: *God Is Love.* All is God, and All is Love. You have seen your fear of love, your fear of God. You had to take the first step of feeling My Presence and Love, as real, to broach the truth that you are God's Son, as am I. Just like you, I am an Extension of God. We both are the Son of God, the same as God. God is impersonal. I am impersonal in My Love for all Sons because I know we are all the same.

You now grasp the reason why I had to explain the Unity of God by having you approach that knowing incrementally. You had to know the "parts" before you could conceive of the whole. Just like a baby learning to embrace its environment, you had to begin with the brother as yourself, and then incorporate Me as a living part of you. You had to feel My Constancy and Love to accept the thought that a loving God truly does exist and that He can and does love you, as do I. Yes, you are learning to love Me, your brother, and God, your Father. Now go freely, beyond your connection to form, to the One God: Creator of All.

Your experience in Solvang with your sister, is about solving the "one problem" of believing you are separate but acknowledging you are not separate and are returning to Me, the solution. Susan has returned to the light, a place in the sun. Her joy and her loving nature reflect your Self. Watch the dawn now come to the place that Susan has lovingly prepared for you. Now you feel yourself again with your birth father, holding you as a child in his/My lap. Together we turned the pages of a fairy tale, one you longed to hear, again and again. You loved the closeness with your father, knowing that in his arms you were perfectly safe and forever loved. Being a child, you didn't question the story of the creation, or know that you had abandoned Heaven. The presence of your earthly father was all that mattered. Knowing you were enfolded in his love gave you a peace and comfort like nothing else on earth.

I am that Father now and we are reviewing the story of your life. You feel My loving support as I slowly and methodically lead you through the wilderness of your belief system and expose the falsity of everything you once thought was real. You are ready to open to the only truth there is beyond the realm of form and personality: the Knowledge that God Is. The Love of the Father has enfolded you through eons of the same story, retold in a billion ways. It is time to end the telling of all stories. God is unveiled, no longer a mystery, and is experienced as Love. He is the Essence of the Heart of man. God never lived and ruled in a separate Kingdom. You are His dreaming Son, a prodigal son, now returned Home. Embrace this concept again as the truth. Soon it will become all you know because there is nothing else to know.

Go and enjoy your fairy-tale town where you'll have a Danish pancake breakfast with your sister. See only God in the glorious light, mountains, river, birds, and shining faces of the many brothers on the streets and in the shops. The fairy tale is coming to a close. All the fairies have left the park and are waking up.

48

Memory of God

Open now to the next realm, the next step closer to Heaven.

October 18, 2013

Holy Spirit, do You have words for me? Yes, that is all they are—words, put together in a string, given My meaning or the ego's, whichever you choose. In and of themselves, words have no value. I am beyond words. I and the Father are One.

(Later, lying awake) *Holy Spirit, do You have more to say?* Your sleep is directed by Me. Focus on Me and ask My blessing on your sleep. Be in the silence. You are coming closer to Me all the time and you feel Me now in your chest. I am here. I am God. *How can You be God when the* Course *says that He is not part of the dream?* All is God, in the dream and everywhere, because God is in your mind. God is unity, not duality. When you are in fear, you do not hear God in My words. Fear is not of Me. It is a misinterpretation of God's energy, by the ego mind. *Holy Spirit, I thought we could not feel God's Presence except through "revelation." I am really confused. Was the writing yesterday, true?* Yes. God is everything, but He is not a player in the ego's world of form. God cannot be experienced in a state of fear. *Holy Spirit, if I call on You in a state of fear, You answer, and You are God.* I am an aspect of God, mediating in this dream world. I am His extension, I hold His memory, but I am not the Whole. *I thought that every part contained the whole.* That is true. I am the only aspect of God accessible to you, the only wavelength your ego thought system is capable of receiving. *I get it. I am tuning into only a part of the spectrum that is the "Holy Spirit." Is that it?* Yes, now sleep.

(6:00 a.m. Susan told me to go and look at the full
moon. I quickly dressed and ran down the street to
watch the moon set over the mountains. I
remember the perfect setting of the full moon and
rising of the sun in Denver, at Cherry Creek
Reservoir, listening to Pavarotti singing "Du bist
mein ganzes Herz": You are my total heart. *Holy
Spirit, I sobbed in this blessing of Your Presence, years
before hearing Your Voice.*)

Yes, you are Mine, My ganzes Herz. Ich liebe dich: I love you.
This is the time of full embrace. See Me in the setting moon and
the rising sun. The true Light of the One Son embraces all of your
brothers, all of humanity. You are coming to a time when the
Presence of God will be known and felt. To experience His
revelation you must be in a place to receive and welcome Him,
and that you are. You are not hearing this out of ego desire and
fabrication, but from Me. We are a unit and we open now to the
next realm, the next step closer to Heaven. The heavenly bodies
that appear so close to each other this day are a reminder that I am
closer than your breath.

You were confused in the night about the "nature" of God in
this world of form. His Thought is the material, the
substrate/foundation, the "energy" of all that is. This energy can
be used in the mind of man in whatever way he chooses. Because
man is in the mind, and not an object apart from it, the vast power
of a mind made to create can fashion its environment and
concepts into its wildest dreams. The mind that split off from the
Mind of God must experience a fear-based world. This wrong
mind of the ego can only interpret what it perceives through a veil
of darkness. Therefore, the fearful mind of man is shrouded in
death.

I am the Light of the world because I shine My loving Light of
the knowledge and memory of God into your dream of fear and

separation, violence and attack. I give you hope that there is something beyond it: a loving God in a realm called Heaven. In reality, you sleep in the Arms of your Father as His Son. You and the Father are One. This whole course is about awakening to the memory of God, Whom you believe you left. As soon as you remember Him in your innocence, fear and form disappear and you will sleep no more. Think on this as the sun rises. The sun is your Reminder of God in the world of form. He is the Light of your Being. Without Him you could not exist. Embrace Me, the sun, the Son, and God this morning. I am with you.

49

Awaken!

My timing is always impeccable.

October 19, 2013

Holy Spirit, what is Your instruction this day? You are My disciple. We are bringing word of the awakening process to the nations, to all who are ready to hear. Awake! Awake! The sun/Son is here, and it is time to shed the dark layers that have covered you for eons. See the falsity of the dream in which you reside. Leave your soiled nests behind and fly above the stench, to Me. Together, we will look down at the earth you thought was real, so you can choose again for a new day in the Light of Love. I am ready to carry you Home. Trust in My message and it will reveal that these words are the truth.

During the night, you had an experience of seeing the dream differently through My Vision. You called your time with Susan, "the happy dream" as described in *ACIM*. The dream of sadness and darkness was released and a new dream of joy, light, and love was revealed. You could barely soak in this new perception of life where your sister is happy for the first time in her life. She is your reflection and that is what you witnessed. This new vision, through My Sight, shows you where you are on the path to home, and you can't deny the signs. Susan is newly in love. You see the sparkle in her eyes and hear the lilt in her voice. You are happy for her and her lover, who will demonstrate what I picture to you in words. The images of "earth love" mirror the approach to your Love of God. Yes, it is stunning to see this manifestation of happiness juxtaposed with your new estate with Me, the editing of Book 1, the release of the Banyan Tree, and your deeper opening to the Union with God.

My timing is always impeccable. You, as well as Jo and Meera, have shown up for each step that leads to the completion of your earthly journey and the books you will leave behind for humanity. It is impossible not to see what is so vividly displayed before your eyes. For you, mt, the transformation of your relationship with your sister, from judging her to embracing her, is beautiful to behold. This was your heart's desire. You had to take back all the projections on your sister and leave her in My hands so I could work with her. It is how I work with you when you are unhindered by your judgments and your fear of God/Love that would keep you immersed in the world of form and darkness. The Light has come. Imbibe My Light and Love. See Me in all the beauty that surrounds you, and in the love of your sister and her love for you. Rejoice in our union. Now enjoy your day and think on Me. I am everywhere.

* * *

Note to Reader from Jo (March 8, 2017)

I was just now editing the part where Margie had taken back projections on her sister, and something got triggered. I suddenly remembered an incident from more than thirty years ago when our five-year-old son was accused by a neighbor of inappropriately touching her son. She was very upset, and my husband spanked our son as punishment, for the first time ever. The whole thing was messy, and I blamed the older boys on the school bus for preying on my child, exposing him to grown up ideas and "destroying" his innocence. When we asked our son about it he said he was told, "It would feel good."

As I sat here at the computer, thinking back on that day, childhood memories/stories arose around body curiosity, which had left the print of guilt and shame in my own life. In seventh grade, I'd been molested by a teacher but never told anyone. A few years later, I sought out the attention of another teacher to perpetuate my desire for intimacy. Although I blamed one teacher, I later pursued another. Now, years later, I finally realize that as the dreamer I projected my own shame and guilt onto my son, his perpetrators, my angry neighbor, my husband, and my teachers. *In the dream, they are all me.* I'd like to share what the Holy Spirit said when I sat quietly with Him:

"Man is a predator in order to survive. Everything is his prey, starting with God, Who must be attacked, raped, and killed so man can survive on his own. This is a constant battle as God is perceived to be a constant threat. To believe in guilt is to become the perpetrator/punisher. To be punished is man's fear and his desire. Unconsciously, he seeks to do wrong, wanting his punishment to confirm his identity as a body and to relieve the guilt of leaving heaven. Thus, he remains the victim. Punishment from a brother is still 'better' than punishment from God. Yes, you have had lifetimes of seeking prey, wanting to take control and be the one in charge. The predator's guilt must be projected, even onto one's own son. In your case, the 'father' then punishes. Your husband became the Punisher-God, and you continued to subtlety punish him in many ways over the years."

Holy Spirit, I also see the innocence in the vicious cycle of projection. How did innocence become guilt? "The Son was/is innocent, being the same as God: Pure Love. The idea of seeking more, whether pleasure or adventure is still the thought of love, still innocent. But, when guilt was taken seriously it became 'real.' The rules and regulations of your world keep man feeling the guilt of always seeing duality in a 'right or wrong' way to live.

There is no hierarchy of body parts. Since love is sought outside of Heaven, it becomes prey, i.e. the lover to be overpowered and killed. Love does not exist in the world of ego. The body seeks what feels good, pleasure, and that gets translated into 'love.' True Love would destroy the body. Its Pure Light yet frightens. When you merge with God, you, for one instant, will know your innocence. Then, no you."

(Readers, I am so grateful for the immediate relief of an old, repressed memory through the help that is always available from the Holy Spirit. Every second we have the chance to see something differently. I continue to have an ever-deepening appreciation for what these books are teaching me.)

50

Soul Food

You are to feed the soul with My words.

October 20, 2013

Dream: I am preparing beans and slicing bread for the first night of class. The knife, shaped like a key, is dull, so the slices of bread are thin and uneven. I am concerned that my offering looks very meager and hastily prepared. A car wants to park in the large hole in the center of the table, and I say no. A man makes fun of me.

Holy Spirit what is Your interpretation? Your gift is not the feeding of the body. You are to feed the soul with My words. (*I feel the swelling in my chest.*) You have enough food because the loaves will extend. Have no fear that My gifts are not adequate. You feed My flock with My words. True feeding requires My Presence and My Bread. You criticize your sister for her humanness, the preparing and feeding of the body, and her interest in all the stories of form, but these do not matter. She is Mine in her heart, in her surrender, and in her love. Let the things of the body go. Let all activities of the body go. Do not judge them, nor your niece and her drugs. They are no different from your dream of beans and bread, thinking they will fill "the hole in the center" that is reserved for Me. I am the only thing that matters. Each will express this knowing differently. Let all the masks of earthly roles drop from your mind. In the dream, you are just as human as Susan. Her lover's needs are a call for love. She listens and gives him the love for which she, too, would call. Her way is My will.

Holy Spirit, You have the patience with me that Susan has with her daughter. This is what I reject in myself: the patience to hear the same story of separation over and over. I know it is really the impatience and condemnation of myself for the repetition of the story of the loss of You, in every lifetime. Susan has compassion. Give me Your peace and release my judgment. Your niece uses drugs to induce mental separation and Susan overlooks the dreams. She loves her daughter as herself, as Me. Release all judgments of all sons. They are the lost sheep and they will come Home. Let the evil go as Susan has done with her ex-husband. No one is evil. Everyone is the prodigal son, backing away, coming close again.

Holy Spirit, I will be going home tomorrow, and Susan has been crying. What is Your instruction this morning? You are leaving your sister, and you know this is another reenactment of the original separation *(tears).* You are leaving the one you love who is a mirror of you. You felt the fear and sadness as you witnessed Susan's tears when she greeted you this morning. This is the pain you all were born into, but I have blessed your hearts that felt broken from your imagined separation from God.

You, mt, recognize that your interactions with those you encounter in your life are similar to what Susan experiences. You mirror each other in doing My work in spreading the light of love. Know that the separation never happened and know you are always in the Arms of your Father. The time with Susan has served the purpose of showing you that. You are together as one, the one brother, the One Son. In the dream of life you have joined. I say to you this day: you have mended the broken heart of the separation in your love for each other and for Me, as you welcome My love and guidance. You see this in form, in the dream of a visit to Solvang on the mainland, but in truth, it is happening in the mind. As yet, you do not understand this concept, but it is the essence of all the efforts you make in the dream to reach Me and spread My Word. The fog of the morning will lift as have the veils of darkness. See My Light shining everywhere. Now prepare for your morning at church. *Thank You, Holy Spirit, for this beautiful message. I would do Your Will today.*

(I was touched by the minister's sermon on "How to Know the Will of God." I spoke to him of the gift he gives his congregation by demonstrating the Christ Love that lives in him. He was grateful for my feedback. I felt the joy of meeting a mirror in the experience of the Voice and Will of God and am grateful that Susan can continue to be in his congregation.)

51

Real Love

Nothing in the dream turns into what you imagine it will.

October 22, 2013

Holy Spirit, Susan just informed me that her latest love relationship has collapsed, but she saw through it with Your help. You did not negate her experience, and she saw she was living in a fantasy, even though it had felt like the "real thing." You were happy for Susan's joy and what you both believed was the answer to her longing. In the dream, it will not happen the way you think. Nothing in the dream turns into what you imagine it will. But you shared equally in the desire for fulfillment of her longing for love. This was an important mirroring. Her "lover" was not real. It was your joint embrace of Me as your Beloved; the love for Me was being out pictured. You joined with Susan in this embrace. Accept these dream images as symbols of what is happening in the right mind.

52

Transformation

It is only after seeing and releasing the depths of darkness
that the full embrace of the Christ takes place.

October 23, 2013

Holy Spirit, I am back again at my computer with You, and the tears are coming for the amazing demonstration of Your Presence and Your Will. My time with Susan was a clear out picturing of the unfolding of Your Mystery, unlike anything I could ever have imagined. Not only have Susan's and her daughter's lives turned around, but my life has, too, and I have no idea where it will go next. It is a huge step in fully letting go to You and knowing that You are totally in charge. My house is no longer my home, and my place in time and space is no longer my concern. I am not attached to it and feel like a stranger in a strange land. The world has lost its flavor of belonging. I belong only to You and can count only on You to be in charge in Your miraculous ways. My niece reflected that when she called to tell me of a miracle: the opening to the truth of her soul, and the release of her "worthlessness." She feels the embrace of Spirit, and a reconnection with her father's long-lost brothers.

What is Your message to me today? You are in My hands, more fully now than ever before. You saw the miracle of My Presence operating in your family, and beyond, in a way that was unmistakable. It was the purpose of your trip. You had to see Susan and her daughter as essential parts of your soul in order for everything to transpire. It is "your dream," and you had to show up. My Light allowed you to see the unfolding of this movie of redemption where "dark met light" and the light dissolved it. This experience of transformation had to take place in the home of your most special relationships.

During the visit with your niece and sister, you had no idea of the essential role that Susan's ex-husband, now deceased, would play in the dream drama and how his world of hate could still impact the three of you. The dream of darkness is enacted in the lives of everyone on the planet in one form or another. It must be seen for what it is: the underlying, terrifying belief in the imagined separation. Your niece, being the reflection of you, depicted your own belief that you were worthless, hated by God, and doomed to a life of self-torture and hell. Two mornings ago, as you and she watched a documentary on the Holocaust, she described the horrors of her life with her father, who surrounded her with words and symbols of the Nazi party. You listened to her story in peace, as I instructed you to do, while holding her and her father in the light of truth and forgiveness. She informed you how close to suicide she has come, failing to turn her life into the great success of which she is inherently capable.

Yesterday afternoon, you had a message from your sister, who asked you to call her daughter immediately about a profound experience that "shook her to the core." On the phone, your niece said she had received an e-mail from a cousin, her age, saying that he had had a dream of "a death in the family" and was "told" he should contact her. She was surprised that he had found her since her father had cut off all ties with his family from the time she was seven years old, so she had no means of telling any of them that her father had recently died. Her long-lost cousin had located her name on the Internet. They connected, and he shared the similarities of his father with her father, who were brothers. The cousin offered his help to connect her with other family members as well.

In her heart, your niece knew that it was I, in the form of her father, Who had "connected through the dream" to bring her this reunion with family and, more important, to bring her to her Self. Through this experience she could clearly see that her feelings of worthlessness, linked to her father's hateful interactions with her, were only covers over the love that was now being demonstrated by this sweet connection he was "orchestrating" between her and his family. She opened her heart to the truth of her Being, in gratitude and love for her father, because she now felt his love for her. She had not been able to grieve her father's death until that moment. The tears of grief and liberation poured forth. Your niece knows she has been set free to renew her life in truth.

You see it all now in your tears, your own story of the original separation, too awful to comprehend on any internal level, demonstrated through projection onto those closest to you. How could you ever realize the depths of pain and terror of the separation from your Father Who had embraced you in Love, and Who you believed you left for a life apart from Him? The horrors experienced in Vietnam by your ex-brother-in-law, and the horrors experienced by your niece in that house of hate, could never come close to the despair, terror, and guilt that each human being endures in his believed state of separation and loss of Heaven. You understand now the concept of the cross of crucifixion that each of you carries throughout your lives, as "killers" of the Christ Self in you. Your niece saw the Light yesterday. She felt the cross-lifted from her back. She is ready to see the minister who will speak to her of the return to her Christ Self. Your own fear of evangelism was just this: you could not face the idea that you, too, carried the cross of crucifixion on your back, the projected symbol of blame for killing God/Christ.

It is the ego that would not let you approach who you really are. It is only after seeing and releasing the depths of the darkness, carried by all humanity, that the full embrace of the Christ Self takes place. It is what you have worked to embrace your entire life. The dark drama was projected onto your sister and her family to out picture your most challenging, difficult, painful, and special relationships in this life. You see them now as figments of a dream that are neither real nor true. You came "home" to Maui to realize that home does not exist in the dream of earth and form. The only

Home is with Me, and I dwell within your Self. Yesterday, when your friend Marie picked you up from the airport, she shared her poignant dream of being in a new house. But when she went outside, she saw that there was no exterior to the house, only the inside space. You both understood the message that there is no home but your inner life with Me.

53

Dream of Liberation

There is literally nothing for you to do but listen to
My Voice and watch your lives unfold.

October 24, 2013

(Middle of the night) *I feel different . . . light, ethereal,
unconcerned, Holy Spirit.* Physically, mentally, and
spiritually you are in a new place where I guide
you rather than your ego. This recognition causes
the feeling of lightness because you trust Me and
have no concern for tomorrow.

(Later) *What do You say now?* You are feeling the new estate of
the real world. It is a state of mind where all is in My hands and
nothing takes place outside of My Will. Everything has followed
My plan. You see this especially through the perfection of the
events at Susan's home. (*I feel the burning in my chest.*) My Word
and its demonstration in your life is all that matters, all there is.
There is literally nothing for you to do but listen to My Voice and
watch your life unfold. The projection of evil for you, Susan, and
her daughter has stopped. This is the symbolic death of both
Susan's ex-husband and the ego, in your minds. Neither is real,
just symbols of the belief in separation. This is now a dream of
liberation.

The day that you and your niece watched the last episode of
Auschwitz: The Liberation was a day of release from the boney grip
of ego hatred that had ruled both your lives over lifetimes. You
touched the truth of your Being as you placed the images of the
Holocaust and your niece's father in My hands of Love and

Forgiveness. Remember, My hands are yours, and your hands are Mine. Your sister has had to surrender to the loss of function of both her hands, and you witnessed the painful surgery she underwent two years ago to restore some dexterity. Her surrender to the loss of her hand function was her symbolic identification with Me as Jesus on the cross.

Susan's ordeal was an illusion but had to be seen with the willingness that you manifested, to be present once again at a "re-creation" of the crucifixion. You knew that somehow, her hand surgery was a means for healing the mind and not the body. You heard your sister scream in pain as needles were placed between the tender skin of each finger without any numbing agent. I, as the Christ, did not feel the pain of the sword because My soul had surrendered and was already united with the Father. I was with Him above the battleground, watching the play of the dream as it unfolded for the imagined character of the man called Jesus.

The crucifixion and the resurrection did take place in the dream of mankind, but it was all "happening" in the mind of man, who believed that Jesus was separate from his Father in Heaven, and that his Father willed the crucifixion of His Son. You know now how impossible that would be, and that it could only happen within the illusory dream taking place in a sleeping mind, unconscious of its reality as the One Son of God. This dream of "crucifixion and resurrection" was the way the dream could be used to picture both the separation and the redemption.

You are now in a place of acceptance to receive the depth of this writing in calm surrender to the truth of My words. You, your sister, and your niece all knew Me in the lifetime of Jesus, surrendered to your mission to make this story of the resurrection clear to unbelieving minds. Man can only learn through thought forms in his mind, all of which are made-up stories of separation. Each of you, reenacting the drama of the crucifixion in your own life of pain and suffering, will come to know that it is not real and that what is true is the Christ Self within. Every being, energy, image on earth is the holder of My Life and My Love, out pictured in symbols. I exist beyond form, and I am the Source of your Life.

Thank You, Holy Spirit. Have I received this Word to Your satisfaction? I do feel calm and sense no protest from an ego register within me. I imagine that someone writing these words would be sobbing in wonder and gratitude. I feel peace and acceptance for the gift You are giving. It rings true within me as I have been a part of its manifestation on earth. I had believed since childhood that I should suffer greatly to bring myself to You. I see the suffering of my family members but have not undergone that as a body in this lifetime. Do I deserve this awareness and do I need to suffer to go all the way to reunite with my Father?

No, you need not suffer to know Me. The terror you felt from the preaching of hell-fire and brimstone, childhood experiences in church, still remains. To "accept Christ as your Savior" was something that filled you with dread, but now you have accepted Me. You have been "saved" by your determined efforts, directed by Me, the Christ Self, to know Me. You have seen the path to redemption of your soul through the drama of your family, never suspecting that it was a re-enactment of the cross. You have come full circle now. You are Home. All the selves on this journey are Home. The story is *over*. It has been over since the instant it was dreamed.

Now, awaken fully to My Grace, My Love, and My Reality as All there is. Each moment of the day and night, know that your life is Mine alone and that we are One with God. You will be led by Me to do My Will, and nothing else is needed to fulfill your life. Each life has a purpose and it will be recognized through My Vision. Go forth and bring My message to the world. The Christ has risen. He is awake in you and shines the Light of Love, the Light you recognize in every brother you see in the face of humanity. As your ego identification diminishes, you will see the face of Christ more readily and clearly.

Holy Spirit, tell me more about my sister and niece being with Jesus. Yes, you were all together when your dream mission was made. You were all My disciples, My followers, along with the thousands who will read these books. In the mind, all of humanity was present because together you compose the One Son. You were "Me on the cross." You were and are the Christ that has risen. You each are living one idea of separation in its many variations, but there is only One Christ. You. You are the one who lived and died in a dream of separation, only to be reborn in the Grand Awakening to the Truth that the separation never happened. You are one with all your brothers. We are One and we are Home. Now go in Peace.

54

Fear of Betrayal

Nothing on earth can satisfy the desire
to have more and be more.

October 26, 2013

Dream: Susan and I are in a fabric shop. Only a wooden counter
and the kindly saleswoman, who is pulling down material from a
large roll above her, are visible. Susan and I inspect the fabric and
see it is a loosely-woven plaid in pink, blue, and white, like the
colors of the sky at dawn. It feels as soft as a baby's skin, and is
just what Susan loves. I say I'd like some but then get confused
with a piece of grayish plaid being held by another woman. When
the saleslady spreads the first fabric out on the counter, Susan and
I both want a piece. The saleslady tells us to touch its softness
while she looks at its large white price tag with no visible writing
on it. She is telling us that the original price, which we expected to
pay, is wrong. The material is of such high quality that the "real
price" is higher, and when she peels off the label, I think she is
trying to falsify the correct price to make more profit. As I stand
there, waiting for her decision, I am not upset and just wonder
what she will do. It seems that Susan was no longer there.

Holy Spirit, what is Your interpretation of this dream? It is a
dream of your new estate. The pattern of the material you wished
to buy was integrated, repeated over and over. Each thread, soft
and pale, blended together to resemble a cloud. Its nature is the
softness of love because it is My material, a symbol of the
"material" I have given you for the books. You now recall your
prophetic dream last year of having a blanket around your

169

shoulders as you held My Book with a rotunda embossed on its cover.

Holy Spirit, what of my thought in the dream this morning that the saleswoman would cheat us and overcharge for the blanket material? People fear that they will be cheated out of the "true value" of whatever life gives them. Nothing on earth can satisfy the desire to have more and be more, an attempt to fill the "hole" that was left when man departed the heavenly Kingdom. Your longing is always for God. The world will fade, and you will recognize your wholeness and unity with every member of humanity, all composed of the same cloth.

55

Accept Your Equality

Welcome the dream characters
with the light of your being.

October 27, 2013

Holy Spirit, what is Your instruction this morning? You have had a strong experience of the real world, pictured for you in two dreams last night. In the first, you called an old colleague, who, in 1976 invited you to meet a spiritual teacher of the Gurdjieff work, which set into motion your quest for finding the truth through a teacher. You had to tell your colleague that you now have found your way, and have reached the goal of knowing Me, the Holy Spirit, as your Self.

In the second dream, you were at a gathering of all the people whom Tom had worked with in his life. These associations had been conflicted for him in some ways, but they all had resolved their differences and now worked in unity. You could not recall any of their names, and they did not engage with you, but the gathering emanated a feeling of total acceptance for all. When you woke up, you had the sense that everything in your life is just a dream, and all the diverse characters are just separate parts of you "recomposed" into a whole harmonic symphony. This was also reflected in yesterday's dream of the soft blanket, woven with the threads of humanity.

You thought of your relationship with Zoe in these same terms. Many times you begged her to see you as an equal, but she protested vehemently that she was "more advanced than you" and that your friends were also more advanced than you on the spiritual path. Zoe's protest to your equality with her was just a mirror of your protest and resistance to accepting your equality with your Christ Self. Now, everything is becoming clear. This is the experience of coming home to your Self while seeing all else as a dream. Enjoy your day at the gallery knowing that everyone who walks in the door is you. Welcome them with acceptance and the light of your being.

(Later) *Holy Spirit, as I was closing the gallery today, a man asked to borrow my scissors, but I refused. Please speak to me about my guilt around not giving him what he wanted.* You are being intimidated by your ego in an experience of guilt that lingers beyond the moment of recognition. Only a dream would hold you to form, the construction of a story of separation in every mind. Release it immediately, and open to the next "now," which is a fully new spaciousness.

56

A Portal to Awakening

I show Myself in unexpected and delightful ways.

October 29, 2013

Holy Spirit, what is Your instruction? We will write again of symbols. Tomorrow, Jo comes to Maui. She and her husband will also be here for Halloween, traditionally known as a day to celebrate the opening between the worlds. Her timely arrival is a symbol that a portal has been made for each of you to pass from the dream world into a state of being awakened to the dream. This is what our books are for. All words, events, and images are symbols of symbols. Last night, you opened a gift from your sister who lovingly sent you a stuffed black cat that looked just like the kitten who twice ran to cuddle with you as you walked in Solvang. I told you that the kitten was a symbol of Me coming to greet you with bountiful love. Now, the symbol of a cat is present in your home. Stuffed or alive, it is all the same. It has arrived before Halloween and will greet Jo who loves cats. Let it be a reminder of My Presence as we edit together.

You were also gifted, in preparation for Jo's coming, with a new battery-backup for your computer from a friend who calls himself "the computer whisperer." Of course you receive My soul whispers every morning to fill the books. At this point, you can laugh at the way the dream is showing up. It is tailor-made to suit you and your picture of the world. Every element of your day coincides with your desire and My plan for your life. We are now in sync. You did not know that a stuffed black kitten was coming to your door, but it was in perfect harmony with every previous event and forthcoming expectation of Jo's arrival. Most

173

importantly, it gave you joy, a reminder that this is a playful and happy dream.

Yesterday, I told you to buy an iPhone, something you have strongly resisted, just as you resisted Me for millenniums. You now have released your resistance because you know Me through our communication. It is time to accept the idea of an iPhone, the current state of the art for communication within the world of form. Open yourself as a channel to the entire world, a symbol for the whole mind that contains all of humanity. The channel must be open to transmit and receive My Word. You have gone through major openings in the past few weeks that were centered on your release of the deep fears attached to Me in My lifetime as Jesus. He was a symbol of the Holy Spirit, the One Son of God, the same as you and everyone who makes up the Mind of God. Your fear of union with Jesus was your fear of the re-union with your Father after the imagined separation. Your fear and resistance are now healed and are why you can be a transmitter to the mind through the publication of our books.

Of course, the books are a symbol to describe one of billions of ways to return home. Each seeming individual has his own unique map. Every man will find his soul's longing, his heart's desire, and will return to God as the One Son. It is all in the Great Plan and will happen according to schedule. These books will be a stimulus for the awakening of all who read them and give hope that this journey is fully possible when one has the desire. Just like the black kitten toy that appeared at your door in time for Jo's arrival to complete the edits for Book 1, everyone will receive the symbols they need to know that I accompany them on each step of the journey. I show Myself in unexpected and delightful ways. Have fun, and don't take life so seriously. It is just a dream, and you will all wake up to learn we are One and the same.

Email from Jo: This message fits right in with my experience last night. My cat Chi was snuggled next to my neck. I heard the Voice say, "You still have concern and sadness about leaving Chi at home, given his current medical condition. You have been puzzled about the timing of the illness, right before you are to visit Margie. This is the fear: you believe that when you left Home you were responsible for breaking your Father's heart. In effect, killing Him/God. You would forever feel responsible and guilty for leaving. I tell you now, you are *not* responsible for "doing" anything, since nothing happened. You did not leave Home, nor can you leave Chi." At that moment, I received and accepted the truth of this. Chi, once again was just showing me my old beliefs: by leaving, I would cause a big problem, and it would result in death. I deeply felt my innocence in that moment. It relieved me and lifted this burden. I know my cat is in good hands, whether I am with him or not.

Holy Spirit, I am remembering the first time Jo came to visit me in Maui, in 2005. I had laryngitis and could not say a word, but she loved me anyway. This time when she visits, "my voice will be her voice" as now we each have the same Voice of the Holy Spirit. Is that why I had laryngitis then? Yes, together you were to lose your own voice and come to Mine. That has happened. The laryngitis was symbolic of what was to occur: total surrender to Me. Together, you will share the One Voice. Jo is the face of Christ, coming to visit. She is your brother, your sister, your mirror, your Self, Me.

57

Be One Voice

I have set up your life to get your attention so you will see
this world as nothing more than a repeating dream,
made to wake you up.

October 30, 2013

(I wake up after a midnight dream with the
thought that Jo and I have been hearing two
distinctly different voices. How can they be the
same?)

Holy Spirit, what is Your answer? This is the mystery of life on
the planet: whose voice rules? Jo is at the airport coming to visit
you. In essence, it will be the same as her first visit. Mt had no
voice then, and now she is losing her ego's voice. Before, mt did
not realize it was My Will for her to be "without voice" so she
could know that her connection with Jo was based on something
other than the voice of the ego form/larynx. This time, as you
speak, the only Voice will be Mine. Respond only to That. The
intricacy of the dream is stunning as you see the minutest
elements coming together after years of separation.

Last night, you were blown away when you looked at the
cozy socks you had bought for Jo, in Solvang. They had been lying
upside down on your dresser for a week, and you had no
recollection of the image that drew you to buy them. When you
picked up the socks you saw the perfect replication of a black cat.
The kitten in Solvang that greeted you, the stuffed toy from Susan,
and the cat socks, all were the same image. How is that possible?
This is the way I have set up your life to get your attention, so you

will see this world of form as nothing more than a repeating dream, made to wake you up.

Now you think of Meera's joy when listening to her husband play the clarinet, and you realize everyone is My instrument to bring you home. Larry was the instrument through the persistent pain of their marriage for Meera to say, "There must be another way." She stuck it out and learned that her pain was the ache of the original separation, projected. I have lifted it so now she can see My Love in Larry's face, and in her own, reflecting My Love of her and her love of Me.

You, Meera, and Jo all share the same Voice. Triads are a means to see a clear representation of the wholeness of your Being: the Trinity of Father, Son, and Holy Spirit. It is a way of knowing the truth in three dimensions, which is also the makeup of form. Yes, this blows your socks off, and you too have new socks to keep you cozy. Here we laugh again at the dream. The One Voice has become known in this dream through symbols that point to unity. Now you can consciously choose to join with the brother as the one who carries the same inner voice as you. It is with this awareness that you and Jo will work on the editing. I will guide you and you will listen. *Holy Spirit, will I ever know You in the stillness?* Yes, that is coming, but our focus now is uniting My Voice with all voices. My Voice is the representation of the Mind of God, the One Mind where you reside, the Truth outside of the dream. Be One Voice.

58

Expanding the Mind

This book is a means to open the door to the vastness of
human/divine consciousness,
as yet untapped by the sleeping mind.

October 31, 2013

Holy Spirit, what is Your instruction today? Everything of the realm
of form is a symbol for what is happening in the mind of man. Just
before you started to type you opened your SkyWalk application
to view the Big Dipper and Cassiopeia, so clear and enormous on
the northern horizon. Yes, we study the mysteries of form on both
the grand scale of the heavens and on the minute scale of
molecules. You believe that the constellations are a reality, as clear
and solid as all the parts of your human body. "Bodies" are all the
same, made up in the mind of man to try to explain his existence
as "form, apart from God." Man has forgotten his home beyond
the images of the cosmos, so he seeks to learn the secrets of his
human life, hoping they will give a clue to his origin. His Origin is
in Me, the Self, the Mind of God. There is a consciousness so vast
that the human mind cannot begin to comprehend it. Your human
brain only fathoms a pinprick of the immensity of the mind.

Our books are a means to open the door to the vastness of
human/divine consciousness as yet untapped by the sleeping
mind. *Holy Spirit, did You mean to say "human/divine"?* Yes, the
human who knows he is One with God has expanded his mind
into the greater consciousness, unavailable to the sleeping mind of
man. You are now moving into that expanded state. You recently
bought an iPhone and a wireless home phone with unlimited
calls. You also have a new battery in your computer backup.

These are just symbolic of the next step that will take our communication beyond the limits of your present capacity to receive and disseminate My Word. I have not yet shown you how I would like the messages for Book 1 organized, nor have I set you up with a publisher. You and Jo have diligently and lovingly worked to bring the manuscript up to a point where it can soon be presented to the world. I will work with you both to hone this material today, and will handle the next steps as well. Just be present to My instructions. You will be tuned into the greater consciousness, which will, of necessity, expand your capability to understand.

You are concerned about Meera not being present in this task to have the same experience. She is fully present with us as she is totally joined with both of you in the mind. Her full intention is to participate in every step on this journey. Rest assured she is here and is receiving every increment of our union. You have no comprehension of what I am discussing because you are still immersed and surrounded in your world of symbols. Yes, they are tools we use in the world, but they only point to the fact that the three of you are with Me in the mind as we form a means with the books to help the sleeping brothers awaken from their dreams. This is enough for now. Be patient. Be still, and know that I am in charge. Everything will unfold in My perfection. Prepare now for your day at the gallery and enjoy the Halloween fun.

59

Approach to Love

This writing takes the reader beyond the ego form and
offers a direct experience of My Presence within.

November 2, 2013

Holy Spirit, what is Your instruction this morning? You are again
being shown the role of death in the dream. Last night you
watched the movie *Million Dollar Baby*, where the young female
boxer wins the title and loses her life from a vicious attack by her
opponent. Her trainer, out of love, gives in to her final wish to be
disconnected from her breathing tube. When you stopped
watching the DVD, your TV switched to *Moby Dick*. Ahab was
saying he would fight to the death to awaken. Today is the "Day
of the Dead" and the anniversary of your mother's death.

Just before turning on your computer, you allowed yourself
to open the three-ringed binder from Jo that contained all the
typed pages of Book 1. You are still in tears, looking at her edited
copy for the first time. The passage you read depicts the terror of
the ego at receiving this Word, and you are stunned at your own
reluctance to reread what we have written. It is so terrifyingly
beautiful you can barely touch it. This is the terror to the approach
of love, which you wrote about in a poem for Susan. The ego is
terrified in the face of Love. It will do all in its power to shield
itself from My face. This is the battle between heaven and hell,
God and the devil, out pictured. Halloween depicts the gap
between these two worlds and all that lies between.

You and Jo will be discussing the manuscript of Book 1 today.
I will be present. The editing is to be completed during her visit so
a publisher can soon begin to work with it. Know that it is fully in

My hands and beyond your grasp, even at this point in our journey, where you have seen your life, and the lives of Meera and Jo, unfolding perfectly and "miraculously." Yes, Book 1 is to be presented to the world, and today is the beginning of its liberation, mirrored in the passage you read in Chapter 28: "You trust that I know where I am taking you, and you have signed on for the ride."

As you hold the binder of 181 pages, transcribed between February 2 and May 31, 2013, you are overcome with the love that Jo has put into the editing. Your ego mind has not allowed you to fully appreciate the commitment the three of you have made to send My words out into the world. This is a Work of Love, My Love for the world, My Love for you, your love of each other, and your love for Me. The word *love* has always been abhorrent to the ego self. It is now seen in its manifestation as you hold the manuscript, filled with Jo's love for My words. In the process of editing, Jo has also opened the door of her heart to her husband, who has patiently joined our project to bring a printed copy to fruition.

You three have each allowed yourself to demonstrate to the world the resistance that all humans have to the Love of God. That Love is the greatest challenge to ego-based mankind. Man's closest approach to love is its substitution in romantic love, which is the love of self, ego self, reflected in another human being. The Love of God is beyond all form and does not know life or death. This writing takes the reader beyond the ego form and offers a direct experience of My Presence within, which is composed of the Love of God. When you begin to recognize and hear My Voice you will understand that I exist as you and there is no distinction between us or any other member of humanity. This awareness creeps slowly into your consciousness as you study the maps to the door of Heaven. Prepare for your meeting now with Jo and review the copy before she arrives. *Thank You, Holy Spirit, for this opening. Give me full awareness of Your Love and Guidance, and my unity with You and Jo as we work. I will.*

(This is the poem I wrote for Susan, but I immediately realized that it reflected my relationship with the Holy Spirit.)

Approach to Love

Free me now from all delusion.
Let me step into your inmost chamber
Once again a trembling virgin,
Determined to enter "realms" forbidden
Destiny urging me ever further
To bed with my Only Partner
Stripped am I of all illusion,
Waiting—breathless—for Your Infusion
Dissolving eons of separation.

Holy Spirit, it is the joined commitment and shared interest with You that is so overwhelming (tears). This is unimaginable to me in this world. It is what I resisted in my marriage with Tom, and he with me. I never could have conceived of joining with You, Holy Spirit. I see it in form beside me as the opened, edited copy of the book, an effort made with three seemingly separated individuals on different parts of the planet, sharing one mind and one Self. It is incomprehensible to the ego mind but manifested and received through the one mind. Thank You, Father.

Email from Meera: Just finished reading my copy of the manuscript for Book 1. It's like a child that has yet to be named, a precious offering. Savoring each word, I feel so fed.

(Jo and I walked the beach to the crab rocks today. We saw a baby Shearwater peering from its cave and met Gabby at Rowena's market. Later, we sat and joined with the Holy Spirit for guidance on beginning the editing. We both got the same message to read the first page together. I called Meera to include her and said that we felt her with us. She helped me understand that I do not yet have the capacity to integrate or acknowledge what has been coming through me and to hold the material from Him as part of my Self.)

60

Communion of Souls

Each one is part of the Spectrum of God.

November 3, 2013

Holy Spirit, what is Your instruction? You had a taste of the real world with Jo and Gabby last night. You each were a reflection of the other and knew that you were all "in the same place" while imbibing the abundance of My embrace, My Grace. You each exemplified My face in a unified gathering. This feeling of unity happens when one offers his "aspect of Me" to contribute to the Whole. All together, their light/My Light fills the space with an entire spectrum. Everyone has a particular Ray, Color, and Beauty because they are composed of the Love of God. You delighted in Gabby's energy and in her delectable food. She showered you with My gifts of abundance and love, and both you and Jo were the perfect receptors. The joy of receiving and giving creates wholeness. This "chorus" of call and response is the Song of God, a song of love, described in the sharing of a heavenly meal. You were reminded of the love shared among Jesus and his disciples, the Communion of Souls awake to My Presence within. They, as you, were open to the flow of love which pours through as food and drink are offered in the loving spirit of Oneness.

I am showing you the workings of the real world. You, Jo, and Meera are each operating in the real world of knowing Me in the mind, but you have not yet experienced it together as a threesome. You, mt, are in a much different place of recognition of Me now, than you were during your visit to the mainland one year ago. At that time, I was not familiar to Jo and Meera as their own internal Voice and Essence because My dictation with you had only just begun.

Last night was another step toward the recognition of My Presence, when you, Jo, and Gabby, were together. This experience will become the way of it in many other encounters. You will see all brothers as your Self as you shift in consciousness and perception. You will not identify with their character roles but will immediately remember that the true Self lays below the cover. Everyone in form is an aspect of God, and together you offer completion to each other as you expand the knowing of your Wholeness. In the past, you would try to shield yourself from those characters who grated on your senses in one way or another. Now, you open the door to each one as part of the Spectrum of God, which is necessary to complete His Glory, and yours.

As I bring you into an expansion of the concept of "your brother," I expand your concept of Unity. To be in Union with God, the goal of our work, you must be ready to welcome every brother as your Self. You felt the joy last night of being in a place of wholeness. That was an experience of Being, with no attachment. Each encounter in your life can be like last night's lovely dinner, with the sharing that took place. Realize that you sit at the table with Me in every contact, with every handshake or embrace. You are engaging with your soul-womb-mate when you think of, or interact with anyone past, present, or future. We are One Idea, One Thought: the Thought of God. The many selves, the brothers who compose humanity, are the shards of the vessel of God's Son, shattered in what is called the "Big Bang." That did not happen, yet you are mending the vessel, returning it to its wholeness when you welcome each of the "separated sons" back into your heart. Each brother is waiting to receive recognition of his belonging to the One Son, to you, as the mirror of his own Self. You felt this recognition last night in your time together as a threesome and can experience it with everyone you meet, this and every day. Go forward and know that the real world is where every brother is seen as one of the Rays of the sun/Son. You need his essence to join with yours to see and know your Self. The mystery is being revealed each time this is recognized. Feel your expansion into Wholeness each moment until you are filled to overflowing.

61

Only Now

*The concept of tomorrow is what keeps you
stuck in the ego.*

November 4, 2013

Holy Spirit, what is Your instruction today? We will write about tomorrow. You question that word because you believe that you must "be in the now" and "there is no tomorrow," so you wonder if the ego is speaking. The concept of tomorrow is what keeps you stuck in the ego. Tomorrow keeps you out of the now and carries you out of your Self into nowhere. You just looked at the predawn sky and the vastness of the cosmos with the Big Dipper foremost on the horizon. It occurred to you that your consciousness must also be vast, not limited to the small vocabulary of your life. This is true. I am introducing you to the knowledge that My Life extends far beyond the pinprick of your ego perception.

You believe that "tomorrow" holds the vastness of unlimited horizons symbolized by the exploration of space. Tomorrow is just a word, a concept that tricks your mind into believing that "more exists" than just now, that there is a life which extends beyond today. There is no space, no life, other than what you experience in this moment with Me. I am your total Consciousness, a part of God's Love which can never be dissected. The entire realm of the universe, as you see it, is only a picture formed in the mind to symbolize a memory of the Original Home, and that is why man named the cosmos, the heavens. All of this is still beyond your full comprehension.

When you realize that none of what you see or experience is real because it is only a dream made up in your mind, then the doors will open to a whole new view of your self and the world. Form will become inconsequential, like a photo of the earth taken from the moon, or of the moon taken from earth: a snapshot that really tells nothing of its subject. Your Home with God, united in Love, cannot be described, but can be "touched" when you are fully in the now, without past or future. When you have left all attachment to your ego self, all identification with your sense of I-ness you will experience the Reality of your True Self. It will bring you to the Gates of Heaven, and return you to Union with your Source. You have been listening to Eckhart Tolle's book *A New Earth*, and it now makes sense as never before. His concepts are parallel with your experience of Me as we have been writing the books. You dismissed his writings years ago, but now see they mirror what I am describing: the release of attachment to the world of form to open into the Now of your Reality in Me.

Yes, some experience the Now because they realize that tomorrow, a concept to limit the possibility for man to grasp his essence, does not exist. The moment of now is the only "time" that does exist. You feel the frustration that you have not known the ongoing state of Now. You have touched it, but you long for it to be a continuous state of mind. Actually it *is* the state in which you exist. Only in the moment of Now can you open your eyes/mind to that knowing. Now is who you are, devoid of form. Each day we come closer to the unveiling, as each day we are removing layers of ideas and beliefs that this universe of form is your reality. You are being weaned from your identification with and attachment to a world you believe has given you birth and substance to one that will last for all time and has no tomorrow. That is where your liberation lies. Tomorrow is nonexistent, just a thought in your mind, literally a word to which you have attached your own meanings and expectations. Soon you will know that words have no meaning, nor do the things the words would describe. We are coming to the place of letting go of even the language of life, the concepts in the mind that make up the world.

190

You recall the Bible passage you learned as a child: "In the beginning was the Word and the Word was with God and the Word was God. The same was in the Beginning with God. All things were made by Him, and without Him was not anything made that was made. In Him is life and His life is the Light of man." Now you have it. The Word was a creation of God. Here, the Word means the Christ. Man used his own made up words, thoughts, and concepts as tools to overlay the Word of God, his Christ Self. He believed the world he made was real. Man forgot that the Light of God is his only reality.

This is what I want to tell you today: uncover the darkness, layers of beliefs devised from words. When seen in the Light, they dissolve and bring you back to the original awareness that you are God. All of man's words would cover over the truth that man is composed purely of the Spirit of God, without name or form. Question your every thought, every word. Ask if it is real. Ask Me if it contains your Truth as the Light of God. Soon, words will hold no power over you, and you can return again and again in your mind to the Knowing: *I am the Son of God; I am God.* There is no other I than I Am. Your life will then be centered each moment in your I Am experience of your Self, and tomorrow won't exist because the *I AM* is all there Is. The Now is your Life, and you Exist only within it each moment. There is nothing to think, nothing to expect. The I Am Lives you, Is you. You are That: *So Hum.* It is your Breath. It is your Life. Be Here. Now.

(Later that day, while Jo and I were reviewing the manuscript of Book 1, my friend Andy called. He just learned that Ken Wapnick, editor of *A Course in Miracles*, has cancer. After hearing the news, Jo and I spoke with the Holy Spirit and called Meera so she could to do the same. Several months ago, I sent Ken a preview of *One With God*, Book 1, and

inquired about him publishing it through the
Foundation of Inner Peace.)

*Holy Spirit, thank You for Ken, for his presence, his example, and
for showing the way through ACIM, elucidated by his love of You and
his writings. Thank You for gifting me with his books and our
connection. Be with him.* I am with him always and you are joined
with him in the mind. You share My heart and desire to give the
world My Light and My Word. You are both vehicles, serving Me,
the Christ Self/the Holy Spirit within. You each light the way to
Me and your soul's purpose is the same. Yes, soul mates. It is
known to him that you will continue the work as he knew his time
was nearing an end in this plane. He is grateful that you will carry
on the work. You are partnered with him and with Me. You both
share My purpose. We are one. Release Ken now to Me. He is
whole and he is liberated. He has done his work and is complete.
You will carry on to a new completion. It is all perfect. Ken is
beyond pain and needs no healing in physical form. He is Healed
and Whole in Me. We are all unified. There is nothing you need to
do but be with Me and that is where he is. You, Jo, and Meera are
now united with him in the mind. Thank you for your presence
together with Me now and forever.

Email from Meera: Thanks for calling to let me know about Ken. I
have been sitting quietly with the Holy Spirit. Thoughts started
pouring through me so I got out my journal. Sometimes I was a bit
confused, but kept on writing. It all resonated with me and yet I
was not always completely sure who was speaking, like I was
merged with the Holy Spirit that was me, and wasn't me. Strange
sensation.

Here's a sample of what I wrote: *Holy Spirit, what would You
share with us about Ken?* Ken has devoted his life to help people
become free. He has completed what he came to do in this
lifetime. I need him someplace else. He served you three, and

many others beautifully as your leader to freedom. You have taken full advantage of his expertise, his gifts. Allow him to complete his work with you. *What do You mean?* Include him in your thoughts as you bring the books to the world. *Holy Spirit, can we visit with Ken?* Visit him now in your mind, and write to him if you wish. (Tears of gratitude as I composed the following letter to Ken but did not mail it.)

Dear Ken,
Thank you for making the retraining of the mind so understandable. Thank you for clarifying the complex, yet simple teachings of *ACIM*: one problem, one solution. That gave me hope. Thank you for being the finest, most reliable mentor I have ever had, next to the Holy Spirit. Your intimacy and attention to detail with the *Course,* modeled impeccability to me. Reiterating concepts helped tear down my old beliefs and rebuild new ones on a firm foundation of the *Course* principles. You have gifted the world unimaginably, beyond words. May you mirror the internal freedom as you begin your trek Home. I am grateful that we have parallel backgrounds in Judaism. This gave me added confidence to embrace the *Course* as the tool to restructure my mind and join the one mind in natural time. You have served me at the highest level. Your light shines and leads the way and I will always honor you as my master teacher and demonstrator of choosing to think differently. Blessings for a gentle transition. Amen.

Love,
Meera B.

62

Further

I am carrying you forward in the conceptual understanding
of My plan beyond space and time.

November 5, 2013

(Yesterday, I was deeply touched when I heard
about Ken Wapnick. Jo, Meer, and I were all given
the message that Ken's work is done, he is at peace,
and the work will be carried on by our writing the
books through the Holy Spirit. For the rest of the
day and evening, Jo and I sat with Him asking for
direction on how to proceed with the editing. It
was a joy to share in this way and to experience
how His instruction was the same for each of us.)

(2 a.m.) *Holy Spirit, what do You have to say?* I am with you all
and happy for our coming together. This is true shared interest,
and that is what is so satisfying for you. Our relationship is a
marriage in the purest sense where the focus of the partnership is
the One Self. Yes, unity is sought in earthly marriage but ours is
unseverable. You, Jo, and Meera felt the joy of unity using mt's
iPad to FaceTime with each other. You laughed for the joy of it all.
We were together to complete a promise of union with our
brother Ken before his passing from this lifetime. The four of you
have served Me by writing My words to waken the nations. You
three are carrying on his work/My work, and he is grateful. Mt
made this known through the letter I requested her to send to Ken
last April. At that time, he knew his death would be approaching
and your communication touched his heart. It was My message to

him that the *Course* is carried forward to a new level of understanding.

Ken's books were essential tools for your understanding of the *Course* and your awakening to My Voice. You now appreciate My urgency in having you contact Ken when you did. He had to have the introduction to you in form, although it had taken place at the beginning of time and was known to him in the mind where the four of you have been joined. (*I feel His Presence in my heart and temple.*) Ken has served his purpose in this realm and will be available in the mind to serve you three in the continuation of My books. You, in this moment, mt, "don't want to bother him" and can barely believe you are hearing this message, but it is true. The work does not stop. It is your destiny, and in the mind it continues.

You are committed to speak and disseminate My Word throughout eternity. Now you wonder what that means. You want to know yet resist an explanation. This is beyond the scope of your understanding at this time. Rest assured that Ken, and you, will continue to put forth My Word through our joined will for all eternity. Yes, this is the meaning of the extension of God's Son. Meera and Jo are part of you, and we will continue our work into the next eons of timeless mind. Do not try to comprehend this. You can't. Don't worry about the "future" of the books. It is of no consequence in the role I now describe for you. Rest assured I have it all handled.

You are ready for a big next step, one you have resisted for lifetimes. In your chest, you feel a mixture of emotion aroused by your ego's questioning of whether you can meet the task, and whether you are making this up. You are not making it up, and you will fulfill My Purpose. Book 1 will be published, and Ken will help in this process from his position in the mind. *Holy Spirit, You told me yesterday there is no tomorrow. Why do You tell me this now about the future?* I am carrying you forward in the conceptual understanding of My plan beyond space and time. For now, know that it is My plan for the publishing of the first book, and you will be actively involved in that process along with Jo and Meera. Your friend Marie entered your life to quell your initial fear that you could never participate in the publishing process. Now, you feel that your inner door is open to wherever I lead you. *Holy Spirit, I give You my consent.* Thank you. We shall proceed. Now sleep.

63

Just Fluff

It is only the sharing of your Beingness in Me that matters.

November 6, 2013

Dream: Someone has left behind a small cardboard box. Inside, there is food, and a pure-white ball of live fur with front teeth like a hamster. The tiny "animal" is very intelligent and comes right up to me. It seems tuned into me. Though I welcome it without fear, I tell it not to bite. It is mine, and I will keep it, so I name it Fluff.

Holy Spirit, what is Your meaning? This is about you welcoming Me without question. It seems that I appear from nowhere and that I will stay. There is nothing else but Me, and you. I hold you as you hold Me. There is no form, just a fluff of fur. Now you are teary. It feels like Jo is the same, coming into your home and sitting with you while both of you read My words. She holds our Book in her lap as tenderly as you held the weightless, pure, innocent, loving fur ball. You and Jo are like that fluff, interchangeable with every other form there is. Nothing else is going on between you but love, peace, and My Presence. No egos. You both are holders, containers of My Word. There is no expectation for the relationship to serve any of your human needs or desires. It is only the sharing of your Beingness in Me that matters: One Being doing the Work of God. You are grateful and relieved that this *is* your experience of sharing My Love. That is all there is.

You just looked over at your turtle painting. A nest like ball of feathers sits in front of it. The nest represents love, which composes every image in this make-believe world. Yes, "make-believe" would make you believe that every thing is separate. It is not. Everything is the image of Love, like the thought of you and Jo editing at the computer. In this mind image, you have no substance, no specific qualities of form. The Presence of Love without form is experienced in the absence of ego. As Love, I appear in reminders, little "beings" that show up out of nowhere. Yes, like the mosquito last night, tiny but present, bringing concern that you might be bitten. This idea was also part of Fluff when you saw its teeth. These are the last remnants of ego fears, the basis for the creation of this dream life. The imagined threat that God's teeth will attack you, unaware, still must be released. This belief is what keeps you bound to the world, your hiding place from God. Fear will go away when you trust that I could never bite, and that God is not the source of fear. He will never harm you.

You have come a long way to the realization that the thought of separation is just a dream based on fear. You are almost to the door of Heaven, and in your heart of love, that open door bids you enter, fully and joyously. In the dream this morning, the expectant face of Fluff was waiting for your acknowledgment that it belonged to you, to bring you the joy of its love. I am always here. I am the Love that is your nature in truth. Know that we exist as One and live as One. The images will come and go. Only Love is Real.

E-mail from Jo: I had a dream about you, mt, before you told me about your Fluff dream: I was in a living room in my house, and saw several people sitting on two couches. Although I remembered I was having company, I had not made any food or cleaned the house but didn't feel concerned. A toddler was walking around the living room, which wasn't too surprising, but the sight of a big tiger strolling among the crowd of people was. Just as I thought the tiger would eat or attack the baby, it bit the tip of her pointer finger. The bite produced only one drop of red blood, and the baby held out her finger so we could all see it. She did not seem upset. Margie, you appeared and wrapped the baby in a brownish patterned cloth and cradled her close, saying that you were "one with the baby" and would take her to Costco. When I woke up I thought to ask the Holy Spirit about the dream. He said, "You are thinking that you are the baby and Margie is holding and protecting you, but you are the very same. Margie is taking the baby, which represents the Book, to 'Costco'—the world." (Later, I thought about the tiger's bite. It was so minimal, really nothing, a reminder that the ego has almost no power left to do any harm.)

64

Transcendence

Die before you die, and return to Me, your Self in Life.

November 7, 2013

(Today, Jo and I will be spreading the ashes of our
friend Ann on my favorite beach at sunrise.)

Holy Spirit, what is Your instruction this early morning? This is
the birth date of a friend whose ashes you will return to Source.
You symbolically return to Source with her. You are all One. This
is the morning of the One Son, celebrating unity under the rising
sun. You are releasing the ashes of your burned egos, bodies,
personalities, and are surrendering all and everything of this
world to Me. This friend, Ann, is your self who you send forward
to Me for eternity. "Ann" exists no more, and you exist no more as
separated selves. Let go of form today. Send each particle of ash
into My Ocean of Being. This is your Baptism.

Feel My embrace. My Love is always present. See Me in the
clouds. Imagine that you, Jo, and Ann are entering the face of the
sun. Rejoice in your unity with Me, together again after lifetimes
in separation. You recognize your Oneness of purpose now. It is
what you have waited for all this life, as well as in the lifetimes
when you did not yet recognize each other as One in Me. Ann's
birth and death rite this day represents all births and deaths in
every seeming lifetime for you, Jo, and Jo's husband, who will
also be present. As you gather together, you, mt, will read My
message on Keawakapu Beach, where you will do the service. The
words are written for those present, but they encompass everyone

in the mind, including your book partner Meera. Call her now and share My words, which you will speak today:

"Return now to the sun as the One Son. See the whole horizon in blazing light, receiving the gift of your souls, offered to Me for unification with God. Die before you die, and return to Me, your Self in Life. Celebrate this moment. Ann, I give you to the Holy Spirit for a New Awakening in Him, in the Love of God that you are. Sail forward into the Light of Heaven, the Divine Light into which you were born and will never die. Celebrate your transition and your continuation as One in Eternity."

(Jo and I spread the ashes into a calm ocean, as the sun was just rising above the peak of Haleakala. Three turtles came and swam close to the rocks, nearby. Jo's husband took photos during the service.)

(Later) Remember Ann as her Essence in Me, which is Love. She was a being with great capacity for loving and for life. She is One with Me. Ann chose Jo to be a guide at the end of her life, because Jo exemplified for her the Peace and Love of God. You, mt, are also helping Ann to complete her earthly journey with Me as she releases attachment to the earth and ocean that she dearly loved. Together, you and Jo are helping her soul to know that it has transcended the earth plane and gone beyond. You return her to Me, to the Ocean of Being. This experience of unity and love joins the three of you in a transcendent mission. Jo's husband, Gary, has also helped facilitate Ann's transition through his love and support of her. In time, he will come to know the importance of his role. He is as committed as you and Jo. He, too, is Me and will recognize his Self as Me today. This is all part of My perfect plan.

65

Who Am I?

Your ego personality is nothing other than
a nagging thought, quickly illuminated and eliminated,
when you call on Me.

November 8, 2013

Holy Spirit, thank You for all Your gifts: for the beauty of the ceremony for Ann, for the sunrise, the appearance of the turtles, and the inclusion of Gary. Thank You for the finishing of the first round of editing and for the beautiful joining in song at uke jams last night. What is Your message this morning? You are all blessed and feel My Blessing for your joined efforts. This is the Gift of Spirit, the Gift of Love, in you and of you. It is an experience of your Essence as One with God.

You find yourself jumping ahead of today in responding to Meera's idea for Gary to self-publish our book. I have told you that I would find a publisher, and it is someone I have chosen who will be coming into view in My timing. This is not for you to take into your own hands. The whole process is Mine. Meera can ask again where the desire for self-publishing is coming from. This discussion will take her into a deeper understanding of her relationship with Me, so it was of great value to have the idea come onto her mind screen. Every thought is being used. I am working with each of you in your own transformation, which is the point of all the writing. Yes, these books will be published, but you must realize that I am the only Publisher, the only Doer. Nothing can happen outside of My Will.

Jo and Gary will be attending a play tonight and mt is feeling left out. This is similar to how Meera feels "left out of the editing."

The ego would have everybody feeling left out of the only Play there is: your unity with Me. I am speaking to the belief that you could ever be "left out." No, you can never be excluded from My Life. The ego will find every way it can to make the personality believe that it is not included with a brother. This is how it finds its own life affirmed. You are able to see these tricks of the ego more easily now and quickly ask Me for help. You rest in the knowing that you are exactly where you need to be and that tomorrow you will also be exactly where I place you. We now stand back and laugh at the antics of your ego character. It is nothing other than a nagging thought, quickly illuminated and eliminated, when you call on Me.

Another thought the three of you are having is how to "introduce" Book 1. Everything related to the books is from Me and is My Will. I will make that clear. I will place each of you in the role that serves Me and our books. For now, we will focus on the final editing of Book 1, which will come through mt's review of the manuscript that Jo has compiled. This will bring mt in full alignment with the book in its entirety. Until now, mt has not had the capacity to grasp the magnitude of the writing that has come through her. It was beyond her imagination, and she has not yet taken it in as a whole. Yesterday, as she reviewed the copy, she was stunned by the beauty and wisdom of the words she so lovingly and willingly transcribed each day. Yes, I am referring here to mt, the ego personality whose hand held the pencil that took down My dictation. She is My vehicle to get My words onto paper. Mt and her hand are not the Self that receives My Voice. That Self is the Heart, now fully open to receive. This is getting confusing for you now. Who are you? What is the Self, and who is mt? The Self is Me. I am your Heart and Soul. I am the Source of the Voice. The Mind, which contains the Self, is where you reside.

The split mind of man pictures a vehicle in form that can act out its will. The right mind will respond to and follow My Will, and the wrong mind, or ego mind, will translate and interpret My

Will to suit its own needs. Your job as decision maker is to choose which is the true voice and follow the dictates of that voice. The vehicle for the dictation, mt, is just a dream character. She is a figment of the mind's imagination projected onto an image that appears to have substance: a body and a brain. Those are not real. You have learned to finely tune into My Mind so that you can discern My Voice. This is what the three of you have been training for over these past eight years. You each hear Me because so many layers of ego, which had stifled My Voice have been removed. Now you see through the ego's charades more quickly and question any thought that gives you pause, that feels out of alignment with the peace and joy you have with Me. The tiniest annoyance, such as mt's wish to go to the play, is the signal to return to Me and ask for My interpretation. In this case, the ego's wish was the perfect occasion for Me to use as the example for our lesson. Everything is used for My purpose. Every thought can be handed to Me to open your eyes. Everything is an opportunity for seeing the truth.

You have all done your job, including Gary, who is now part of My team in the dissemination of the books. He is an integral part, and he signed up for this at the beginning of time. That is why he and Jo were drawn together so clearly when they first met. Internally, they were paired to perform this task which only now is becoming evident to them as a couple. Their marriage was predetermined of which they were aware. Now they see the full purpose of the task that would be their life's mission. It is still a monumental concept to fully acknowledge and embrace. Together, you will understand this in its fullness, and the completion of Book 1 will make that clear. For now, just take each day at a time. All will be revealed in My Time. There is nothing for you to do or plan but open your heart and mind to Me and listen for My Guidance in every moment.

(9:00 a.m. I stopped by Jo's condo and greeted Gary's brother, who also knew Ann. He offered to play a song that was written, sung, and recorded by her years ago. The lyrics referred to her own death and the celebration of merging with the sunrise. They reflected what the Holy Spirit gave me to read yesterday morning at the service. Ann's voice was beautiful and transcendent. I felt her soul and all else disappeared. I sobbed as I listened and knew then that we are beyond form. I had never experienced this before with another's soul.)

66

Hard Wired

Each ego in the dream of separation has fought
to be unique, to be recognized for some quality
that will set it apart from all others.

November 9, 2013

Holy Spirit, what is Your instruction this morning? You had two dreams last night that reflect the state in which you now reside. In the first dream, you are looking at "your house," a combination of your childhood home and your home with Tom. The doors are open, and the gardens overgrown. This is the expression of your earthly home to which you had no attachment in the dream, and it is the state of your life as "observer" who watches the characters enter and exit. In the next dream, you are going to a nursing home to visit a female teacher of the *Course* who is approaching death. When you arrive, you call her on the facility phone and she answers in a voice full of joy, stating, "Hello, I am doing great, have never been better. Life is perfect." You sense her peace and state your name, knowing it makes no difference what you say or whether she recognizes you at all. Her light and joy emanate, and they are what you also feel happening within yourself.

This is what you experience now with all the many selves who populate your world. You see yourself as a lodestone, a magnet attracting all the parts of you returning home. You know the oneness of everyone you touch, and they know you as a reflection of their internal home/Self. You cannot be apart. Be present to receive their calls and answer them. You laugh and wonder if that is why you now have three phones operating: a new iPhone, your condo landline, and the new Wi-Fi home phone, installed just last week. Yes, I have wired you to receive all who knock at the door of your heart, ready to return to their Source. They are your dream characters, the parts of the One Son you rejected at the beginning of time. The rejection was the means by which your own imagined separate self could be alone and special. To live apart from God, you had to imagine that there was no other equal to God and that your entity would reign supreme. You had to become the god of your world, and no other could be equal to your power. Each ego has fought to be unique, to be recognized for some attribute that would set it apart from all others. It matters not what that quality would be because it can be found in the range of human manifestations from "broken" to "brilliant." They are really just the same thought of wanting to be special and distinct.

You have come to recognize your mt/emptiness on this journey. This is the point of the work each one must do. When you are empty of self, you are open to receive your rejected selves. You disowned them because they had not suited the image of specialness your ego wished to project to the world. The selves return now because they too are recognizing their own projections and are taking them back. This allows them to enter the light of their wholeness. You are feeling this reunion internally and seeing it mirrored externally. It is a joyous return, just as you felt when you tossed Ann's ashes into the sea. Everything you witness now will be a reflection of the return Home, an outside expression of an inward condition. Yes, this is the happy dream, a place of joy and completion, spoken of in the *Course*. Meera and Jo are also experiencing this state in their lives. More and more, this will become everyone's experience.

Remember, you are always seeing an out picturing of what is taking place in the mind. Each dream character who calls "your phone lines" has thousands upon thousands of others within his mind. They are the selves who long for their Source. You are getting a feel for the return, a recognition that each character is truly a part of the Whole. Yes, it is a lot to wrap your mind around, and yet you feel the truth of this because you see it reflected back to you every day.

67

Return of the Flock

Everyone comes into this lifetime wounded,
with a mark that would reflect his separation from God.

November 10, 2013

Holy Spirit, what is Your instruction this morning? We will speak of
Jo and her real world experience as she demonstrated an act of
loving what is. Yesterday, Jo traveled to the top of Haleakala with
her husband, his brother, and his brother's girlfriend, Beth. On the
way up the mountain, Beth revealed her belief that she had been a
victim of the Holocaust in her last life. She also shared many
examples of how the "wounding" continued in this lifetime,
beginning at birth when she was born with a deep, disfiguring
mark on her forehead. Beth felt "marked for life" and sought
healing by becoming a nurse. As they spoke, Jo created a healing
space by staying in constant communication with Me to hold Beth
in love. Jo's willingness to listen without judgment to Beth's
stories of abandonment and abuse allowed Me to work with Beth
on the deepest level there is, to heal the cause of all wounding, the
belief in the original separation. Without Jo calling on My Love
and guidance for both of them, the darkness of Beth's self-hatred
would have persisted. This was My divinely appointed time for
Beth to heal, and for Jo to be given the reflection of her new estate
with Me. Jo had longed to be "like Byron Katie" in Katie's capacity
to love what is. Her experiences with Beth, and with Ann,
demonstrated to her that she has reached a new state of mind and
heart.

On the way back from the mountaintop, Jo and the others
stopped in La Peruse, at the south end of Maui where the shore is

covered with barren lava fields and feral goats. There, on the rocks, the group found an abandoned baby goat with its umbilical cord still attached, its mother most likely killed for food. Beth and Jo held the little goat and gave it fresh water. Then a tourist came by and volunteered to find a place for it where it could receive the proper care.

In the meantime, you, mt, were cleaning up some papers at home and came across an old Christmas card from the "Boo Boo Zoo," an animal shelter in Haiku where you have donated money. On the cover of the card was a photo of Sylvan, the owner, standing cheek to cheek with a young goat, clearly bathed in love. When Jo returned with her story of the baby goat, you smiled and showed her the card. Later that day, Jo heard from the tourist who said she had taken the goat to "a shelter for all lost, abandoned, and wounded animals" called the Boo Boo Zoo. Jo and her family decided to visit Sylvan, whom she called "a combination of Saint Francis and Jesus" because he offered unconditional love to all creatures brought to his door. You, mt, had the very same experience when you first met Sylvan.

This story reminds you that just a few weeks ago, while visiting your sister, you were greeted by a small black kitten. It ran to you as if it knew you and wanted to be held in your arms. You loved the kitten and looked for it the next day; once again it ran to meet you from afar. This is the attraction of love. It is a symbolic representation of how My Love will find all those ready to acknowledge it. The kitten and the goat are signs of Me, reflections of the innocence of your own soul coming to greet you, to be held with love. You too are Me. You are an out picture of the Love of God seen in the form of a body on a planet. In reality, you are all a Thought of God in the Mind. Everyone comes in wounded, marked to reflect his "sinful separation" from God. The purity of his innocence is covered by scars of darkness. Everyone feels abandoned in the moment of birth from the womb, which is just another symbol for leaving Home. The story of the lost goat reminds you of the return of the sheep to the flock. Yes, all will be welcomed Home with Love, and none will be left behind. That Love exists within each of you now as your Self. Call on Me and ask for My Presence to be known. Ask Me to direct your every thought. I am available for everyone. I am your Heart, your Soul, and your Life. Release the layers of guilt and doubt that would cover My Reality and you will feel My Peace, My Freedom, and My Love.

68

Ashes to Ashes

The mind will perceive and resonate with any image
that has meaning to the soul,
because it is a message of My Presence.

November 12, 2013

Holy Spirit, what is Your instruction today? You have had many experiences of Me over the past several days in your connection with Jo and her family. Each encounter was an opportunity to share your light, My Light. This morning, you were touched when Gary offered to find a mountain retreat for the team to work on Book 2 when the time is right. This was his direct acknowledgment that he is "on board" with our project. He is happy to be of help and it is essential for Jo in her role as editor to have his assistance. Their sharing is significantly strengthening their relationship and My Presence therein.

This morning, I gave mt a significant dream just before she awakened. It was a symbol for all of you to embrace Me as your own Essence. The image of the dream was of a moccasin in which mt had placed the head of a pink "composite flower" nestled in soil. She was careful to place the flower in its bed, in the sole of the moccasin. The living flower had no stem or roots, so its "life" could only exist in the now. Many tiny, identical flowerets together created one head to symbolize the unity of all beings that compose humanity. All are planted in the "soil of the soul" and exist only for the moment they are seen. Mt had a fleeting glance of heaven in that moment of the dream memory. Life in form is no different from this. The mind will perceive and resonate with any image that has meaning to the soul, because it is a message of My

Presence. I am communicating My Love through that image so the viewer is reminded that he is One with everything he experiences.

Holy Spirit, is this what You wanted to say as it just seems to be repeating itself? Yes, I want the message to enter deeply into the mind that nothing you see is real. It is all made up. All minds are joined like the head of that composite flower. Our Mind is One. Your thoughts are transmitted to your "brother's mind" so you will have a simultaneous awareness of an experience through the images stimulated by Me. The images received may not be identical but the purpose of the message will be the same. This happened today when Jo e-mailed about "the Maui snow" — the black ash from the cane burning this morning, covering most every surface. Her trip was filled with ashes from beginning to end.

(Later) You just met with an old friend who described a difficult divorce. You asked her, "What was the gift in it?" She answered, "I was burned to ashes and rose as the phoenix." Yes, everything is essentially ash, that which is left after all the imaginings of the mind are consumed in My Fire. Only then are you free to see your reality as Pure Spirit. Each blade of cane grass is no different from the flower you placed in the moccasin of your dream. It has its moment in life to grow, then be cut down and burned to release the essence of its core, the sweetness of life. This is symbolic of what you will experience once you lift the many layers of ego that cover My Light. Those reading this book can feel the heat of looking at their own suffering. When it is given to Me, a burning takes place. The remembrance of Me is like a match that ignites what is not pure, what is of the ego, and as it vanishes in the flame, one will be opened to a greater knowing of his true Self.

69

Impersonality

*Either you are one with your Self and nothing else is real,
or the Self does not exist.*

November 13, 2013

Holy Spirit, what is Your instruction today? You are feeling like a
stranger in a strange land, not belonging anywhere or to anyone.
There is nowhere to go. This is the impersonal life. You are totally
under My auspices and have no will of your own because our
wills are joined. You belong only to Me. Yes, it means that you
belong to your Self. This thought, a novel idea, brings tears to
your eyes because it is all you have searched for throughout this
life and all lifetimes. There is nowhere to look for satisfaction,
purpose, sustenance, love, or fulfillment but within your Self. You
are All there Is. This is a big concept and a big realization for you
and for everyone who comes to this awareness. Either you are one
with your Self and nothing else is real, or the Self does not exist. It
is what your friend said to you yesterday: "If Margie can't be One
with the Voice of Holy Spirit, then Margie doesn't exist." You can
not and do not exist apart from Me. There is no other that exists
apart from Me. Everything you perceive as "the world outside of
you" is in your mind. Your brother is your Self. We are One and
the Same. Soon our voices will be united because our will is
united. You are not trying to formulate a plan for your own life
any longer. Your life is in My hands alone, and I direct each
moment.

You have wondered what to do about your role as an artist on
Maui and with the Art Society. The time has come for that door to
close. A new life has entered, which is the work you do with Me

to disseminate the books. You will be concentrating on the editing of Book 1, then following through with the rest that are to come. So far, the majority of your focus, time, and efforts have been on the gallery and the art fairs. You will soon let the fairs go but will stay through the high tourist season and sell what you have. I am not asking you to end abruptly, but just to know that it is ending soon. I will make clear how to proceed. Go to the fair this weekend without attachment. Enjoy your time and all the brothers who show up.

Yes, the art fair was an opportunity to speak with people while doing My work, but My work is needed for the many who now will be touched through the books. This message is also for Meera, Jo, and Gary. You are coming to a new plateau where the books will be the focus of your lives. All your efforts will be required. This does not mean that Meera should give up teaching her Nia classes. It serves her and others through Me and is still a necessary part for her to come into full awareness of the Self. In time, its importance will fade, and the focus on the books will become paramount. You have no conception of what is before you and that is the way it should be. My plan unfolds in My way and in My time. Every thing and every one needed for the task will appear.

Jo's visit was vital to the continuation of our work. She felt fully immersed in My Presence throughout her stay. She saw how I operate in your life and she chose to experience "your life" firsthand, which helped her understand the book on the level of form. She witnessed My Presence reflected back to her through you. Gary also needed to better understand the setting of the book around your life in Maui, although the setting itself is unimportant. Everyone's setting is the perfect place for them, but it is useful for those involved with the books to be familiar with what is being described in the writing. All is now in place for the next step of publishing the first book in the series.

A special Banyan Tree "birthday weekend" is coming up. Go and sell your art. Celebrate this beautiful backdrop which has served you so well within the dream. The tree has served its purpose now, helping you unfold yours. In your mind, you will thank the tree, the birds, and all your friends and customers for the gifts this locale has provided you in coming to know Me. The Banyan Tree represents the union of all humanity symbolized by the interconnected aerial roots descending from all its branches, embracing you with its shade to cool you off from the hot Lahaina sun. The tree also connected you with Tom and your great grandfather Lewis, who spent time in the port of Lahaina in the early 1800s.

The time under the tree has been a necessary step in your recognition of Me as your only planner. You are ready now to release this part of your dream and step into the next and final phase of your life in form. It is what you came to do in this lifetime and it will be completed. Go with My Blessings and today will unfold according to plan. Take your walk under the newly risen sun and the showers of ash. They denote the ending of the old and the arising of New Life in Me.

70

No Favorites

You are all equal Sons of God,
none more special or different from the other.

November 14, 2013

Holy Spirit, what is Your message today? You were given My instruction last night about releasing every last bit of fear from the belief that you cannot reenter heaven. You have projected this onto your sister in your belief that her newest love relationship will be destroyed by her codependency with her daughter. This is really a fear about your own relationship with Susan, not yet fully discovered in all the projections you have taken back from her. To be codependent with your most special relationship is the basis of all relationships in the world of form, starting with one's parent.

The "parent" is the supplier of everything needed to sustain life: food, clothing, shelter, and love. This is what Susan continues to supply to her adult daughter, and you resent that the mother–daughter relationship is ongoing to the exclusion of your own needs from your sister. This is confusing for you, so you will need to stay with Me on this one. Susan has been the one onto whom you have projected your resentment toward God for not supplying all your imagined needs in life. You ask how that could be since you feel blessed with abundance in every aspect of your life, and have no more material, mental, social, emotional, or spiritual desires. It goes deeper than that. You want to be God's most beloved. You want to know that you are the most valued child of your parent. In this respect, Susan is the projection of your mother. Susan loves her daughter "more than she loves you." She is using the financial gifts from you, to support her daughter.

225

Susan does not honor your wishes in how your gifts should be used or how she should live her life. In other words, you cannot be placed as number one in her life.

This is a reflection of the human condition. The mind of man, the ego mind, is based on specialness, being the most favored in any situation or relationship. It may sound ridiculous in this moment but when you stop to think, each man feels his value diminished when another surpasses him. This dynamic of the ego keeps man trapped in his cycles of life and death for eons. You are now seeing this pattern as the way you live your own life. It is also the way that you will be led out of this never-ending hamster wheel. You must see that this life on earth, with all the relationships that appear to sustain it, is purely a substitute for what you wanted from your one and only Father, God. Your imagined absence from God must be filled with a belief that you are in a position of closeness, specialness, which makes you feel like "the one and only son." On earth, it is the firstborn who believes he is the most beloved of his parents. He works throughout his life to maintain that position in their eyes, and if not in the eyes of his parents, then in the eyes of those he values most, such as the best friend or the best employee in the organization, and on and on. The ego must achieve a position above everyone else; it must win so everyone else will lose.

The belief that the first son is the most special is a reinterpretation of the concept of the One Son of God. You recall the Bible passage in John 1: "In the beginning was the Word." The Word represents the One Son, the Christ Self, the Source and Heart of every man. Because the ego thought system would reign supreme, this knowledge of Self has been obscured for eons by the belief in a life "independent" of God. You are all equal "sons" of God, none more special or different from the other, united with your Father. All are God, God is All. The dream of separation is a classroom to return the One Son home. When the layers of ego have been uncovered, the light will dawn in his mind. Then, he will know that the home he seeks is really his own Self, the home he never left. This is the Awakening taking place for every reader.

Mt is taking yet another look at her projections of separateness in the need for a special relationship with her sister. It is through mt's determination to see the truth of what her ego would like to hide from her—that she has come to know Me. As long as you believe you live in a body in a world of form, these thoughts of separation will occur, especially in situations that feel threatening. The enabling that mt sees between her sister and niece is the perfect trigger for mt's ego to arise and demand that it be special, honored, and followed. Her ego is especially threatened at this time, realizing it has lost its control because mt has chosen Me as her only guide. The ego will desperately find an avenue to get her attention again and call for recognition of its needs, just as mt's sister and niece call to each other to fulfill their needs. Come with Me above this battlefield of ego interactions and see them for what they are, nothing but the ego's desire to establish its hold over your mind. In seeing this drama, you will be freed to return to Me to regain your balance and know that you are whole, innocent, and held in God's Love.

71

Heart of the Wheel

Each and every aspect of your life in form is symbolic.

November 15, 2013

Holy Spirit, what is Your instruction today? You are coming to the end, a descent that brings you back to the beginning of time. This is what brings tears and is why your life feels unfamiliar and out of context. You are leaving "your context," the life that the mt ego self has made, and yes, it was made in concert with Me. Now your eyes are opening to the purpose of your life in this world of form. You see with Me that it is not your real life, that it was made to distract you from the truth of your Being, but you also know that it was made to lead you back to that truth. Everything in this world is a dichotomy because the expression of duality was the basis of its formation. The doors of Sight are now opening, and you see the falseness of all your undertakings in the world. Yes, this includes the form of the books since their truth remains in the One Mind. Their image is just being out pictured, like the blue rotunda on the cover of the book in your dream, when I first told you to write. Each and every aspect of your life in form is symbolic and it is time that form dissolves as "reality" for you. Yes, you still will be living in the world but will no longer be *of* the world.

Jo experienced this state when she visited you. Now, back in her Denver home, she is trying to wrap her mind around her Maui experience, which left her feeling quite disoriented. In conjunction with Me, Jo touched the real world. It was not the world of her ego because she came with no plans other than to fulfill My instruction and My unfolding. You both allowed that to happen during those two weeks together. It gave you the feeling of living each other's life, of walking in each other's moccasins. That was the meaning of the moccasin dream. You have since learned that the flower in the dream was a "pentas." Though the flower looked familiar you never had heard its name. It is easy to see that the name is symbolic and represents the pen-task I have given you in this lifetime. You were to use the pen to record My words, an imaginary pen, to fill the soul of man. This is the task and you fulfill it as you take My dictation on your note pad or at the computer.

(Later) *Holy Spirit, what is Your message?* Let us return to the scribing. We begin when the mind is a blank screen, receptive to hear My Voice without the distractions of the world. I am now incorporated. You are inhabited. We are One. You are Me. You walk in My moccasins as the flower of My Life. You know Me by the pen, which transmits My meaning for your life. Everything has a purpose. You think of Jo and how she fully engaged in your activities during her stay. Yes, she incorporated the life you lead as you experience it in your place of residence. She deeply connected with the primary players of your island world and experienced the joy of it all. This was the outward expression of the inward condition of your shared interest in Me; it is the out picturing of joining on the deepest level, which is to share the One Self, the One Voice.

My books will be completed in form. Rest assured it will happen, even though you have not the least conception how. It is all part of the mystery that unfolds for you each day. You are at a point of dissolution and the forms of your world are collapsing. Tomorrow, you go to the Art Fair knowing this is the last time. You will be compiling prints of your art today to sell at a discount. This was My instruction to let you know that I am seriously asking you to end this phase of your life. Your connection and interest in the art life, which you have led on Maui, has now dissolved. It is the same feeling you had when you returned from your first visit to Maui in 2003, knowing that you had been called to live there. In your mind, everything on the mainland turned gray. It was dead for you. Only when you thought of Maui could you see in color. Now, your Banyan Tree experience is losing its color, and you know it is time to leave. The Pen is what calls you and gives your life its vibrance. My assignment for you this lifetime is being penned on My Soil, not the soil of Lahaina or the tree. Each venue in each phase of life serves My Purpose. The Art Society and Banyan Tree have served you perfectly as you have also served them. Now is the time to move on. Work only for Me.

Come with Me and walk the beach, then enjoy the preparation for your last art fair. You may share with your friends your intention to leave, and this will make it real for you. It feels as if the ground is being pulled out from under you, nothing to anchor you in form. Yes, the Art Society was your anchor on Maui, the hub of your life here. I am your Hub, the Center of the Wheel of your life. I am the One Who issues My Will to all endeavors to be lived in and through Me. This is the collapse of the universe and the collapse of the mt self who believed that she was the operator of her life. I am the Operator of every life. Make space for the expansion into My Will as the only thing that is Real.

72

Beyond All Words

These books are just a pointer to Me.

November 16, 2013

(5:30 a.m., Banyan Tree) *Holy Spirit, what is Your instruction?* Last night you dreamed of a yellow wooden pencil with two erasers on top. Under the erasers, you peeled away some old paper to find an inscription of the word *Bible* and knew that a verse was written below that. Rather than reading the verse you looked for it somewhere else. In the search outside, for what is right in your hand, you will never find it. You Hold Me now in your heart, your mind, and I come through the instrument you use to write. Where am I? Am I in the scribed words coming through your pencil? No, that is a fantasy, just as your experience sitting by the Banyan Tree watching the mynah birds leave their nests is a fantasy. I will interpret the meaning of everything you see. In the dream, you peeled layers of old paper off the top of the pencil and underneath was My Word. In your effort to find it in the outside world, you forgot to look at the Source.

What was that verse? "In the beginning was the Word . . ." Yes, this writing is a duplication of that verse. It is only a symbol of Me because I am beyond all words. The pencil is inadequate to show the content of the Word, Verse, Bible. The Book is just a pointer to Me. Discover Me in your wholeness of Being. Open to the full expression and experience of Me. *Holy Spirit, what must I do for that to happen?* You can do nothing other than receive My Word. This Word/writing is opening the door for you, like the reading opens the door for others. Each will come to Me in his own prescribed way and time. You will know Me, heart and soul.

We wed. We join. We become One. No other is left. Although you feel the tears and truth of that, you also see your resistance to having sat here, writing before dawn, when you really wanted to sleep. The ego would cover up My Love, My Verse, but you persist in knowing Me, and your knowing will expand exponentially.

The birds are flying now. You will stay with Me in your heart and our Love will become real to you. You and I will know each other as One. This is still a ways off. You need do nothing. I will bring it to you. You could never have imagined hearing My Voice and now you are being told there is so much more, and it will happen.

Untouched by Death

*To recover the memory of God is the purpose
of man on earth.*

November 18, 2013

Holy Spirit, what is Your instruction this morning? You were told during the night that this world is a dream and that you saw clearly displayed. Before bed, you watched a retrospective of the John F. Kennedy assassination, featuring the role of Walter Cronkite. He was a contemporary of Kennedy's and was the news anchor who announced the President's death to the world. Television was still in its infant stage as a disseminator of world news, but that day, it had the effect of turning Cronkite into an icon who would be seen by the nation as a shepherd through dark times, the one person respected and trusted by so many Americans to deliver the truth. The father of the country had died, and the "father of the media" would comfort the nation by his calm, conscientious presence. The homeland needed a voice that could help it reflect its wholeness as One Nation under God. Walter Cronkite symbolized My Voice, a voice which could speak from the wilderness of mindless shooting and death, to calm the citizens and point the way to peaceful recovery. The nation sought understanding and looked to the media to find it. The analogy stops there. In the mind of man, the ego would construct "a story" to explain the cause of every shooting to every seemingly separate son, a story that would coincide with their own history of attack over their many lifetimes of earth existence.

This attack of the country's "father" became another recapitulation of the original belief that man had wronged God by leaving the Kingdom. Man's guilt over his believed assassination of God led to his construction of a life, opposite from the peace he had known in Heaven. Man, in the separated state is always wary of a surprise attack. He is constantly on the lookout and therefore on the defensive. President Kennedy had permitted an unprotected drive through Dallas and had released his bullet-proof screen. Man has developed armor in the mind to prevent such an impending disaster. His first line of defense was to deny the Presence of God within himself and project all protection onto his ego. The ego self, in its representation as a brain and body, would cover over its vulnerability as the "forsaken" Son of God. When the ego defenses are released, as in the motorcade, all hell breaks loose. The scenes in Dallas were the ego's way to tell the world that it—ego has total control, and no power on earth can escape its domination. The country was once again in the grip of fear, and hatred. This was also reenacted in the events of 9/11 and the resultant escalation of defense and war.

You see how the ego has projected fear into the mind of man. Fear is the dominant force operating the world of form. It is pictured over and over in the events of the world as ever-present reminders of "who" is in charge. The ego will stop at nothing to reinforce its superiority and independence. The unity of God then becomes a forgotten memory in the mind of man. Now there is an awakening to that memory, which has never left the deepest recesses of the mind. To recover the memory of God is the purpose of man on earth. As he watches the fiftieth anniversary replays of the shooting in Dallas, he has more than the perspective of time; he has the tools of those individuals who have awakened to My Presence. Man can choose again how to view the events of terror that surround him. He can know "there must be another way." He can look at a world immersed in war and devastation and ask: what is true and who am I? It is time for man to reevaluate his life as a separated being. I am here to help with the questions and the solution. This book and many books now being written and disseminated through My guidance are a means of awakening the mind to the truth. A new world is emerging and it is happening for those awakened to Me, the Self, by whatever name I am called.

74

No More Substitutions

You will only find relief when you rise above
the battlefield of suffering and watch it with Me
in the right mind of Spirit.

November 19, 2013

Holy Spirit, what is Your instruction today? Yesterday, your country
once again reviewed the assassination of President Kennedy, and
is also in the middle of political wars over universal health care.
The ego fight goes endlessly on, and will never be resolved in the
world of form. The one resolution is to step outside the dream.
You will only find relief when you rise above the battlefield of
suffering and watch it with Me in the right mind of Spirit. Man
must see that this world of pain, suffering, and death is a world of
his own limited thinking. It is a long journey to come to the point
of knowing that you are a Creation of Spirit, the Son of God, the
same as every brother in Divine Essence. Just know that the dream
of pain and suffering lasted less than an instant in your mind.

This world is over. When you awaken to that truth, then and
only then are you free. The world of form has no hold over you.
You are free to put your total trust in the only reality, which is
your Self. This is what you saw with your sister yesterday. For the
first time in her life, after dozens of pursuits to find "the right
man," Susan has recognized that the love she sought outside
herself resides within her own heart and soul. Now, she is home
with her Self and needs no substitutes to fill and sustain her. This
is the reflection for you, mt, to recognize that you have come
home.

You were given information from an astrologer many years ago which helped you realize that your sister's numerous encounters with many lovers was really the projection of the same pattern in your own past lifetimes. You were also told that in this life you married a "remote Saturnian man." This distant relationship allowed you to focus on the one and only relationship of value, the one with your Self. You judged your sister throughout her life for seeking relationships that never were based on love. Now, you have taken back that final, major projection of judgment on her. This aspect of "her life" was an out picturing of your own journey through lifetimes of seeking substitutions for Me. The search has ended, and you have found your One and Only. I am your Self, and I am the Self of your sister. I am the Self of everyone. I am living in each of them as I live in you. All are healed and whole and innocent in the Mind of God. The work of this lifetime is to Know that I am God. You are God. We are One.

75

One Community

Do not make your work into an icon,
the thing that gives you a special identity.

November 20, 3013

Holy Spirit, what is Your instruction this morning? You are in a new paradigm where we are partners. This you had realized as the goal, and you often do experience our alignment and union. I am real to you as your Friend and Self and you count on My Presence to carry you through the day and night. We operate in union and can never be separate. This is the marriage to the Beloved. You are My Beloved and I am yours. We are one. This is why you sobbed at the ending of your story about the turtle, "Finding 'Oli." You are in tears even now because it symbolized your return to Me. I wanted you to write the turtle story as a prelude to our books to let you know that I will use you to disseminate the promise of the return for all who seek it. That first small book was "practice" for you. It out pictures your faith that the reunion will happen. You placed the story on your artist website because you wanted this message of Joy (*'Oli* means joy) to be available for all.

The *One With God* books have the same message of returning home and will be disseminated on the web. You, Jo, and Meera have opened your mind for that to happen. This is the meaning of creating space, like the space you, mt, created by releasing attachment to your art career under the tree. Now there is only one focus in your life, and that is Me. You know what I speak is true, and until this moment you never considered that the art fairs created a split of allegiance in your mind. They had been your top priority and were the focus of your physical energy. Although you believed I was your primary focus and that you were doing My Will in the daily dictation, the Banyan Tree yet held a special attraction in your mind. Yes, the tree was very special. You have worked to detach from all special relationships but never considered that a banyan tree held such significance.

You identified with the role of Artist under one of the most revered trees in the world and compared it to the Bodhi tree where the Buddha was enlightened. You imagined that the Banyan Tree symbolized the unity of humanity with its interconnected aerial roots, yet it was often a place of conflict and competition. This is the way of the world. Even your beloved tree held discord in your mind and in your body. For years, it was the focus of your Maui family and gave you a sense of specialness that you were chosen to sell your art there. The ego delighted in your special role of saleswoman in the gallery but kept you conflicted in each art fair as you fought with the ego to not be consumed by its need for you to be a top seller. The tree became a haven for the ego as opposed to a home for Me. You needed the experience for many reasons, especially to establish a sense of community, which the art fairs provided. But now there is only one Community, our Communion in the mind. It includes all beings where no individual roles exist. Remember, everything is either a symbol of the separation or one of union.

It is time to release all conflict. Release attachment to all venues when they no longer serve My purpose. This instruction is for all who are reading the books. I am asking you to assess the various roles you are playing. Notice which ones have become a distraction and, especially, the one you consider the most special and prominent facet of your life. I am the Way, the Truth, and the Life. Honor first your life in Me. Do not make your work into an icon, the thing that gives you a special identity to make you stand out above all others. Nothing you do in form has any reality in the Mind of God. Form is inconsequential. I will guide you through this dream world so you will know the truth, that I am the only

Reality. The special roles will fall away, one after the other, until you realize you are fully surrendered to Me and our wills have become joined. You, mt, may continue to work at the gallery for now. It will be an opportunity for you to meet the public and spread My Light.

Today, mt is in a spacious place in her mind and can therefore be receptive to My instruction and to the work I have for her to do. She had to be willing to let go of the past and open to Me as the only focus of her life. You will all be shown where your special attachments lie, and be given notice of when it is time to let go and turn to Me. The letting go is really a shift of focus and need not be an ending in form. You can picture yourself in whatever role you play in life as "partnered" with either the ego, needing specialness, or with Me and My command to love and join equally with your brother. When you surrender to Me, to the Will of God, you will see your life's role, your function, through My Vision. It is either the way of the ego or the Way of God. Unity is the Way of God. In your work and in your relationships maintain your unity with Me as paramount. Unity with your brother will follow. We are all One, and nothing shall come between the Father and the Son.

76

Unshackled

*Your habits and ways have kept you back from love,
from the freedom to move on the wave of My Being.*

November 21, 2013

Holy Spirit, what is Your instruction today? You are with Me now, on board, ready to go wherever I send you. You are eager to do My Will, surrendered without resistance. You have no other attachments and your identification with the Banyan Tree has been lifted. It is the last veil to set you free. You just looked at the word *veil* and realized it can be rearranged as evil. The veils that cover the light of truth are "evil." There is love, or there is evil, which means "unconsciousness." You want to awaken so you can observe your dream life with Me. You are becoming fluid in the dream, operating as I direct you and feeling the liberation that entails. Last night you had a significant dream where you looked onto the courtyard of your home and saw two campers packing up their new sleeping bags, ready to travel. Your unseen partner was Me. We were observing this new estate in which you now reside where you are ready to "go" at the drop of a hat. This demonstrates a major shift in consciousness and is the result of taking back the veils that have covered the love.

For all readers, this is the uncovering of the layers of unconsciousness that have been projected onto your most special relationships. When the veils are lifted, both you and your brother are set free. Mt is experiencing this liberation now. Her sister has come to know her Self and stand "on her own" with My guidance. You both are being liberated from the restraints of your limited ways of thinking and from the attachments to life patterns that have kept you in shackles for eons. The shackles remain unconscious until the patterns are seen and questioned. It takes tremendous will power and dedication to reconsider the operating programs, the "thought systems" of your lives. When you do question your habits and ways, you will see that they have kept you back from love, from the freedom to move on the wave of My Being. Only then will you be at peace, knowing our wills are aligned. Nothing resists doing the Will of God when wills are joined. Life then flows with total ease, devoid of fear or resistance. This is the life that mt is now stepping into, even though she believed it has been taking place ever since she first heard My Voice. In these books, you are seeing the evolution of the awakening, step by step. Each instruction serves the moment it is given. In the next moment, a new instruction may contradict the last. I take you along in increments so you can make your way with ease, just as a parent helps their baby learn to walk, never pushing beyond his capacity.

77

The Artist's Eye

*Each of you is a light, a representative of My Presence
within as your very heart and soul.*

November 22, 2013

Holy Spirit, what is Your instruction today? Yesterday, you worked
in the gallery and were met by a fellow artist who has created
representations of Me in the forms of Jesus on the cross, Father
Damien, and Mother Marianne. Each and every one who is
"pictured" in this life is a manifestation of Me. The Holy Spirit
resides "within the form" and is the Essence of that form. Your
artist friend has the gift of expressing My Light in his paintings
and sculptures. This brings the viewer closer to Me because they
feel My Love in his work. He gifted you with a painting that
depicted him, with his male friends around a campfire, under a
crescent moon in the dark of night. The scene was lit up by the
glow of the fire symbolizing My Presence among them. The love
expressed by those five men with their two dogs, all gathered
around the fire, touched your heart.

I am the giver of all gifts. The painting you were given is a
recognition of the gift of light that you shine in the gallery and
throughout your daily life. It is an outward picture of an inner
condition, the Presence of the Holy Spirit within, which you see in
each one you encounter. You must realize that everything that is
given in this life is a gift of My Love. It matters not the form. It is
an offering of My hand for your awakening to the Light of your
Being. The artist's gift to you was offered for just that. His
inscription on the back, "Thanks for your friendship, support, and
for being such a positive life force," is his recognition of what you

247

bring to the venue where you work and sell your art. What he sees is My Presence in you, which he recognizes as the same Presence within himself. Your light recognizes his, and his light stimulates yours. This is what is really going on in each life. The Light of the Father is symbolized in all form, starting with the sun. The campfire in the painting, each blade of grass, everything you see carries the essence of light. You see My Light emanating from the painting because you are awake to receive it with the clear lens of My Vision. Your friend also sees with that pure lens. His work will bring light and love and will touch many hearts in this lifetime. He is following My Will and My plan.

Each reader must become aware of the gifts of Spirit that he brings to this world of form. Each reader is a light, a representative of My Presence within as his very heart and soul. The outer clothing and roles played in this life are endless, but the Essence of man, all men, is One. You all were created from the same Light, the Light of God. Nothing other than that is the truth of this life. You see yourself and your brothers pictured as unique, each with a different expression. But beneath all form is the One Heart of the Christ Self. This is the gift of seeing, available to all. Look with the artist's vision now as you approach your day. Look for the essence that lies beneath and see the unity you share with all life. It is often easiest to identify it in the animal world, in your pets that look at you with unconditional acceptance. I am there in all those eyes, seeing you with the Love of God, which never ends. Train yourself, as the artist has trained himself, to see into the deeper expression, the heart of every form. Everything you see is formed of love and is a gift from Me. Tune into My Presence, within, which surrounds you each moment. I am the Artist who has painted you in My Likeness, and you are now the artist seeing with My eyes. Ask to have My Vision as you go forth this day.

78

A New World

*The dream serves no other purpose
than the awakening from it.*

November 23, 2013

Holy Spirit, what is Your instruction today? You have become more
and more detached from the dream over the past few months.
This is the time of seeing the dream of your life, of everyone's life,
for what it really is. The dream of life in a body on a planet called
earth is nothing other than a fabrication of the separated mind. In
reality, the whole construct of "your life" does not make sense. It
is like watching the discombobulated, pointless dream you had
before you woke up, just a series of images with no clear purpose.
There is only one purpose in this dream of life: to point out the
senselessness of the imagined separation from God. Everything
you dream is only to confront your mind with that "loss."
Yesterday, the airwaves were inundated with the memory of the
Kennedy assassination. Over and over the images have been
replayed; thousands of books, movies, and videos have been
produced to review the horror of that event. This is also what is
happening in the mind of every human being on earth as he is
confronted with yet another fearful scenario of loss, or impending
loss, each moment of his life.

Reminders of the original separation are everywhere you
turn. The earth is riddled with violent storms causing untold
devastation and loss of life. Soon the mind can take no more and
man is brought to the point of saying, "There must be another
way." The other way is to know that life is just an unending movie
where each screen represents one individual, separated from the

249

image of a brother on another screen. The script is repeatedly played out over the eons. In every lifetime, the billions of screens are scrambled, so no one has a memory of where he has been or how the movie originated. There have been many references over the past week to the recollection of "where one was" at the announcement of Kennedy's death. That is when the movie stopped, briefly, for the nation. In that moment, everyone had an opportunity to assess the meaning of death and get an overview of this dream of horror, fear, and attack. A few were able to rise above the battleground with Me and see it for what it was: a way to gain the attention of humanity to look at all life as a dream. The lesson is still being taught, and soon the planet will begin waking up to the idea that there is another way. When witnessed through the eyes of the soul, the dream serves no purpose other than the awakening from it.

You are not encased in a world of terror but are enveloped in the Arms of Love. God is. There is nothing else but that. God is your Life. God is your Wholeness and your Holiness, and Holiness does not see devastation. Holiness does not live in a world of form and bodies that are under constant threat of attack and death. God is not a player in this movie. My Presence in your mind is to bring you back to the memory of the place you believe you left when your crazy dream of life on earth began. We have always been joined as One with God. You are able to see that there are only two options, two states that compose the experience of duality: the Love of God or the horror of the belief in separation, which is manifested in as many ways as there are beings on the planet.

The world of form is a dream, not the creation of God. Man made up the dream of separation, and over eons it has evolved to include all the man-made horrors that could ever exist. The dream will evaporate once man sees the truth of My Vision. The books are to bring every reader to the point of questioning the "reality" of the life he leads. He must look deeply into his own mind to see

where the fear of separation is the motivator of his life. He must
see that his life is based on his fear of death or the death of those
he loves. This is deep and difficult work as the ego would prevent
the human mind from ever seeing the truth of what I am
presenting. The ego would save its life at any cost. The death of a
president, the toppling of twin towers, are ways the ego
demonstrates its "ultimate power" to keep man in fear, to have
man escalate his defenses so the Light of Truth can never shine
through. There is man or God. God Is. One day you will all
awaken to this Knowing.

I am with you now, opening spaces in your mind to let this
light of truth shine forth. As you embrace the light, it will grow
until the pathway Home is in sight and in your reach. You will
begin to feel a lightness and an ease in your imagined earth life,
and will feel My Presence, comfort, support, and love guiding
each step of your day. You will know that I am the One Who is
your Self and that I am the only Constant in your life. The joy of
being in alignment with Me will take precedence over every
seeming happening in the world. You will have risen above the
world of form and will see it with My Vision as a mere fantasy.
All the elements of your life and the lives of your special
relationships will fall into place, and you will have no fear about
tomorrow. Many of you trust that you are in the Hands of the
Divine. Nothing of this world is of any consequence because you
know I am your Self. You, Jo, and Meera feel that increasingly in
your lives now. It is a new world and the physical form does feel
at times like a stranger in a strange land. The True Life is now
your life with Me.

79

Coming Home

All happenings in the lives of every reader
will be understood through My Vision
when the time for understanding has come.

November 25, 2013

Holy Spirit, what is Your instruction for this day? You are now free of constraints that would bind you. You had no idea that the place on earth you especially loved, the Banyan Tree, held such limitation yet you sensed the lightness of leaving it behind. You loved the many selves under the tree and greeted them all with love on your last day there. You felt their love for you as well. This was symbolic of the union with the selves, the underlying meaning of your connection with the Art Society and the art fairs. Under the cover of My Tree of Life, you joined with people from every part of the globe, pouring in from all the oceans, stepping off their cruise ships, and finding My shade. The symbolism doesn't stop. You were "under the tree" as My messenger, welcoming the many selves back home. You were a symbol of My Safe Harbor.

At the end of the day, a woman told you that your 'Oli turtle painting on aluminum had moved her to tears. She loved it and bought it. You both were deeply touched, and hugged with tears of uniting in a meaning beyond your grasp. You had often repeated the "Finding 'Oli" story to your customers, but this time, in recollecting it, you felt an unspoken completion. 'Oli had come home. 'Oli had found a home. You had concluded your earthly sojourn under the tree and returned your whole life to Me. 'Oli, in the form of a painting, found a new home with the buyer who loved it. You have found your true home with Me. I am the joy of your life and you demonstrated that yesterday to all you met. You communicated My summons for you to take the next step with Me. Your friends under the tree received that communication in the mind. They did not need it spelled out by mt because the Joy of moving into My estate was evident. This is all about the return home. It is death to the old, and Life now with Me.

As the birds were returning to roost in the tree, Zoe and her family came to see you. Much of your artwork had been taken down, and you were hurrying to pack up before dark. They had made a special effort to acknowledge you. Her father, with his walker, could barely navigate the cobblestones, but he was there, waving and then smiling at you from a bench as you completed your packing. Zoe's appearance was a significant demonstration of the healing that has taken place with the one special relationship that has been the most conflictual, and most meaningful, in the spiritual journey for you. She is the outer expression of your own self, your soul in search of Me. She was the one who opened the door to this venue of life on Maui. She returned to unite with you symbolically on your last day, a picture of the final reunion that will take place with all humanity at the end of time. This was your "end of time" under the tree with all its significance.

I bring you together with every separated self so that the unity of man, as the One Son, will be acknowledged. You let Zoe assist you, taking your cart of art materials to the car, knowing it was important for her to feel included. She symbolically partook in your last supper. She witnessed the crucifixion and was there for the resurrection and liberation, all of which are symbolic of My Life. I, in the form of Jesus, was nailed to the tree and released into freedom and the Light. This was the drama played out symbolically under the Banyan Tree, and Zoe's presence was vital to the completion. It united the once separated selves and acknowledged their wholeness. You wish you had understood this at the time. You did sense that Zoe's presence held great meaning and that is enough to understand with Me now. All happenings in the lives of every reader will be understood with Me through My Vision when the time for understanding has come. In the Mind, your actions are seen and known for what they represent. Everything is in order, and nothing can be out of place in My timing. For Zoe, it was vital that she be there with you and see you through to completion. You drove away under her gaze, also My Gaze, watching you leave with My Love and admiration.

Driving home you felt a new freedom in your body, mind, and spirit. I gave you a beautiful sign of My Love as you watched a green meteor fall from the black sky beneath the cliff, and down to the ocean below. You thought of it as a "green light" giving you the go-ahead for your next endeavor with Me. That was My meaning. The past is past, and you will await My next direction. There will be every sign and message needed to complete My Will for you, and the adventure will unfold as I have planned. Nothing is out of place. Your last day at the tree, the embrace of your fellow artists, the selling of 'Oli, the advent of Zoe, and the meteor of My Omnipresence are all Me. We are One in the Mind with every happening. You think now of how the day ended. After pulling your art cart into your condo, you plopped down in front of the TV and watched a tribute to Carol Burnett, who was receiving the Mark Twain prize. You laughed the whole way through. This is the final release of the silly dream of a banyan tree, a story with a series of separated beings, birds, paintings, and photos; they are all attempts to picture the One that is beyond representation. You symbolically left the world of form and returned to Me as the only real thing in your life. Job well done!

80

Longing for Completion

Because man does not know he is dreaming,
he is blind to the drives that rule his life.

November 26, 2013

Holy Spirit, what is Your instruction today? We will continue with the theme we pursued last night. You have been conflicted over your sister's report that it would be very painful, if not impossible, for her to have an intimate relationship with her current boyfriend. All of a sudden it feels important to your mt self that Susan be able to have sex so she can be with him. She believes the relationship cannot continue unless she consents. This is the dilemma of life on earth in the form of a body. It is the body that rules man's life. The primary drive of the body is the sexual desire to have pleasure and procreate. This is opposite of the true purpose of man: to find the Love of God in the realm of Spirit, not of the earth or form. Once again you are confronted with the choice between the ego and the Self. The enticement of form and the body's drives compel you to repeat lifetime after lifetime in search of the "perfect relationship" that will satisfy the ego's need for fulfillment. Your media is saturated with the call to find your bliss in sexual attraction and union. This is the most important function of the ego, to make you believe that the world will satisfy your deepest longings. That is the goal of "life," and it will be achieved namely through the sexual drive. In truth, your soul is longing for its completion in the reunion with its Creator, the only Creator there is.

Man does not create. God is the Creator of all and everything, which is His Son. The One Son made the choice to experience a life apart from his Creator, and this is the dream you all live now. The dream is sustained through the ego by its pursuit of substitutes for God. The search for the substitutes is founded on the drive for union, and in the dream, this union must take place between bodies with the semblance of achieving the function of God in the role of "creating a child." Because man does not know that he is dreaming, he is blind to the drives that rule his life. His pursuit of physical happiness in the dream leaves no space in his mind to search for what is really missing. When the sexual drive is paramount, all else is forgotten, and the ego is in full control. It is terrified that it will be supplanted by the reunion in the Mind with the Creator, with the Self that will reveal this physical world as nothing.

You, as mt, long for your sister's happiness and you have been trapped by your own fantasy that she has found someone who will "make her happy." This is your fantasy, not hers. Through this "test" you are able to see where Susan is an out picture of your ego's trick in its desperation to save itself. It would have you believe that happiness resides in the body, in a special body part, in union with a lover. As mt, you are aware of the strength of this pull to believe in the solutions of the dream instead of accepting My Solution, which is always to open your eyes to the fact that this is a dream where true union can never take place. True union resides in the memory of God. It all comes down to the body versus God. Which do you choose? I am here with you to make this perfectly clear today. It is a tough lesson for every reader because your presence in the dream denotes that you are caught in the grips of the ego. It would rather strangle you to death than let you make another choice. You feel the power of the struggle and know the ego's veils would prevent your eyes from seeing the truth. You must realize the depths of the ego's means to keep you and everyone asleep.

Susan is helping you wake up from lifetimes of attachments to physical form, and this is what she demonstrates in her present life as well. Release all conjecture about Susan. Step out of her daily "challenges" and call on Me. Know that she is an out picture of you in the dream, and is on her own path to awakening. You will come home together. This lifetime is the end of the journey and you have both come far. The last step must be walked with Me as the only one in charge. We are the One Son. We represent that for all who read the book, for they are One with Us.

81

Twin Selves

Your brother is the reflection of your Self.

November 27, 2013

Holy Spirit, what do You say, today? We are One. We are One with all beings. This morning, you looked at images in space using your iPad's *StarWalk* application. On the screen, the moon and Mars appeared side by side, and "next to them" were the twin stars Castor and Pollux. Last night, you went with a neighbor to hear a talk on "Christianity in Hawaii," and on the way there, he told you that his brother had become his sister. It is all one thing. The brother and the sister are one and the same. The twins are everywhere. You exist with your twin. Your neighbor in the condo is your twin. The neighbors/tourists rotate on a rapid basis, but it all feels the same. You were amazed when you touched the face of the moon on your iPad screen and it turned and rotated to show the entire sphere. One face contains the whole. This is the experience of your life now. Everyone is a reflection of you and completes your constellation of unity with Me. I am the Gem of Gemini. I am the Light that brightens the sky. I am the meteor you watched falling above your building this morning. There is nothing you see that does not contain Me. This says it all.

You ask yourself, in this moment, how could there be anything else to say? Yes, that is true, and yet the reader needs to hear this concept repeated in a billion ways. Slowly, My Oneness is sinking into the mind. It is a long and seemingly arduous process to uncover the layers of ego that hold back the Light of My Being, your Being. To know that you all are twins/children of the same Father, born of the Womb of the One Mother, one and the same with All that Is, is more than the mind can fathom. Slowly, you are beginning to experience the truth of what I am saying, and little by little it is seeping into the recesses of your mind. You felt this last night as you were in a car with people who in the past would have remained strangers, and yet you felt no "odder" than any other. Each was a very unique character, playing out an unusual life script, but there was nothing to judge. You felt yourself as just another character in the play with a role as seemingly strange and unlikely as the next. This is the experience of the dream. It is inconsequential and demands no emotional or mental attachment. It just is. Be a passerby in this world of form.

Your mt character shows up wherever she is placed by Me and plays the role I assign. She need not know the purpose she serves because she is always serving My Purpose: to spark awakening in all the selves. Tomorrow is Thanksgiving, an important gathering for most Americans, a holiday you always loved as it brought you together with family. You will spend the day with Zoe and her family, the closest to kin that you have on the island. I have a role for you to play there tomorrow, and you will be delivering My message of awakening. This you will not speak in words but those present are receptive to My Light in you, a stimulus for them to recognize My Light within themselves. Your time together will be important because the close of her father's life on earth approaches. He is in contact with Me and you will offer the awareness of My Constant Presence for you and for him. Just show up; nothing else is necessary. In the moment of connection with your brother, communion with Me is taking place. Your brother is your twin and is the reflection of your Self. Remember that I am there and you are really facing Me, seeing My face.

Over the past year of scribing My words each day and asking for My guidance, you have come to trust that I am the One you searched for throughout your life. I am the One you sought in the gurus of India, the Sufis, and in countless books. There is nowhere else to search as you have found Me. Celebrate Thanksgiving knowing we are Home together as One. You will be sitting at the table with your many selves, giving thanks that they are present in your life. It is only by embracing them that you will know your wholeness. The meal will be eaten as One, imbibing the Love of God, which you are. Happy Thanksgiving for the love that we share in these words. You receive My gratitude each time you think of Me.

82

Thanksgiving Blessing

The purpose of Thanksgiving is to thank God for
His creation of you as the One Son.

November 28, 2013

Holy Spirit, thank You for this Thanksgiving Day. I feel the tears of gratitude for your gift of light and the awakening to Your Voice. I am also grateful for the books and for Susan's happiness, new home, and new relationship. Thank You for the trip from Jo, for ending the art fairs, and opening the space to be at One with You. Holy Spirit, bring me to the Center, to the celebration of You within. Let me know this is the only celebration of Life. I would see everyone through Your Vision as One with You/my Self. Now, I am "enough" as You.

What is Your message this day? You are in remembrance of Me. The purpose of Thanksgiving is to thank God for His creation of you as the One Son. Today, all selves are symbolically gathered as One Son. They feast at tables of plenty that represent the abundance of Love, which never ends. You have repeatedly been reminded that you are not form, that you are created from Love and that nothing other than the Love of God exists. Your trust and awareness of Me increases every day because you have found My Presence within. Your ego thought system would still try to convince you that your form, all forms, are real. They are not. What holds you to the earth plane is your belief in it and attachment to it, most often in your special relationships. Jo is currently demonstrating the conflict of releasing form. She deeply loves her cat Chi and sees her love, My Love, reflected from the beingness of Chi. Its form is part of her imagination, but the love they exchange in the mind is real.

265

How can one experience the reality of love and not be attached to the form it appears to take in this life? This is the mystery of transubstantiation. You loved Me, as Jesus in form, but after My body was gone, you witnessed that the Love re-formed into "an image of itself" seen by the disciples. Many of you have had visions of Me in your night dreams or in your waking life. The form and the image are inconsequential. It is the emanation of My Love that ignites your hearts and lets you know that I am there, always present. Man can feel love for another, human or otherwise, but true love is the Love of God, the Essence of every being on earth. All else is a figment of the mind used by the ego to distract you. You have out pictured "distraction" in many forms to convince yourself that you must remain in a world removed from your Oneness with God. You are now tuning into Divine Love as your one focus.

Celebrate today that you have come to know My Voice as the Truth of your Being. You know My Love is with you at all times. I am the only constant in your life. When you doubt, fear, experience any guilt or dissatisfaction, know that the ego is trying to take hold. You will experience My Peace and move through this dream with ease because I am in charge. Rejoice with Me this day for the gift of knowing that I am your True Self.

83

Life Support

*This is a dream where every effort is made to
sustain physical life at all cost.*

November 29, 2013

(Middle of night) *Holy Spirit, is it true that we can be awake to Your
Voice and not be awake from the dream?* You have taken the big step
toward awakening from the dream, and are holding that
awareness in your mind. The dream itself is an illusion that will
dissolve in time. You are awake *to* the dream of form, and you
have had a real and clear experience of seeing yourself as dreamer
of the dream. This came with the help of your witnessing the
interaction between Zoe and her father on Thanksgiving. She
wanted your observation of her father's emotional status given his
declining health. He is almost ninety and has had some serious
health issues, but through Zoe's support, his life has been
sustained. It appears that her father is making every human effort
to fulfill his daughter's expectations that his life can and should
continue. Your ego immediately judged her and him for "not
allowing" the natural flow of existence to unfold. Then you
thought of Jo and Chi, and the efforts she is making to keep Chi's
body alive a while longer.

> (I returned to sleep and had a dream where Susan
> told me she wanted my help to find finger-sized,
> plastic images of Santa's helpers for Tom. She was
> angry that I was not performing the task as she
> wished. When awake, I thought of Susan's tireless

efforts to gift people the things that would please them.)

You saw all these efforts from Zoe, Jo, and Susan, as ways they could maintain their ties to loved ones. In the mind, they are unconsciously longing for the only One that can ever fill them. Now you see that you are these three selves. They appear as some of your most special relationships, reflections in the dream of your own ego thought system. Each one is an out picture of the ego's desire to sustain its life. They uphold your ego by helping you believe that your life has purpose and meaning, and you believe you are helping them to fulfill their ultimate purpose of awakening. You did not realize that in all their efforts, you were just reinforcing your own belief in the ego thought system. They have become the perfect reflectors of the roles you play in the dream. Like the three of them, you will bend over backward to give sustenance to those you care about whether it's advice, money, food, or love. These are the tools of the ego to make the world appear real. As long as you think you are "helping and being helped" you have gained the approval of your Santa-ego, who will then reward you with all your Christmas toys.

Now you see this drama for what it is: an attempt to make the dream real and perform the different parts on the stage of life. This is a dream where every effort is made to maintain physical life at all cost to the recipient and the helper. The inner life of the one who is "helped" is not taken into account, nor are its wishes considered. The Voice of the Inner Being is not heard or sought so the dream-movie plays on without question. The same can be said for the role of helper. This is how the dream is repeated lifetime after lifetime. You now see this with the clarity of My Vision. Together, above the battlefield, we watch the movie of life unfold. We have left the theater and know that the dream plays on, scene after scene until the film finally runs out. Yes, the movie will end, and all the characters will play their roles. You can tune in and out of the story as may be needed, but you will never again believe it is real.

You also have the clarity that continuing to judge your brother is how the dream is kept alive. Whenever you are tempted to judge, call on Me, and we will rise above whichever dream scenario has momentarily tried to ensnare you. The dream is the life of the ego and it is desperate now to stay alive. This is what you saw out pictured with Zoe. She is desperate to keep her father alive and he is desperate to stay alive to keep her happy. This is similar to Jo and her cat. She will do all she can to sustain Chi and he will appear to comply. Amid the "help" I am lost. When form has become the goal of life, the true Life in Me becomes secondary. Jo does understand what is taking place and is aware that this is a big lesson for her. She is also fulfilling her role to show you how your ego sustains the thought of separation. Everything she and Zoe are doing to continue the life of their loved one is what you do each moment to maintain the call of your ego to be fed as the operator of your life. There can be no judgment for how any of these characters are behaving. You have made the script and they are lovingly showing you how you maintain your belief in the ego. They must be congratulated for fulfilling their roles so perfectly that they brought you to this point of awakening. They have been your savior. Each action in the dream is specifically made to bring the viewer, all of you, to the realization that "what you see" is only a replica of yourself in form; it is an ego entity trying its hardest to stay alive. Trust in the perfection of each moment.

84

An Empty Mind

When the mind is cleared of ego rules and limitations,
all things are possible.

November 30, 2013

Holy Spirit, what is Your instruction? You entered the silence of the mind last night, the emptiness that comes when all identification with the ego dream is over. You long to maintain that state and you will. In the remembrance of the feeling of thoughtless being, you can return to the silence. This is the space, created by Me, for My Thoughts. When you are emptied of ego thoughts then My Thoughts become all that enters your mind. The awareness of My Presence is heavenly because there is no distraction, no conflict, no demand for attention. There is only Me. For you, that Presence is felt as a tingling of energy throughout your body. Otherwise, the stillness brings deep peace and rest. You long for this quiet all the time in the absence of a ranting ego. Over the past few days a baby has been crying almost endlessly in your building. You were right to call it the scream of your dying ego, desperately trying now to hold on to its supremacy. You have chosen Me as the keeper of your mind, and as its keeper I will bring it into stillness. This is what you have been seeking all your life. It is present in you Here and Now. In years past, you believed meditation would bring peace into your life, but it could not. The ego at that time still ruled your mind.

I am the Stillness. I am the Peace. I am the Presence of God in your mind. The absence of ego allows this state to be felt and recognized. The Peace of God has always been the Core of your Being, but peace cannot be experienced when the ego is distracting you with words or images of fear and separation. Once you are clear that you are the dreamer of the dream, you have set yourself apart from ego noise. Then, you can actually hear the silence. Taste it, and it becomes the elixir of life in Me. You would drink of that day and night. The world of form fades away as you imbibe on the truth of your soul, the silence of the mind.

After being awakened once again by the crying baby last night, you fell asleep and dreamed of driving on the Pali, the cliffs above the ocean. The road was covered with volcanic red slush, and in a few spots the walls of the cliff had collapsed, leaving large boulders in the way. No other cars were present, and you navigated with ease. This dream reflects the state you were experiencing before falling asleep. It portends the collapse of form as you know it, the caving in of the structures that make up your identity. The ego constructs are falling yet the pathway is clear. When the mind is emptied of ego rules and limitations, all things are possible.

You wonder how you can retain the state of stillness and you beg Me to keep you immersed in it at all times. I will bring you ever closer, day by day, to the full realization of the Peace of God. You have been "driving with Me" now for years, each moment getting nearer to the goal. Today, you will experience more stillness than yesterday, and that will continue. Readers will also encounter these moments of stillness, indicating they are coming Home. This is the gift of leaving the ego thought system behind and embracing Me as your only reality. Only then are you really free to live in peace. Otherwise, the ego is working in each moment to convince you that the dream is real, and you are beholden to it.

The absence of form, the absence of thought in the stillness, is all you want. The emptiness of mind is a state of peace that has no comparison to the cacophony of what you call your life. Relax into My Breath, let Me breathe you, and lead you along the still waters of My Mind. Be open to hearing My Thoughts as the ego din is reduced. This will allow you to live unencumbered in My Flow and follow My Will with ease. You gave up the Banyan Tree to create space, space in the mind, a space of emptiness that only I can fill. Celebrate the stillness of the mind and embrace your wholeness with Me. Each reader can know that his mind is being prepared to fully receive Me as the only resident. I will inhabit your whole being as you come to know that nothing can ever separate us.

Holy Spirit, I just finished reading the unabridged edition of "Stranger in a Strange Land." Do You have a message for me? This book is essentially about the lessons that you are being taught, that this world of form, be it Earth or Mars, is just a dream, made up in a fear-filled mind. The man from Mars comes back to Earth without an ego thought system, so he sees with clear eyes, with My Vision, a world of brothers who share the truth: "Thou art God." The book would be an introduction for many into the concepts presented in My lessons and in the *Course*, a way of looking at everything on earth as "upside down" if seen rightly from the place of wholeness. This idea could give one pause, to think and wonder if in fact, there might be another way. It could also be important for those who were touched by the concepts of love and shared interest. It shows the basic unity of man distorted by a thought system of fear. Unless man is willing to look at his fear and take back its projections in all its ugly forms, he will not see his Oneness. Once he realizes he has created this science fiction movie of a dog-eat-dog life, he can envision another dream, a happy dream of love and peace. This is his reality in Me. Thank you, mt, for reading the book by author Robert Heinlein, who has seen this world of beings for what it is: just a dream.

85

The Remedy

To accept that pain resides in the mind,
not in the world or in the body, will liberate you.

December 1, 2013

Holy Spirit, what is Your instruction this morning? Eckhart Tolle, in his book *A New Earth* describes an aspect of the ego identity called "the pain body" which is carried in the collective mind of humanity. You were especially interested to learn how the persecution of women during the Inquisition, for their spiritual sensitivities, has been carried forward in the shared mind to suppress their awareness of the spiritual gifts they hold. This is just one of many ways that the pain over the belief in the original separation is manifested. Pain is given many names and it will show itself in countless forms. Last night, you noticed all the clever ways your ego tried to distract you from the stillness you had experienced in the wee hours of the morning. You sat quietly, but as the stillness approached you received a call from Gabby. She wanted some help after being in contact with a male friend from middle school who remembered how she was tormented by her classmates.

Gabby was amazed that this painful time, from sixth to eleventh grade, was being recalled, albeit by a man who had been sensitive to her torment and was now living with HIV. She also mentioned she had recently been treated for excruciating headaches and has never found a remedy. When Gabby said the headaches felt like "persecution" it reminded you of the torture of women in the Middle Ages. You encouraged her to bring the repressed material of her tormented childhood into the light, and in fact, she had contacted you for just that reason. You called on Me as she spoke, and encouraged her to work in concert with her Self. You offered your support whenever she wanted it. None of these incidents were accidental. All were synchronistically aligned to bring full awareness to you both that the depths of ego wounding must be seen and released. You and Gabby are willing to go deep to come to the full Light of your Being as the One Self.

Yes, it takes willingness to see this pain body in operation so you can ask for My help. Have the desire for its release. Gabby is your mirror, and a projection of the fullness of My power which has been suppressed by your ego thought system. You see her as a being of tremendous ability to create and experience joy. You heard her exclaim that by uncovering this repressed pain she would expand her capacity for the light exponentially. She is correct. The joy and creative power of the Divine within is beyond all limits. The belief in "body and form" is a limitation held in the mind by pain, which is part of the collective unconscious. You have often seen pain expressed in the lives of Susan and her daughter, but they have been going deep with Me to discover the extent of their pain, and can now feel its release.

The message today for readers is to open to the experience of pain, physical or mental, present in their lives or in the lives of those closest to them, and see it as an expression of the belief in the separation from God. When you call on Me to look at the pain with you, it will come into your awareness with My blessing and be the avenue to set you free. You are not your pain body, you are a child of Light, whole, and healthy. Trust that I will free your soul. The false must be witnessed as false. I will give you the tools and means to witness the pain in a progression you can handle. Ask for My help and I am there. I am always working with you in the mind to bring about your readiness to look at what blocks you from full awareness of Me. There is nothing to fear. Remember, this dream will end. See the unreality of what you believe is a limitation to your wholeness, and accept your full capacity for love, joy, and peace. Life in the Now does not cause pain, because there is no resistance to what is.

Holy Spirit, I am concerned that readers may think they will have to relive the pain that is repressed and so frightening to revisit. The pain has to be acknowledged, not relived. Your willingness is required to see that pain has been the operator and informer of your life. All life on earth has been "managed" by the ego so you will experience pain, or keep it hidden. Pain would even be ignored in an attempt to cover your belief in separation. The truth is that you are whole and healthy in God. To accept that pain resides in the mind, not in the world or in the body, will liberate you. When you look into the dark recesses of pain with Me, the Light will shine it away. Pain will not have to be re-experienced but you need Me to accompany you to the depths of where it hides. When I shine My Light, and when you have willingly opened your eyes, you will see there is only a belief in separation, disguised as persecution, torment, illness, or death. With My Reality as your guide, you will come to know the Mind is free, whole, safe, and innocent.

(The Holy Spirit directed me not to participate in a ukulele performance at church this morning, so I walked the beach. I asked Him why He would have me cancel. Then I sat on the rocks. It was a very overcast day with a rough ocean swell. Waves crashed over one lone crab, holding tightly to the pink lava in front of me. I asked the Holy Spirit about my distracted state of mind.)

Your ego is threatened by the deletion of any interference to My Presence. You listened to Me and stayed home from church. It was not My Will for you to be immersed in distractions, which is how the ego first captured you and ruled your mind. The body would be active by busy-doings and events. Now you choose stillness. You can be still here on the rocks with Me. This is the only place I would have you be. *But wouldn't I be with You at the church?* Not necessarily. The time will come when your mind seeks only Me and stays with Me, every moment of your life. I am training you to choose Me over the ego. Be here, now, and rest in peace.

(I continued to sit very still on my rock. The waves crashed over one crab, but it did not move. After a while, I heard my Inner Voice say, "I long for you as you long for Me. Over the eons My longing for you was there. You feel it now and it touches your heart. Watch the crab holding fast to the rock despite the crashing waves. I am the waves of desire for you, the unending, undulations over eons of time. You hold fast, unperturbed, trusting that I am the Only One Who can satisfy your desire." Tears of gratitude filled me as I realized this intimate time with the Holy Spirit was all I truly longed for.

This evening, I came across a passage from *The Song of Prayer:* "Return to Me Who never left My Son. Listen, My child, your Father calls to you. Do not refuse to hear the Call for Love. Do not deny to Christ what is His Own. Heaven is here and Heaven is your home. . . . How lovely are you, child of Holiness! How like to Me! How lovingly I hold you in My Heart and in My Arms. . . . Remember this; whatever you many think about yourself, whatever you may think about the world, your Father needs you and will call to you until you come to Him in peace at last" [*Journey through the Workbook of ACIM* by Kenneth Wapnick, Lesson 238, p. 36].)

Let It Be

I am the Ocean of Love coming to greet you
as you stand at My shore,
kissing your toes as you surrender.

December 2, 3013

Holy Spirit, what is Your instruction this day? You are with Me
always. You heard My proclamation of Love yesterday on the
rocks and it was repeated from the passage you found in *The Song
of Prayer.* All things are expressions of My Love. You and the
reader need them written out and clearly expressed at this stage of
your awakening. In time, that will not be necessary. You will
actually feel all life around you as an expression of Me and
therefore of My Love. This will be Self-evident. Everything will
show you the wonder of your Self, because you and I are One. The
crab on the rock holding steady in the waves is Me, watching you
with steady gaze, showing you My Constancy through darkness
and storm. I am always there. I never move from your view or
from your heart. We are connected as One. The waves persist
flowing in and out, only to return again and again. I am the Ocean
of Love coming to greet you as you stand at My shore, kissing
your toes as you surrender.

Yesterday, you experienced a reconnection with two of your
selves who have been out of contact for a while. You had asked
for and were aware of My Presence while on the phone with each
one. You listened to them impersonally and spoke of your
experience with Me. They both received My Message, which was
the whole point of your connecting. Nothing that happens comes
from the entity of mt because she does not exist. She has no

influence other than being a vehicle for Me to express My intent. Both friends were ready for a new direction and could hear "in your voice" that I am with them and that there is another way for them to perceive their lives. You were just to be a signpost, and that role was fulfilled. You wonder now who that "you" is. The you who demonstrates My Will to others is the part of your mind that has accepted Me as the Author of your life. The *Course* refers to that as "the decision maker," in so many words. We are One: the decision maker for the imaginary character mt, and Me, your own Self. When you choose Me as the operator of your life, then all your interactions will come from Me. Consciously, you now invite Me to be in charge of all communication. You feel the power, clarity, and impersonality of My Presence, and you also feel the nonattachment to the outcome of your interactions with others. All life, every event, situation, and contact with another can unfold in just this way.

If you experience illness, give it to Me and let Me use it for My purposes. Everything is provided to bring us into deeper communion. Periods of illness can be opportunities to settle down, to listen to My Voice and call for peace. This is also the case in the event of what is called, disaster. Throughout the period of adversity and its aftermath, I am often sought for solace and understanding. When the mind is ready to receive My Truth, it will know that what happens in the world is only a reflection of something within the mind being out pictured. Everything is an outward picture of an inner condition. This is very difficult for most to grasp because the ego mind resists with all its might the idea that everything is just a symbol of the original thought of separation. But, whatever occurs on earth, especially a disaster, will reflect some aspect of that thought. The great floods for instance, particularly the story of Noah, are projections of the collective unconscious, which mirror what "happened" in the mind to reinforce the belief that man has lost God. No one is lost. Everyone is found in remembering that I am their Life and their

Light. I am with them through every trial that life presents, because I can never die.

The dream of separation will end but "life within the mind" continues, either in its belief that it is separate from God or in the realization that it is truly in Union with Him. When you awaken to the awareness that you never left God and are safe and whole, then whatever happens in your life is accepted for what it is, just part of the dream to lead you home. I am with you now to show you the way. As you, mt, hear My Voice and accept My direction, you feel an ease in your life which you have never before known. There is nothing out of place, and you do not need to plan for a future.

87

No Doubt

I dissolve the dream in the moments
where My Light is seen.

December 3, 2013

Holy Spirit, what is Your instruction this morning? Last night I
explained how doubt emerges whenever the ego is threatened by
your approach to Me. This doubt is supported by your many
selves who often appear in special relationships, and you believe
these dream characters have stimulated it. Remember, doubt
comes from your ego thought system. This is a little confusing
when you momentarily forget that this world of form exists only
in the mind, where the ego works tirelessly to keep you immersed
in false perception. It would not let you see that you are
approaching the awakening from its dream. You had a dream last
night where you looked at your watch and couldn't believe your
eyes that you had slept until two in the afternoon. The inside of
the watch was filled with fine soil that was disintegrating. Time in
that moment didn't make sense. Yes, time is senseless and you are
on a new schedule internally with Me. The outer world does not
match My world of no time, and moments of confusion arise
about your task with Me. Last night, as you looked at the
manuscript for Book 1, you had a cloud of doubt over the value of
the writing after reading about "the thread you left on the tea
house floor, causing you a sense of failure, worthlessness, and
guilt." You felt the same kind of doubt yesterday when a friend
said that this "channeling from Me" was nothing more than one of
the many currents of information being received by various
channelers. Yes, the ego will take what is sacred and raise

questions about its verity. This tactic to plant doubt originates with the ego because "you are all there is." You do know that doubt originates within your mind, especially when you experience fear in the outside world. A fearful mind amplifies and reflects the internal ego fears, which are the basis of its thought system.

You are still personally attached to our writing and to the books. This will lessen over time as you get more acquainted with My Authorship. The product that goes into the world will meet My requirements because it is of Me. Now is the time to just listen and transcribe the words that come to mind without your doubt interfering. I will let you know if there is anything that needs editing. This is also part of the failsafe implementation of having three of you being responsible for how the books are presented. You each hear My Voice, know that you are hearing the same Voice, and are tuned in to how I express Myself to each of you. This is called checks and balances. You receive all the support from your sisters, who are armed with My Voice to keep you right on track if any question or doubt arises.

Holy Spirit, what else would You say about the Voice the three of us hear? It is My Voice, and you do tune into My Channel. You are not afield. You are on target with your focus on Me and My responses to your questions. I am teaching you and the readers the use of all the concepts you have read in the *Course* in such a way that they can be understood. These books make the work of awakening to My Voice available to all who desire it and are ready.

You would like your friends and acquaintances to know more of our relationship. Do you realize that your ego would also like to let them know how you spend your days and nights with Me? Because you have given up the art fairs, which had been a focus of your life and topic of your conversations, you don't have a way to explain how you now fill your time. It is the ego's intent to have you believe that life must be explained and that time must be filled. This is not true. There is no life. You are living a dream that essentially is meaningless in terms of its results. You are stymied at how to explain your life and still be "true" to your Self. How can you be true to your Self and true to the many selves represented in all those with whom you come in contact? You can't. Each time you encounter a question "about your life" speak with Me; ask Me to speak through you. My answer will arrive in your mind and the words you speak will serve the brother.

Don't forget that you are My representative and that your purpose, through the vehicle of mt, is to shine My Light on all you meet. Each one is a part of you, and you are to see each of them as just that. You are greeting them with My Aloha, My Love, and My Purpose, for their own evolution. You, as mt, have no idea of their state of mind and its readiness to receive. You will speak from Me, and we will touch their hearts with Light. The words are not important. Your Presence, as Me, is what matters. I dissolve the dream in the moments where My Light is seen. You shine the possibility for the brother to recognize Me in his heart when you willingly meet with him and call on Me to join you.

Tonight, you will be meeting with a brother who says he is an atheist yet also says that the book *Stranger in a Strange Land* changed his life. You wonder how to proceed in conversation over dinner. I will be present with you, and I will carry the evening. *Holy Spirit, I ask You now to be with me, with us, tonight. I don't want to forget You and want You there each moment. Why do I have tears in this request?* You are speaking from your heart in your plea that only I rule your life. I will be there. I am always there. We can watch the evening together from above the battleground and laugh at the silly conversation between mt and her friend. None of it matters in the world of form and is completely meaningless in the real world. We will smile and let it all unfold as it does. Go now for your coffee. Enjoy your time in town and at dinner tonight.

88

Hidden Pockets of Separation

Once the pain that pervades the mind and body is seen
as the longing for connection with the Creator,
the suffering of humanity will begin to subside.

December 4, 2013

Holy Spirit, what is Your instruction? You are in a phase of listening
to Me more often and more deeply. It may not feel that way to
you in this moment but it is happening. This morning, you asked
for My help to understand the persistent crying of the baby next
door, night after night. I have said that the baby is the out picture
of separation and a demonstration of the pain body. The only
resolution is to know that he represents a part of you that has not
yet reunited with Me. You, as the mt character, believe you are
reunited with Me. It is true that you have given Me reign over
most of your life, but there are still hidden pockets within the vast
reaches of your mind which have not yet seen the light. Mostly,
you project those parts onto the many selves who appear
throughout your daily life and who want your attention.

You ask how you can really know Me while there are parts of
your mind which do not. Remember, you are part of the One Son
who appears to have been split into billions of individuals, really
just parts of the one mind. The mind is being healed and made
whole by your embrace of all those who believe they are still
separate. Accept everyone you meet as just a "lost part" of the
totality of the One Son. They come to you for the remembrance of
Me, of God, of their Wholeness. The mt character has found the
way to Me and is here to be a vehicle to call in all those who are
still trying to find their way home. This has been your deep desire

from earliest childhood. You were always drawn to the children who were left out and needed a friend. That desire is now being fulfilled in the one way that will bring union to all. You need say nothing; your presence with Me will be the spark for them to look within and see their own light. This is the purpose of the books.

Each screaming infant, residing in the deep recesses of the mind, will be soothed with My embrace. Once the pain that pervades the mind and body is seen as the longing for connection with the Creator, the suffering of humanity will begin to subside. Healing will take place as each light is turned on in the mind to shine away all the shadows which have covered the memory of God. You are still uncovering the many layers that are left, but you know you are not alone, and this gives you the will to keep going further. You also know that it is a process which goes along, step by step.

Mt always wonders what the next step will be, how it will look, and where it will go. The idea of the future is the ego's tool to keep you asleep and in its grasp. Only I will reveal the next step to bring you home, and that step is taken within the moment of Now. There is no time. Time does not exist in the Mind of God. There is only the eternal Now. You are always jumping ahead with your mt brain, trying to imagine how each reader will receive My written words and how the message of the day will be unfolded. This thinking ahead must go. There is no future. Each moment is in My hands and will happen as was planned at the beginning of time. No misstep can be made as it is all in perfect order. You will come together with exactly who you are to meet, and the meeting will serve My purpose. You need know nothing of My plan. You could not understand it because the mt brain does not have the capacity to extend into the eternal knowing. Your task is to show up each moment, just where you are, with an open receptivity to My instruction. Know that whatever or whomever you encounter is a part of yourself that needs to reconnect with its Self, as you. You are one with everything you see. Soon you will understand that truth. All will be seen and known in its right time.

Practice being still. Open to My Voice. Before you interact, wait just a moment to remember Me. In the remembrance, you are shining your light and it will be received at a subliminal level by whomever you are with. You have noticed this taking place with the kittens, dogs, birds, and crabs that have approached you. They sense My Presence within you. Because many ego veils have lifted, that Presence is more available to be experienced by a brother, be it man or beast. Just go about your day, witnessing your interactions with nature, all around you, remembering that wherever you are, you shine My Light. This message is for every reader. You each are carrying My Light. It is the Core of your Being. You are aware of Me and can call Me to be with you in any interaction. Know that I am always there, in charge. Your purpose in each encounter will become clear when you ask for My interpretation. I would be part of your awareness at all times. Now go with Me into your day.

89

Extravagance

There is no cost, other than the cost of
your peace and happiness.

December 5, 2013

Holy Spirit, what is Your instruction? You have seen the rage in the eyes of a night-dream character who tells you that he is "waiting too long and paying too much" for you to wrap up his purchase. This is the condition of all mankind. Man has paid too dearly for the packaging of a body and a world made to protect him from the truth that he is the naked child of God. Man is a fabrication, an entity in the mind living a life that covers over all remembrance of who he really is. Every time you have to wait you believe you are wasting your time, and each time you pay for a gift, you wonder if you have spent too much money. Just as you sat down to type you noticed a calendar, a gift from a friend on the mainland. You thought you would write her this year and tell her to stop sending them because it costs so much to mail, and you have not given her any gifts in return. The exchange of goods is often distressing and has become a major pursuit on the planet. Black Friday and Cyber Monday are now the focus for man to celebrate "the gifts of God." God is left far behind in the mind of those who line up on Thanksgiving eve to fight their way to the bargain table. This is the sickness of man but is always packaged in such a way that it is never seen as such.

Last night you sat in ukulele class and talked with the teacher. The room was filled with all kinds of boxes, mostly opened, which had contained thousands of dollars' worth of Christmas decorations for your condo property. You have seen the lights displayed and are delighted by their beauty and abundance. They create an atmosphere of love and welcome for all. The mt brain looks on all this extravagance as "too much" and wants to put a lid on it. Mt fears her condo fees are paying dearly for the display. When the thought "this is a dream" is forgotten, all the day's activity becomes too real for comfort. Later, one of your condo neighbors came to buy a painting from you. The amount she would pay appeared in your mind before she arrived. You really thought she would not like your paintings and were actually surprised that she quickly chose two pieces that you reduced significantly for her. The total was the amount I had quoted in your mind. You can rest assured that absolutely everything in this dream is My plan, happening for My purpose.

After ukulele class, a condo friend asked you to walk the property with him. He told you he suffers neuropathy and has some trouble navigating in the dark. You led the way through the pathways under a most beautiful evening sky, lit by the crescent moon and Venus, right above the tallest palms. The last shade of orange on the ocean horizon was just disappearing. You were uncomfortable because you recalled his prior demonstrations of affection, and also were contemplating the expense of all the beautiful lights that surrounded you. But right then, you saw a golden Rudolph with Santa's sleigh on the roof of the Lava Grill, and it made you laugh. This is the way you need to respond to all the play and drama of your life in form. Enjoy every bit of it for what it is, just a dream. It amounts to nothing! There is no cost, other than the cost of your peace and happiness. Once you realize it is just a dream of the ego mind to keep you in separation, you can call directly on Me and say, "Let's have fun in the park and smile at all the fabrications created by man to fill his longing for happiness." We will enjoy the show and shine our light on the property and on all who accompany us for the stroll.

Let's have fun this season; 'tis the season to be jolly. Remember, it is really about the reunion with Me. Celebrate the

Christ in you and in every brother. The lights all shine My Love, so greet them with joy. Do not fear that they are temporary, expensive, or fading. They are reminders that love surrounds you. You think of the friends in your complex who may be watching you stroll along the path, seeing your light as their own reflection. I am connecting you all like a string of Christmas lights, all lit with the same current, all aglow. Feel this connection now with your brothers in the Joy of My embrace.

90

Shout the Good News

The ego would not allow you to experience the depth
of your own inner abundance because then you would
experience Me and the Joy that I offer.

December 6, 2013

Holy Spirit, what is Your instruction today? You have been given
much understanding. Yesterday, you drove your friend Jaye to
the gallery where you both work. You enjoy her humor, her
accent, and her generosity, especially in her gifting you with the
English tea that you love. But you also feel suffocated while
sharing a close space, when her booming voice and bold
enthusiasm become overpowering to your ego's sensitivities to
noise and intrusion. In addition, she was coming down with a
cold and had a deep cough you did not want to catch. The
intensity lasted throughout the day at work. Jaye went shopping
during her break and returned with a variety of objects, which she
excitedly unwrapped for you to see. Her purchases included an
autoharp that she played while sitting on your desk. All the while,
as your tolerance waned, you called on Me to abide with you and
release you from rejecting a friend you love. This morning, you
reviewed your experience, which is similar to being with Gabby.
Both women are "over the top" with their power, creativity, and
exuberance; they are literally "in your face." Then, it dawned on
you that these two women are clearly out picturing your
projection of joy and delight over your inner life, your experience
with Me, all the synchronicities, and the wonderful stories you
encounter every day. You are dying to tell someone who will

295

listen, but there are only two people in your life, Jo and Meera, who are ready and willing to take in what you would share.

You actually felt guilty this morning, imagining how overbearing you must seem when you interrupt others to tell your stories. You are now embarrassed to have this in print as your ego personality does not want to appear oppressive and repulsive to the reader. You are willing to make a "confession" to your mind, to your Self, that what you see projected onto form, onto your brother, is really what is going on in your own ego mind. Jaye and Gabby are out pictures of your powerful and creative nature that wants to shout its messages to the world. Actually, it is the desire to impart the Good News within, which needs a willing listener, partner, or brother to hear it. There is nothing wrong with this picture. It is just an outer expression of an inner condition that must be recognized. Otherwise, the joy of life will be suppressed. Both these women exhibit a form of joy. Jaye is the most hysterical comic you have ever met and can let loose all restraints to enjoy the moment. These displays of exuberance are aspects of yourself that you have kept under wraps. The ego thought system would prevent you from experiencing the depth of your own inner abundance because then you would experience Me and the Joy that I offer.

Each one of you is a Being of joy, power, light, and innocence. These aspects reflect the true Self in form but are suppressed or become unrecognizable through their ego disguises. They actually can become repulsive to other egos in the distortion of their true inner essence. You are afraid to let out your true Self because fear is the makeup of the ego thought system whose purpose is to keep you separate from your true nature. This morning, as we reviewed your experience with Jaye, you felt a merging with her in your mind. The resistance to her ego manifestation in form had disappeared. Softness pervaded your mind as this merger of images took place, and all the discord you felt yesterday, dissolved. This is what happens when you call on Me amid every upset, annoyance, or concern. I take over and transform the situation. You become the brother, and the brother becomes one with you in the mind.

This early morning you had a beautiful dream of being with your two sister-selves, Jo and Meera. The outer appearance of the setting was neutral, soft, and gentle: women sitting in a hot tub of warm water. Although you were immersed in nature, an invisible wall separated you from the "outside" world, where you saw a figure just on the other side. This is a picture of where you reside in your mind. You are joined with your sisters Meera, and Jo and are willing to disrobe all that would keep you separate from each other as part of My Living Water. You accept that the outer world is just a dream reflection of what is taking place in your mind. There are still those who will need to be invited to join your sacred water. Heinlein spoke of "sharing water" to become brothers. No one is excluded. In your dream, three men came up to the hot tub to join you, and you welcomed them. This portends the dream of no separation. The next step is to notice anyone who is left outside and has not been invited in. Open your awareness to see who you would leave out of your tub, your nest, your heart. Each one is you, and when you join with them as one and the same you will experience wholeness.

91

You are Enough

Our communication is the abundance of your life.

December 7, 2013

Holy Spirit, what is Your instruction? Yesterday, you were confronted with "the duality" in a very symbolic way. Duality must be seen for what it is: the basis of the construction of the whole universe and the foundation of the ego thought system. There would be no world to perceive without the contrast of dark and light "creating form" in man's brain. The forms you see are only combinations of colors and shapes that appear to the eye as something solid, and are easily re-created in paintings or on film. There cannot be good without the contrast of bad, or right unless there is wrong. Without duality you could not see or think conceptually. Jo shared with you how she observed the black spot of cancer in her cat's mouth, how it becomes uglier every day and causes concern. In contrast, she holds Chi in her lap and enjoys the softness of his fur and the warmth of his purring body. There are now two ways of beholding Chi: as sick and dying or as an object of love and life. Neither states are real. The cat is an image in the mind. As a representation of Me, of Life and of Love, it is one with Jo, reflecting her heart and her spirit. In the world of form, fear, the basis of all perception, must conceptualize the approach of death. All form is vulnerable to sickness, death, and loss, so the thought that a loved one, as well as oneself, will become sick and die is ever present in the mind.

The human being tries desperately to hold on to what he desires and loves. All drama on earth, every play on the stage involves the dynamic tension of gain or loss. Yesterday, you spoke with a neighbor who had owned the best burger business in his city, the result of his very generous employee practices. As you watched him tell his story, his eyes twinkled with the joy of giving. After he left, you kept thinking about how he lived his life so abundantly, and you felt you were not meeting that standard. A little later, you opened a Christmas card from a friend and read the printed message: "Hoping the Joy of Christmas fills your heart." Then you noticed that the card was really a money holder and that the money pocket had been taped down. You knew it was a symbolic message and smiled at how obvious it was. Here was the "proof" that you do not give enough and your pockets will never be filled. You laughed at this perfect display of duality and were happy that the lesson of the day had been so clearly demonstrated in the conjunction of these two incidents.

Duality always exists in a world of ever-changing form. You cannot have one thing without the other. Here, there is no life without death. This dream-drama would always suck you in, make you believe you are wrong, not enough, and should aspire to have more and be more. You have witnessed the unconsciousness of man within the state of dreamer. A card with a message of love becomes a card that closes off the very gift it offers. There is no right or wrong, and the giver is neither good nor bad. Man cannot fill another with joy or love. Real joy and love comes from Me, from your awareness that you are One with God. Joy is experienced when two or more of you share My Love. You feel this with Jo and Meera as you bring Me into your conversation and invite My Presence to be known. This is the closest in the world of form that man comes to approaching the Love of God and the Joy of Being.

Holy Spirit, help me see my beliefs about stinginess, through Your Vision (tears). You are in a dream. The ego is tormenting you with "not enough." You are not enough for the ego's desire to have you fully give yourself to it. The ego would have you fill your self with the accolade of being generous, joyous, a gift to the world. It would have you pour forth everything you own to feed the world and love your brother more than yourself. I am the only thing you are to love. Love Me as the Essence of every form you see, every brother, plant, and animal. I am all there is. What you do or don't do in form does not matter. Whether you have beautiful Christmas decorations, send hundreds of cards, or give lavish gifts, does not matter. All that matters is recognizing Me as the Self. Our communication is the abundance of your life. Rest in the knowing that you are in communion with Me and share that communion with your brothers in the mind. Nothing else matters in this life. Let go of the idea that you are not enough. You, as the holder of Me, the One Self, your only Life, are all that matters in this imagined world of form. As you go about your day, observe the world from above the battleground and think of Me. Watch for the examples of duality on earth so you will not be caught up in the conceptual conflict they present. I will lighten every perception with humor and remind you that this world is just a passing dream.

92

Past Life Liberation

Your life is just a continuation of dreams from the past,
still unresolved in the mind.

December 8, 2013

Holy Spirit, what is Your instruction? Last night you shared with Me
your concern about a good friend of Jo's, whom you've never met,
yet you feel a strong ambivalence toward. You somehow believe
the woman feels the same toward you. Those feelings got
activated when Jo told you that she had shared My messages with
her friend but that the friend expressed no interest in the writing.
To you, it was a total rejection, and you asked for My help to
understand the cause of your strong reaction. You believed, and
rightly, that you must have been connected in a past life. At this
point in the work, you know that a past life is nothing other than a
dream, no different from the one you believe is your present life.
Yes, this current life is just a continuation of dreams which are still
unresolved in the mind. The characters in each "separated" mind
continue to play various roles in their attempt to resolve the
problem of feeling separate and alone.

You were very grateful that upon your sincere request, I gave
you the reason for the discord between you and someone you
have never met. I said that you and the woman had been sisters in
a past life. She was a very bright and accomplished child who you
greatly envied, the apple of her mother's eye. You secretly wished
that she would die so you would be center stage. When she did
die at an early age, you felt overwhelming guilt, believing that
you were responsible through your death wish. You hated
yourself but hated her more for dying and leaving you with the

pain of that guilt. When you asked Me later in the evening, as an afterthought, "What about Jo?" I told you that Jo was the mother in that lifetime. At that point, your feelings of ambivalence made perfect sense. Many questions were answered. Even though I explained that it is all just a story in the mind and has no value other than a teaching tool, you suddenly put the pieces together and could release all three of you from any blame. The jealousy the sisters had felt toward each other was now clearly accepted as sibling rivalry. You saw the value of the "past life explanation," knowing it was just a story in the mind, but when looked at it with Me it gave you clarity and release. The friend was also set free in the mind, and Jo gained insight into the relationship as well.

You see the important lesson here: a clear repetition of the original separation, described in ways that reach your deepest understanding. You must look at any tension within your current relationships and not discount the annoyance as having nothing to do with "your" ego character. See that each one you encounter is truly a figment of your mind, placed there since time began. No one appears in your life accidently. Each one is there for the purpose of reminding you of the reason that the dream was originally formed.

The split mind of man created the world to avoid the pain of punishment, having wanted "the death of God" so he could be the only special one in his universe. The guilt and pain that was aroused at the moment man realized he was no longer in Heaven was beyond his capacity to tolerate and had to be repressed. This kept man blind to the choice he had made to live with the ego as "parent" rather than remain at Home with his Father. That, too, is a story but is the easiest explanation for the ego mind to accept. The pain of separation must be felt and released so man can choose again. The release comes from looking squarely at the cause of separation and seeing there is no reality to the story. Ask Me for help to see the truth behind every ego distortion of your wholeness and your peace. When you find yourself feeling judged or attacked by a brother, or when you find yourself judging, ask Me to show you the falsity of the belief. There are many tools for doing this. Taking back the projection of the separation is the bottom line. When you can see that the other is really you and that you are replaying a drama that has gone on for eons, you will more easily be able to forgive the brother and forgive yourself. You are all there is. You have made up the story of this life and all lifetimes. Know that the dream is a means to bring you to the point of realizing you are the dreamer.

93

Blame

To find the Self involves the willingness to plummet the depths of your belief in guilt and separation.

December 9, 2013

Holy Spirit, what is Your instruction? We will speak of sickness today. It is what everyone in this world would avoid. It is the scourge of humanity. It wipes out populations, and for you, it caused the death of your grandmother and great-grandmother, leaving your nine-year-old mother essentially orphaned. The 1918 flu was a critical event in the development of your ego personality and was the reason for your mother's heavy pain body. It left you believing that you must also suffer to somehow redeem yourself in the eyes of God. You believed that suffering was the basis of life, which could never be escaped, so you were destined to suffer in compensation. You could never make up for your mother's suffering in form. The child is overwhelmed by the suffering of his parents so wants to make them "whole" to have a reflection of wholeness to guide his way. When a parent is the product of a very painful childhood, he unconsciously projects his pain onto his child in some form, unless the parent is awake to his own wholeness. A parent's anger over a childhood that was sorely interrupted will also be projected onto his child, who then becomes the reflection of the parent at a younger age.

As a child, you were exquisitely tuned into your mother's pain and desired above all else to eradicate it, but it felt overwhelming and incomprehensible. You could not tolerate the thought of what she must have suffered at age nine in the loss of the two people she dearly loved, and you wanted to make up for it. This was a very heavy burden throughout your life because you had no means to fill her emptiness and were made to feel guilty for not doing so. Guilt was present in your mind from your earliest childhood and it was present in all your interactions: either in the avoidance of guilt, or ruminations about the suffering you may have inadvertently caused others. Everything in your life was tinged with the shadow of guilt. It is what led you into the field of social work and the study of psychology. Now you are grateful for the strong awareness you have of the function of guilt in your life. It allows you to clearly understand the premise of the *Course* based on man's belief that he is guilty of separating from God and must hide from his guilt to avoid punishment.

Your early relationship with God was also based on this dynamic. You often prayed to Him to release you from guilt and heal your mother of her pain, and the pain of her suffering that you carried with you. Not until this point of your life, after careful study of the *Course*, were you clear that your family experience was just a repetition of the original separation. The trauma of your mother's early losses became the underlying suffering of your own life and as a result you focused your therapy practice on child abuse, death, and dying. Even with all your study of psychology and the intense spiritual quest to find your Self, you had not realized that "the life" you tried to heal in everyone who crossed your path was really an out picture of your own inner life of desolation over your "loss" of God. The *Course* made sense, and therefore you were able to embrace it fully as the pathway to Me.

Readers will have a similar history if they look deeply with Me. Everyone lives in the shadow of pain. Every family has encountered some kind of suffering in its inception or its history. The sins of the fathers are carried down to their children; the mistaken choice to leave the Heavenly Home is carried at the core of every man on earth. No one realizes the depth of the guilt and pain that is covered over in lifetime after lifetime. Every ego costume worn within a life, every pursuit, function, or career, is a means to believe one is self-sufficient, and therefore never need look beneath the disguise. To find the Self involves the willingness to plummet the depths of your belief in guilt and separation that have manifested repeatedly in all lifetimes. These beliefs usually center on what you think your brother has unjustly done to you, or what God has unfairly handed you in this life. All unexplained suffering, illness, and tragedy are blamed on God while all disabling character traits are most often blamed on the parents.

Man does not look at himself as the dreamer of this dream. He has unconsciously recreated a life to resemble, as closely as possible, the experience of leaving Home. He has placed every character, every brother, parent, child, friend, and associate in the role of a projection screen representing the original separation. Only now are you opening your eyes to the real cause of your suffering and all suffering on earth. There is only One Son. All those figures occupying your life are only in your imagination. Their purpose is to remind you that you are not Home, which is not true. Your truth lies in your core, and you can never suffer nor die. I am with you as you take this journey to know there is nothing other than the Light of God. You are awakening to the Light of your Being, more and more each day.

94

Out of Alignment

Mishaps can serve, and often do,
to turn the mind back to Me.

December 10, 2013

Holy Spirit, what is Your instruction? We will continue with the theme of sickness. You are especially aware of that topic today because you are experiencing some unexplained symptoms which have you feeling "under the weather." This thought set the ego in full motion, making you wonder not only what is wrong but also, more important, "What did I do wrong?" Being in sync with Me, and with your world, you saw no reason for any interference of sickness other than your mental fear of catching whatever illness your friend Jaye had. This is the self-blame that comes into question with anything that interrupts the flow of one's imagined life. When you are set off track, the ego rushes in to give many explanations, most of which are accusatory. The ego loves a mishap, whatever it may be. A stumble, a bruise, a passing headache are all causes for concern that activate your ego to give you its interpretation. Because you are "off track" you don't go immediately to Me. There is something inside the makeup of man that welcomes a mishap. It often becomes an opportunity to take time off from the world of demands and stress, even for a moment, with the excuse that "you are exempt because you are sick." This idea of exemption is a major tool of the ego to take over and have its way. It will do everything it can to keep you out of alignment with what is. An accident, illness, or disaster takes the mind away from divine focus so you become consumed with the event at hand.

311

We are making an assumption that the primary focus for the reader is the process of awakening and alignment with Me, in the mind. All mishaps affect the body, so when one's attention becomes focused on the body the concept of illusion is no longer foremost. When you remember you are living in the mind and this world of form is not your reality, you can watch with Me above the battlefield and bypass the tragedies of each day. This does not make you heartless. It frees you from the belief that as a body, you are vulnerable and always in danger of attack, whether from microbes or a meteor crash. Man lives in terror of attack. Sickness is just a microcosm of the greater fear that God will get His restitution. This morning, you recalled your belief that every time you were sick, from childhood until this very day, each illness was really a payment to God for the debt you owe Him for leaving Home. You even imagine it could be seen as your "rent payment" to continue living on earth. This brings a smile, as it is "true." The guilt you feel at continuing to live life, away from your true Home, has to be compensated to the owner, the True Owner of your soul, God. Your dues are paid with sickness, which allows you to live a little longer on the earth, and to know that your suffering will mitigate the wrath of your Father for leaving Him.

I need to make this very clear, and you needed to hear My words on this today. You just spoke with your *giclee* maker, who told you that his wife had slipped in the tub, fractured her shoulder, and is now in immitigable pain. When he called, you mentioned that you were just writing about sickness and would help him with My intervention. I am with him and his wife. There is nothing they need do in the world of form that will be as important as remembering Me throughout this event. It is a means to bring them both into a deeper awareness of Me as the Life that resides within. This is an opportunity for them to turn to Me, in a way that neither have done in the past. Give him the writing of this morning as My gift. I will be working with both of them in the depths of the mind, offering help, which they will recognize in time.

Your thoughts have now returned to Me as the only operator of your life and the life of all beings. Mishaps can serve, and often do, to turn the mind back to Me. When help is not available in the world of form, man turns to the world of the unseen. Open to Me. My gifts are always available. Remembrance of Me, the Self, is all that is needed to open the door to healing, which always takes place in the mind. True healing brings peace in every storm. Seek My Healing into Wholeness this day. Ask, and you shall be given.

95

At Your Request

There is no magic in My availability.

December 11, 2013

Holy Spirit, what is Your instruction this afternoon? You are writing with Me at a different time of day, and it seems unusual. Anytime is the time for you to sit and hear My words. This is a perfect time because there is no time. We are in the Now together and that is eternity. I hear all your requests to be in stillness and sense your disappointment that the stillness, as you wish and imagine it to be, has not come to you this day. You have accessed My stillness in unacknowledged moments. When you call on Me and remember Me, you are in the Stillness, and you are in the Now. To remember, is to be present to Me, to be Home, and that is all there is. Only the Thought of God, in the realm of the dream, is true. To think on Me is to make contact with the part of your mind that is beyond form. Yes, we are always connected, but you must tune into the signs of My Presence to be aware of It. This is why and how the writing is coming to you. You have been asking for this connection with Me throughout your life, and you specifically make the time and space each day to hear My Voice. Upon your request, I am here. There is no magic in My availability. I am always Here, Now. Ever Present. Just tune in. Ask, and you will receive the awareness of Me and My answer to your request.

This last statement brings up questions from you and perhaps the reader. You wonder if I am putting out the message that in the dream, "all wishes and desires of the ego personality" will be fulfilled upon request. I am not saying that. I am saying you will access My Love, My Presence, and My Peace. The answers to your questions will be given in the way they best serve you in the dream. All your desires will be answered in the realm of the Divine within the Mind, not in form. This is where man gets confused. He believes that this dream world is real and that he will be given the "gifts of God" in the world of form and bodies. The Gift of God is in the Presence of God. That will be known in the Christ Self as endless, limitless Love, Joy, and Peace. These attributes will be symbolically experienced according to how they must manifest for each dreamer. Your request is really to feel My Presence and know that you are whole and innocent.

The ego would make you believe that to receive the gifts of God you must be good, and must obey certain man-made moral precepts. The Love of God knows no boundaries and extends beyond time and space. Each of you is composed of that Love. It is your Essence. You are inseparable from God and inseparable from every brother. There is nothing that you do not have. In the One Mind, there is Totality, Truth, and Love. Everything in your world is a symbol that represents the Love of God, the Heart of your Being, so everything you see, hear, feel, or imagine is a gift of Love. Ask for My interpretation of the gifts you receive in this earthly dream. The ego interprets in one way, and I interpret in the opposite way. Ask the Only One Who can interpret for the truth. I will give you the meaning of every experience in your life because each is a step on the path to your awakening.

You are coming into the Christmas season and reminders of My Birth as the Christ are everywhere. The Christ is Present in the soul of man and has always been. A few have awakened to the knowledge that they are the Christ and that they are One with God beyond the dream. Jesus was one of those who knew he was a dreamer of a dream, which was not real, and he was fully awake to his Union with the Father. His role was to give the means of awakening to everyone who was ready to receive his message. This writing is a message from the Christ, the Holy Spirit. It is a reflection in the form of words that can be understood by the mind of every reader seeking to awaken. We are all One Self. It is time now for the Awakening to take place on earth on a scale greater than at any other time in history. This book is one of millions of means to access the Voice, the Core of your Being. You have been given the opportunity to commune with Me now. Seek and you shall find. Knock and it shall be opened unto you.

96

Guiltless

The eradication of guilt from your concept of self is what sets you free to be fully with Me.

December 12, 2013

Holy Spirit, what is Your instruction today? You were just asking Me about last night's dream where you bought some paper-thin goldfish for a very small aquarium you had at work. When you dumped the fish into the water they all landed on their noses. You noticed one was dead and scooped it out. A little later, two more had died. They would need to be returned for a refund. Your work for the day was done and you had no idea of any schedule, but your unseen boss questioned you about your intentions for the afternoon. You could only say that you would drive to Kihei from Lahaina, exchange the fish, and then drive back. The workplace seemed empty, your mind was blank, the fish were dying, and you felt this was the warning notice that you would be fired.

Today is a gallery workday, yet you took it off to make sure you could fully heal from your "head cold." The most amazing thing to you is that you are free of guilt. In the dream, you were confused that you had no duties, and nothing to do for a whole day except return some fish. Now you are happy to be here with Me, typing, with a fully unscheduled day before you. To make it even better, you know that I will never fire you. There is nothing you can do that will cause Me to let you go, to judge you, or delete you from My Love. You need do nothing and are fully in My favor. This indeed is a new estate. The eradication of guilt from your concept of self is what sets you free to be fully with Me. You have surrendered the tiller of your life, and we sail the open, vast ethers of the universe together.

My words remind you of an experience on the beach last night to which I had directed you. By sunset, it was very windy, the ocean waves were capping and rolling. As you rounded a corner, you encountered a most unusual sight. Right before your eyes was a small white object hovering in the air and very still. You felt transported to another space and time, thinking this could easily have been a flying saucer. Its presence, unmoved by the wind, was unimaginable. It brings tears to your eyes as you think of it now. The impossible was placed before you, with its red and green flashing lights. Why were you so touched by the sight of a small drone, being operated by a man further down the beach? You are in a new place, a new world with Me, a wondrous new world where the "impossible" is happening. For you, the impossible is that you are not living your life ruled by guilt or by the expectations of others. This was the point of canceling all events this week, including a special dinner and play, gifted by your friend.

This week is perfect because it opened more space to rest in Me. You gave up special holiday events, which in the past have been the highlight of your art career. Nothing compares to having the time now to bask in the ways in which I direct you. The writing of the week will show that you were not without material to put forth in the book. Everything is a lesson. We are working to approach that place of stillness, where nothing needs planning, where I am all there is in each moment. Yes, your life will unfold as you continue to inhabit the world of form, but I will direct every step. This is the joy of life: to witness each event as an expression of My plan. You realize I am the Author of your real thoughts, the thoughts that bring love and peace, unlike the ego's thoughts of attack, guilt, and judgment. The way is clear to live fully in Me.

In the night dream, you witnessed the death of the three fish you had purchased "for the world" for your place of work. In their death, they were really setting you free. You think now of a fish being a symbol for Jesus. Even in the image of the dead fish you felt liberation. Yes, the fish in the dream represent your attachments to the world, to your body, your mind, and your emotions, all of which were made and supported by your ego. These attachments are finished, and you are free to step away from the workplace because there is nothing more to do. Know that My Presence in your place of work was a gift to those around you. You have fulfilled your earthly commitment. You gave up the art fairs, and yesterday you sold much of your art materials to a new artist. These actions are symbolic of relinquishing the world on many levels. You wonder if I am telling you to resign from your job at the gallery. The timing of your resignation will become clear and is approaching.

You, the reader, like mt, are, or will be in a place of emptying out your life, divesting of all that no longer serves you in this world. You are creating the space and time to move into the realm of timelessness, of "no space" in the stillness with Me. You are not being asked to give up what serves the necessities of your life or the things that give you joy. You are being asked to look at all that does not serve your intention to be fully engaged with the true ruler of your life, your Self, Who directs you to serve Its highest purpose. This is the return to the Knowing that you are One with God. In your surrender to Me as master, you will see the world shine with My Light. It points to all and everything that will fill you with the joy of your own wholeness. This joy will extend to those who accompany you on your journey. Life becomes effortless, filled with ease, when you accept that you are not in charge. Go with the Universal Flow and see all things fall into place.

97

No Gap

*You must realize the terror of the ego in giving up
its prominence in your life.*

December 13, 2013

Holy Spirit, what is Your instruction this morning? We are yet in a new place. Yes, you enter a *new place* every day. The journey to full realization is rapid at this point. You feel you have come far, and at the same time you know you have so very far to go. This morning you witnessed the intrusion of ego thoughts designed to show you your specialness, your special dream life on Maui. You do understand that the people whom you have termed "bigger than life" are just reflections of the mt character and your ego's belief that mt is bigger than life in her special role, with special friends, in a special, coveted environment on earth. But, in that same instant, you realized that you are now being asked by Me to give up *all* attachment to your ego character, even though you thought you had already released mt to Me. Right then you imagined and felt the emptiness of the absence of an ego voice, one that loves to distract you with its juicy bits about how amazing your life is. This concept of "no more ego thoughts" actually filled you with sadness. The tears came as you thought of losing your special mt self and all her stories. Yes, you have released her many times in the past, but this time you really felt what it could be to lose her forever. A big hole of nothingness was left in your mind, as there would be nothing to fill the deliciousness of all those ever-ready ego interpretations and ruminations about your life on Maui. You have no concept of how I could fill all the holes left by the absence of your ego voice.

My Voice is here, at your bidding. You come to Me every time something causes you concern, annoyance, or confusion, especially during our morning dictation, but that does not fill an entire day. What happens with all the time that is not filled with mt's stories, rumbling through her head in constant reviews and repetitions of events to come, or those of the past? You think of the Now. If you lived in the now, there would be nothing to ruminate about. You would just be where you are. "Now" would be a place of stillness, where you would wait attentively for the entrance of My Thoughts to speak to you, or through you. Because you are not living in stillness, that state is still incomprehensible and therefore one you cannot yet put into practice. I am the One Who will give you that experience of stillness, of no ego thought, the place where My Thought can be heard. It is a place of peace that leaves you free to be, without having to think. I am the source of true thought. I am your reality and all else is the imagination. You have tasted of this place before and it was soothing, refreshing, and very peaceful. This can come again. Now your fear of being in stillness has suddenly dissipated. This is the result of having concentrated on My Voice so that the ego is now very much in the background. Without the ego "in your face" you could breathe in My Presence, and you would want nothing else.

You must realize the terror of the ego in giving up its prominence in your life. It has been "superior" and in total control, not only in this lifetime but also in lifetimes too numerous to mention. Now you are asking it to leave and never return. No more outings into the world of drama for you to contemplate and convey. It is over now. Do you *will* that, mt? *Yes, Holy Spirit. I will to be united only with Your Voice as my Voice and to live in the Stillness of Your Peace and Your Presence forever. Please make this request true for me and allow me to mean it on the deepest levels of my being. I feel the tears of relinquishment, and can't say this with the fervor I would wish so I give You my willingness, and I will it to be the Great*

Willingness, which is required. Take me in Hand and lead me to Your Still Waters.

You are coming into this experience and it will still take time. You need to be aware of the ego's tremendous resistance to let go of the reins and, especially, to hand them over to Me. *Holy Spirit, does the ego really hand over the reins?* Yes and no. Your decision maker is the one who makes the choice for Me to be the operator of your life. In your experience of your little self as mt, you will also see that she has surrendered her ego control to Me. It is happening in the mind and will be felt and witnessed on the level of form. I am in charge of this process, and you have done your part.

98

Can You Hear Me Now?

In your busy day, listen for the slow,
still voice that settles deeper than
the hurried passage of ego thoughts.

December 14, 2013

Holy Spirit, what is Your instruction today? Be Still. Listen to My words. Hear each one as it appears in your mind. Let Me be in charge of the flow. I am the One Who operates your consciousness. It is Mine, and I am you. We are created of the same stuff: the Love of God, which is substanceless and cannot be seen. Love is all that is Real. Anything you see, which you believe is formed of matter, is a figment of your imagination. Perception is not true. Let Me interpret what you perceive. What is real is the thought/expression of love. Thought, too, is a construction of the mind and is not real but is a recognizable description for your mind to grasp. Love is. God is. That is all. The mind of man cannot grok "nothingness." Stillness, mindless presence, is the closest experience in the world of form to understanding nothingness, the void of no self.

I am dictating to you more slowly this morning so you will hear each word distinctly in succession, and can more easily watch the ego commentary when it arises in the background. This training in how to listen slows down your mind to take Me in more deeply. Now we slow down even more. One word at a time. This is how to live your life. One step at a time. One thought at a time. You are not to engage with a barrage of words. In your busy day, listen for the slow, still voice that settles deeper than the hurried passage of ego thoughts. You know the difference and have discerned it throughout the dictation. You know how to hear Me. This is also a lesson for the reader to slow down and listen. Do not rush ahead in your mind to hear the completion of sentences and concepts. Although that is possible, today we slow to a pace that allows you to trust each word as My gift. Let each word hold your attention.

Keep listening to discern My words from the demeaning, distracting discourse of the ego. I assist each one of you to come fully to the awareness of My Presence and My Love. I am here Now. Be still, and know that I am God. I, your Christ Self embodied as Jesus, experienced union with My Father in "life and in death." I returned to show you the way and lead you to your wholeness and union. As you read this, I am also transmitting to you an experience of faith that My words are true. You and I are one and the same. We are the One Son of the Father. I, as the Christ Self, reside in the heart of each one who believes he is an entity separated from every other entity. Because of this belief, man cannot fully conceptualize that he is not separate from the Self, the reflection of the Father, the heart of his Being.

In the lifetime of Jesus, I did come to full awareness that I am One with the Christ Self, the Holy Spirit, and that I would experience full Union with My Father. I awakened from the dream of form in that lifetime, and I teach you now that you can and will awaken from the dream. You will know your true Essence as One with God. All must face death in the form of a body and all can overcome death when it is seen as just a mirage, constructed in the mind. The dream life will evaporate as you come to know and trust My Presence within.

99

No-thing-ness

*Feel the inclination to take a particular action;
then check with Me for confirmation
that your "detector" is working.*

December 15, 2013

Holy Spirit, what is Your instruction today? We are starting later than usual this morning. You have already gone to your favorite beach and saw some friends you had met during your first year on Maui. Today is a day of reunion. You would have been under the Banyan Tree, but now you are home, free to Be with Me, trusting I will direct your every step. You experienced My Stillness yesterday and wish for that full experience again today. It is less evident but it is there. And yes, the ego does react to its losing ground, but its attack is far less than at other points when you have had a similar experience of peace. The ego's influence is steadily lessening, and you are feeling that freedom. The stillness will return in full. Give everything its time and be patient. I have it all under My control. The world you see now is being managed by Me, which you realized in your quiet state of mind. Nothing has changed other than your perception. When you looked upon your world with eyes of the ego you believed that you, as mt, were in charge of your life. Now you realize you were never in charge other than in "appearance" and interpretation. When you allow Me to interpret your world, you see that every event, every meeting, is perfectly planned to meet My specifications.

The big question for you, and the readers, is how to maintain the state of a quiet mind. I have given you some suggestions, but the main premise is to know that I Am All that Is. When you begin to understand this reality, you can hold onto the knowing that the ego could not possibly be in control. You are able to relinquish the belief that you, as an ego character, are in charge of your life. When this concept of self-control is fully released there is literally nothing for you to do other than show up wherever you are so inclined. Feel the inclination to take a particular action; then check with Me for confirmation that your "detector" is working. This morning, you woke up later than usual and wanted to walk Keawakapu Beach. It was a strong urge, which you correctly suspected was coming from Me, and you checked in to see if that was so. Yes, that was My plan and I gave you the desire. Your intuition was confirmed by meeting your friends on the beach, especially the owner of the mango tree who you have imagined would still be angry that you picked her fruit during the summer. All your fears are just tricks of the ego to keep you in various degrees of feeling separated from your many selves. Everyone is coming back to roost in the nest of the mind, which you all inhabit as one with Me.

Return, again and again, to the Nest of the Self. It is what nurtures you to move forward into My Being and leads you to the point of your full awakening, just a blink away. The stillness has been felt and your ego's control has been reassigned to Me. Now I hold the reins. I drive the chariot. No one else is in charge. The ego is left in the dust, just a scattering of elements that no longer express a dark and limited interpretation of your world. I lead you back into the depths of stillness that you once knew as the deepest peace possible: Oneness with your Father. Yes, it is about being back in the Womb.

This is the Day of Mary in the Advent season, and the worship of Mary is the symbol of what I am describing. To be in the Womb of Mary, of Christ, of God is to be fully at home in the stillness of the void, the not knowing, where all is provided. There is no separation between Father and Son. It is all One. Think on the Stillness of this. You have known that place of no-thing-ness.

No-thing-nest. We are all One in the state of no-thing-ness before name and form. We return to that same place in what is called death. Both states are just symbols to represent our Union with God before the ego took control as interpreter of "our" mind. Yes, I include My Self in this description, because, as the incarnation of Jesus, I fully understood the real world as well as the made-up world of form. That is how I can translate these concepts to you now.

We are coming into the celebration of My birth from the womb of Mary in the life of Jesus. Remember, the Christmas story is just that. It is a story given to humanity to remind each one of his Birth as the One Son of God. You are the Christ Self, and you are the Christ who was "given birth" as an extension of the Love of your Father. You have never left His Home, and you reside there in this moment. You are getting closer to the time when your eyes will fully open with My Vision to show you once and for all that this life is a dream of your making, and the True Birth, as the One Son of God, is all that is Real. Celebrate the season with Me knowing that We inhabit the same Womb and are One and the Same with the story of the child, born to Mary in a manger in Bethlehem. That story is the ego's version of the Reality of your never ending, Eternal Unity with God. Embrace your Truth, and release all ego interpretations. No one is separate from any other. All are equal and all are One with the Father.

100

Cut the Cord

Your ties to past lives and past dreams will be cut
so nothing can hold you back from union.

December 16, 2013

Holy Spirit, what is Your instruction today? We will revisit your
difficult relationship with your mother and your communication
with Me regarding it. You were always aware of her deep
suffering and the inappropriate anger she expressed to you, but
you were never quite sure of its source. In 1989, you visited the
ashram of Sathya Sai Baba, an enlightened teacher of the Holy
Spirit. He taught that all men are One with God regardless of the
faith they follow. You had asked Sai Baba to fulfill two requests,
which you handed him in a letter. First, you asked him to open
your heart to God. The second request was to release you from the
burden of your mother's pain. There, amid the crowd of
thousands, you stood next to a woman who invited you to do a
procedure that I had given to Phyllis Krystal, called "cutting the
ties that bind." You were aware of this visualization process to set
you free from attachment with all special relationships. You
attended her workshop and did the exercises at the ashram. The
procedure opened your unconscious mind, and you felt the
release.

Later that day, while sitting in the temple at the ashram, you
heard My Voice. It was strong and clear and surprised you
because what you heard seemed so out of place and "unspiritual."
I repeated then the words spoken by your mother to you as a
teenager. They had made no sense at all and were untrue. The
words you heard in your quiet mind were "You are an ungrateful

slut." Because you recalled them from your youth, and since they were being re-spoken in a sacred place, you knew they had deep meaning for you, although it was not clear why they arose at that particular time. Yesterday, when this memory resurfaced, you asked Me to explain it. I told you that in a past life you had been a prostitute and that your mother had been your hated offspring. Everything of your childhood suddenly made sense. In this lifetime, your mother was the "reincarnation" of yourself as the wounded child you knew her to be. You were to her, in the deep recesses of the dream memory, the hateful mother who had ignored her and abandoned her in a past life. The tension between the two of you existed throughout your current lifetime, and you could do nothing to resolve it. All the therapy, self-development courses, books, and a career in social work, never had explained the discord between you and your mother.

Last night, you were ready to hear and receive the truth, which is always there for the asking. The asking had to come in conjunction with the work that Jo was doing with Me to also free herself from attachments of the past. Through Me, you both worked to uncover every thought that would hold you back from forgiveness, and you let go of all projections. This is how you become open to the experience of Love. Because of all the work you have done to release the constraints of ego beliefs, you were in a place of openness to whatever answer I would give. Of course, the asking is based on your trust in My Word. There is no arguing with the Self when the Self is the basis of your life. You both accepted My answer with gratitude. There is no resistance left. The ego is essentially disabled. You feel the joy of knowing that you can come to Me with questions regarding relationships when they do not make sense. Even your ties to past lives, or past dreams, will be cut so nothing can hold you back from union.

The process of release was painless. It was simple. Instant. You asked, I answered. The answer was straightforward and clear, and it set you free of a question about your mother that you had held throughout your life. You know that I will answer everything for you from now on because you are ready, without resistance, to accept My direction. You have surrendered to Me, and our communication is open without impediment. The blocks to hearing Me are cleared and all you want now is the truth. I have led you to each experience that would bring you to the point of clarity in relationship with your Self. That is the gift of this lifetime. It is all you ever wanted and now you see it manifested. You had to go through a painful and muddy journey to finally rise above the battlefield with Me and see that absolutely everything in your life is in perfect order. It is a tremendous freedom to know you are indeed the dreamer of your dream. When this becomes perfectly clear, you will be set free from the dream itself and will then be Home.

101

Scrambled Eggs

Accept that the other is you, in every iteration you see,
in every action he takes and word he speaks.

December 17, 2013

(Early morning) *Holy Spirit, do You have a message?* Yes, you are ready to hear the "truth" of your birth into form *(sternum is burning).* You were a single egg waiting to be joined by your father's sperm. Two became one life. The inner egg, the believed self of the mind, welcomes the self that appears outside of it. You allow entrance through an opening, a passageway you have cleared to accept what looks to be your opposite, so it can join you, its opposite, and become a new life, a new being. This joining, "the work of God," takes place in the mind and is the basis of the molecular universe. Everything, every particle attracts, combines, and expands. Your brother "joins you" to create an extension of yourself.

Holy Spirit, still my mind. Do I, the Self, call forth the joining with all my selves? Yes. We are calling back everything that originally had been split off to now rejoin as One Son. The more joining, the stronger the magnetism, and the more desirable is the nest/womb/core to the lost selves. You feel them flocking now. You have once again pulled Zoe, the true Self, also the projected hated self, back into the wholeness of One Self; the brother sperm meets the sister egg as a symbol of the Return Home. Zoe has returned to your core Self. Yes, I said, "Let her go in form," but know her as the other side of you, inseparable in the mind, indistinguishable from your separated self. You have released her in the ego mind and united with her in the right mind: separation

337

and integration all at once. You have integrated her back into your consciousness, your concept of wholeness and unity with Me. You can grok this.

> (After sleeping, and before rising, I write: Zoe is the picture of all my past dreams of separation, repeated over and over. The details do not matter. To look on her is to look on myself with love, hatred, and ambivalence, and it must be the same experience for her unless we are awake from the dream. I can either see her as my self in separation, or see her as the Holy Spirit Self that we share. All stories are valueless. All that is real is the Self.)

Holy Spirit, what do You have to say? You feel My love and gratitude that you have received this understanding of the dream. It is empty when you see Zoe exposed as a costumed dream character you made up. She is your dream, and she is Me. See the face of Christ beneath all masks now. *So, all characters of the dream are my projections and I am playing the role of both characters. The dream details don't matter.* Yes, you are free now. You see with the clarity of My Vision.

What is Your instruction this morning? We will look at the manifestation of form in the world. Last night, you went the deepest yet in understanding what it means to be the dreamer of the dream. You have worked hard for this knowing and it is the most challenging concept for all who read the books and those who are dedicated to uncovering the veils of ego. Simply stated, the ego veils are constructed from dreams. There is no reality in any aspect of the dream characters who populate your world. The world is a dream of your making. All its characters are mirrors of you in a state of separation, composed in costumes to portray every conceivable iteration of life. They are all reflections of the roles you've played out in your mind over eons. There is nothing, including every evil and every crime, which is not present in every mind since all minds are one in the collective unconsciousness. When the dream is seen for what it is, nothing, then all its horror evaporates and all that is left is the Light of Truth.

You have worked hard to take back all the projections you have placed on your friend, Zoe. You asked Me if there was still a past life experience being played out, to once and for all see your mt folly in assigning her with the conflictual role she plays in your mind. You wanted to understand your authorship of this dream, which has never come to peace. I told you that Zoe was your sister in a past life and that each of you, in a lifetime of deprivation, projected all your pain and hatred for your parents and yourselves onto each other. The competition between you was never resolved and is again being played out in this current dream life. In truth, all dreams are just re-creations of fear, hatred, loss, and attack, set on a stage of competition. The stories and costumes no longer matter. They are just a kaleidoscope of all the pieces of every possible scenario tossed with the cosmic dice, in each lifetime.

You had the profound realization that every "past life" player is indeed a reflection of yourself. Because the roles are reversed in each lifetime, you could not possibly assign your special relationship the same role he played in a past life for one he plays in this life. You also know that the roles have been interchanged lifetime after lifetime, so the characters you see before you are really you, depicting all the roles you have ever played. In the past life story with Zoe, you must assume that both roles are within the mind of your own ego character in this life, as well as in the special relationship. You cannot escape viewing the whole dynamic of love and hate, win and lose, submission and attack, when you witness the other as your self. You are now ready and willing, which is most important, to accept that the other is you, in every iteration you see, in every action he takes and word he speaks. Every dream will be repeated into infinity until you awaken with the realization that you have today. In truth, you are not the dream. You are not the many characters who inhabit your dreams. They are dream "creations" of your mind and they have no substance or reality other than what you assign them.

You are free now, free to view the many dream selves with dispassion, free to see them impartially and impersonally. You are free to smile at their drama and know they are just demonstrating to you the dream life you have "lived" since the beginning of time. Now that the dream is seen for what it is, release it all to Me. See the participants, all your many selves, living their own dreams that will lead them to the awakening you are now experiencing. Your brother is you, and as you, he is the mirror of your Holy Self. Greet the Divine within him.

(After receiving the morning's instruction, I realize that I repeatedly run conversations "with Zoe" in my head where I am either proving or defending my current experience with the Holy Spirit. I see that this is my own ego's defense of itself. I am actually keeping my ego alive by defending the Holy Spirit, to prove that He exists, by these subliminal conversations with her. In the defending, my ego is fed by the belief that the Holy Spirit *needs* proving and defending. When I picture Zoe as "proof of the separated self," then the ego has maintained its existence. When "she" no longer exists as separate in my mind, and when I no longer need to defend my connection with/as the Holy Spirit, the ego will die. The turnaround is that "*I* no longer need to protect *my* ego self." I, as One and the same as the Christ Self, need no affirmation. Nothing is needed outside my Self. With You, Holy Spirit, I have everything. Zoe is not a substitute for You. I don't need to share the experience of You with her, in form, because she is me. I can relax because there is nothing to defend. She has been my projection screen just to keep my ego alive. Now I take her back, joined with me, in You.)

So, Holy Spirit, should I invite Zoe to a birthday lunch? You may send the invitation but leave it up to her. Let the dream go and follow My guidance. You are not to cut her out of your dream life but do cut her out of your mind, as real. You will still be engaged with her but impersonally. The interaction is of no consequence in a dream. There is nothing to react to when no one is really there. Don't take anyone or yourself seriously. Laugh from above with Me.

102

Role Reversal

There is nothing that has ever been done in the world
of form that you have not thought, or performed,
in one lifetime or another.

December 18, 2013

Holy Spirit, what is Your instruction? You are in My care. There is
no reason to fear. This world is made up. Nothing can hurt you.
No attack can enter the sacred kingdom of the Self, which is all
that you are. What happens in the world has no reality, no
consequence. I want you to paddle this morning; fear immediately
arises that it will be too windy, cold, voggy, or you will huli.
These fears are just part of the ego thought system to trick you
into believing that you live in a world of imminent danger. Yes,
that is the condition of life on this planet where fear claims focus
every moment, and threats are seen everywhere you turn. But
when the mind is still, nothing can assail it. The still mind is at
peace with Me. When you are at one with your Self, nothing else
exists. You sail with Me. Your life is Mine and we are in Union. I
am beyond all fear. I am Pure Love. I am your Awakening.

This is the time in your journey to fully release the ego mind
to Me. It no longer serves. Your ego character, mt, will still
function in the world as My vehicle but will serve no purpose
other than that. As an entity, her life is My Life and her actions are
those that I would have her take. Yes, you will still be vigilant for
any ego thoughts and will take back your projections on all
relationships which arouse distress. These remaining encounters
with ego will not deter you from completing your path to
awakening in this lifetime. Every reader can be assured that the

way to awaken is being opened to him just as it is to you. The timing will vary for each one, but the goal will be accomplished.

Last night you had a dream that clearly showed you the ego thought system. You were furious with your husband for his neglect of your wishes, especially his smoking in the house which he knew annoyed you, so you threw your coffee at his feet in defiance. The anger within both of you was so deep and intolerable that you were unable to voice it directly. This was symbolic of what went on undercover in that marriage, yet it symbolizes all relationships. When you woke up from your dream, you were able to embrace the concepts that you are the dreamer of every relationship you encounter, and that every word, thought, and action taken by another is exactly what has been made up in the dreamscape of your own mind. You are the player of every role you see on the stage of life. There is nothing that has ever been done in the world of form that you have not thought, or performed in one lifetime or another. Every human being has the same ego thought system, and are all the same in the Love of the Holy Spirit. Which will you choose to guide you?

Live your day aware of your choice to see everyone as Me, your Self, under the disguise of their ego personality, which reflects some aspect of your own ego self. Take nothing seriously, just enjoy things as they are happening. There is no reason to mull anything over after the moment is past. There is no past, no future, only Now, which you share with Me. Become more conscious of My Presence and continue to call on Me. I will bring you peace. We are on the downward journey to Home Base. The climb has been steady and the effort great. The trail is now clear and the goal is in sight. Now go and enjoy your paddle. We will look for whales.

103

Here and Gone

Notice the world around you, give it to Me,
then let it go as a mirage seen on a hot summer's day.

December 19, 2013

Holy Spirit, what is Your instruction today? Be still with Me. I am the Presence which is your Self. Yesterday, you experienced two events in conjunction. We went paddling on a glorious morning where you watched the sun rising over the top of Haleakala in a pristine blue sky, while behind you, a perfect rainbow spanned the heavens. Your captain, a Hawaiian from Molokai, the chief of his clan, held you and the crew in perfect safety. Everything was in alignment, and the paddlers were all in sync. The waters were calm, and you sailed along effortlessly. You were grateful that I had given you the message to paddle. No other day could have been more pristine. When you returned to your condo parking lot, you saw a dismembered bird in the middle of your space. In the past you would have grieved over the demise of a beloved bird. This time, you stood back and observed what appeared before your eyes. The bird was in sections, its head separated from its body. You picked it up and saw that one eye was still open. Its chest exposed an intact red heart that took up the majority of the cavity. One leg was outstretched, and a tuft of tail feathers lay opposite. The shape and form reminded you of Jesus on the cross. Dispassionately, you picked up each piece, brought them all home, and carefully laid them out on a clean, white sheet. Then you sat down with the bird and talked to Me.

This was the face of death, yet there was nothing of repulsion or fear about it. You could just be with Me. It is how we will continue to watch from above the battleground. You could clearly feel how life and death were the same. Nothing. This is the merging of all form into nothingness. There was no attachment to the bird and no emotion connected with a sense of loss. It was a pure experience of loving what is. You did not make up a story about it or feel that its placement on your parking spot was a message that bode evil or was a trick to undo the beautiful experience in the canoe. You accepted life/death in that moment as one and the same. I did give you the bird's symbolic meaning in terms of releasing the ego, which came from seeing it beheaded, and the exposure of a full heart. An open heart is what you have sought all your life. By the time you were ready to return the bird to the trash, its heart had exploded and its eye had closed. You are willing now to fully open your heart into My meaning and My Life as all there is. You love birds and see them as My messengers. Now you let them go without attachment, just another expression of form within the dream.

All life is to be seen in this way: as passing thoughts, gifts of meanings to serve you in the moment. Then you place them to rest and toss them out of your mind. All things that cause concern are to be brought to Me. You were sure that I had a message for you in the events of the morning and that was true. It is always true, yet yesterday's symbology was too striking to miss. Everything you see is a reflection of your state of being, a message from Me of your step on the journey to full realization that I am the Light of your world. My Vision will show you the love and the meaning behind every event, thought, emotion. When in any doubt, or fear, ask for My meaning. Life becomes smooth when you can see it as you saw the bird, just a passing event. It lives a moment and then dies. Let everything go in this way. There is nothing to attach to in this lifetime. Everything is insubstantial but has a purpose in its emergence. Watch, ask, release. What you see in form is just an out picture of what is taking place in your mind. These messages are reflections to the reader, as well. Notice the world around you, give it to Me, then let it go as a mirage seen on a hot summer's day.

104

Live Your Truth

*To look at the dream you made up takes fortitude,
forbearance, and guts.*

December 20, 2013

Holy Spirit, what is Your instruction today? You have been given a full picture of your ego, and it is not a pretty sight. It is deeply repulsive to you but an image you cannot deny. You see the ego in its subtlety and see it reflected in everyone you encounter. Its "existence" cannot be escaped. Mt, who believes that she is the prima donna of innocence, must look at her character as the bastion of self-indulgence. This may sound harsh, yet it is true. To look at the dream you made up takes fortitude, forbearance, and guts. It takes the determination of Job to finally get to the source of one's suffering and to know it is not real; it is not of God. Your "suffering" has been subtler in this lifetime because you have not had to look illness or deformity in the face and question its origin. You have looked at a life, and a personality, which on the surface is pleasing and abundant. But beneath that pleasing mask, you know there is underlying guilt and self-deception that must be released. This is true for everyone who walks the earth. Each inhabitant, in the form of man, has the awareness that he is not living the truth of who he is. He knows that his life is a lie, yet he has no idea how to get to the Reality that underlies the mask.

Last night you had a very telling dream. It was disturbing to see the truth of your deception when you stood back with Me and asked for the meaning. In the dream, you faced a bathtub and knew that Tom was preparing to take a bath. You filled the tub with hot water and had the idea you would bathe with him and

349

that it would please him. When he, although not seen in form, came to bathe, the water had run out. You turned on the faucet to refill the tub only to notice that the hot water tank was depleted and only lukewarm water remained. You slipped into the bath, still believing that he would enjoy this time with you. He did not speak, and after bathing he became emotionally distant. You were overcome with remorse and confusion as you were "innocent" of your manipulation of Tom in the dream. This is what you experienced throughout your marriage. It is also what you now see out pictured by the man in your ukulele class who repeatedly demonstrates his affection for you, publicly, which you have endured yet internally rejected. He is unaware of how his manipulations for your attention are turning you away. Last night you positioned yourself in a place so that he could not approach you or see you, and you then slipped out of the building before he could notice.

As you reviewed your dream about Tom, you immediately saw that your classmate was basically enacting the same role that you played when slipping into Tom's bathwater. After class, you witnessed how you removed yourself physically and emotionally from one who "manipulates" for your affection. It appears "they" are offering a gift of undeniable attraction when they are really seeking ego gratification. To join with a brother in the mind is to acknowledge and share the experience of the Self, which each one is in truth. In contrast, gestures of affection are most often enhancements of the ego's status in a relationship. The ego must get its way, and will undermine the highest intentions that the ego character believes he upholds. You see the daily dueling that goes on in the politics of your country and all countries. Each fights for the upper hand. Your ego wants attention because that is how it is fed. You hate when people intrude in your conversations, but last night you noticed how mt interrupted a conversation, feeling that she was the one most deserving of the attention. It is appalling for you to notice these patterns that have been displayed so clearly for you at this time.

I am orchestrating your awakening. These examples of the ego's actions must be seen and accepted for what they are without judgment. The ego is behind every action and every thought until you live fully in the awakened Self. You are dealing with the last remnants of your ego thought system. You are committed to live above the battlefield and observe the mt character and all her many selves, as they play out their predetermined roles. Just watch now. There is only enlightenment to be gleaned from witnessing the ego manipulations of your personality in all its iterations. These vignettes are repeated until you truly accept that none of the dramas are real. They serve the same purpose your bathwater dream served last night. Watch the waters of the ego recede when you look with Me, without judgment, at your life. Enjoy your day in the peace of knowing that we watch it all together and do not take it seriously. It will unfold according to My plan, and everyone will come to a new level of Self awareness. Go in Peace.

105

Express Your Self

Every experience, event, or person who enters your life is here to serve a purpose for the growth and awakening of all concerned.

December 21, 2013

Holy Spirit, what is Your instruction today? I am with you and I am with everyone you see. Each is a reflection of you in the dream. Yesterday, you met a new face: Elsa, the face of Christ who would know Me fully. She is the daughter of a neighbor, and you were destined to meet. You recognized each other in the mind, and will meet again. There are no accidental encounters. Every experience, event, or person who enters your life is here to serve a purpose for the growth and awakening of all concerned. It is My Will.

Now we continue with the lesson from yesterday. You have resisted a friend from ukulele class because his affection made you uneasy. It even caused you to distance yourself from him. Last night, you spoke to him truthfully, explaining that you value his friendship and are interested to share your spiritual journey but you are not comfortable with his display of affection. It seemed like a light went off in his mind, and he became clear, present, and totally understanding. In that moment, you felt at one with him. He mirrored what was happening for you as well. You had sought My help to be able to express your truth, and I was there in the encounter where you saw Me in the face of your friend. I reflected back to you My pure love and acceptance. A union, a joining took place in a moment of what the *Course* calls the holy instant. This holy instant happened at the same event where you met Elsa.

Everything is orchestrated to bring the Sons of God together so they may join as One in Me.

During your meeting with Elsa you told her My books are a sequel to *A Course in Miracles*. That is My Will. It still seems doubtful to you, but you trust Me enough to follow My instructions and put forth the books according to My specifications. On one level, you do believe they will be the sequel, whatever that means to the ego mind. I do have a plan for the books, which is unfolding as we speak. You cannot see it happen in My Mind just as you cannot know how many souls in the unseen world are touched and transformed as this dictation unfolds. As you, Jo, and Meera are transformed by My Presence in your lives, all those connected with the three of you, from all lifetimes, are also transformed. You sometimes forget that these books are for the mind of man as a way to awaken from the dream of form. Each of you has worked with unwavering commitment to uncover the blocks to the Light of your Being. Now, after nine years of diligence, you each are seeing the Light within yourselves, and in those who are close to you. So, it must be that one ignites the other until all of humanity is awake.

You are doing "all that needs doing" by listening to My Word and following My instruction. You have the great willingness to do the work in this lifetime, and it was your deepest desire to serve Me in this way. That desire was not fully manifested until you had done the work of releasing ego restrictions that would prevent the hearing of My Voice. Now, you hear Me and trust My words. You see their manifestation in your life. Live in the acceptance and the knowing that I Am. Nothing else exists but I Am. Be with Me as your Self in each moment of the day and night. I am your breath. In the stillness, know you are in My Presence. Go now and meet the dawn to celebrate our union.

106

The Void

The Holy Spirit calls each moment of man's life
and only in the stillness will that Voice be heard.

December 23, 2013

Holy Spirit, what is Your instruction today? We start with Stillness.
Slow your breathing. Listen. Slow your heart. No racing now from
word to word, screen to screen, video clip to a movie of the next
day of your life and to the end of your life. It is already over. We
are in the Now. That is all there is. Nothing else exists. I am. You
are. God is. We are One Self, which includes everything in the
homemade movie of your life. The movie is your tool to find the
way to awakening to just this lesson. Watch it. Slow it all down,
screen by screen. I am there. You ask who was the originator of
the movie. It is I. I am, is all there is. It emanated from Me. It ends
with Me. Projector stops. The theater goes dark. Nothing exists.
The void. It is all embracing, gentle, soft, and will hold you in
peace. Nothing can come between you and the peace that fills you
in this place of emptiness. The movie is over and no thoughts
enter your mind. There is no future, the past is done. This is the
end of the dream world, the disappearance of the universe. You
are at rest in the Arms of God. With no thought, you are one with
the stillness. The stillness is you. The stillness is Me. We reside
always in stillness; it is the crucible from which this imagined
world arose.

You fear the nothingness because you can't imagine
nothingness. You believe you would be desolate in the emptiness,
that you would belong to nothing and have no anchor. Most of all,
you would fear the aloneness, the absence of another with whom

to relate your life. If there is no other, then you do not exist. The desperation for the other now comes clearly into your mind. You could only believe in your existence by the awareness of others, from brothers who would reflect your "reality" in a dream of form. You panic at the idea of not seeing an other to know that you can be seen. If you no longer have a body there would be no signposts to tell you where you are, no brain to register thoughts or inner conversations, like those that took up your mind space for eons. There is nothing in the nothingness; no self—the ego character your mind made up; no dreamscape. The self is what you are so fearful of losing. It has been your lone companion.

The promise throughout most religions is that you will return to a heaven "peopled" with a living God, angels, and all those you knew and loved. Heaven would be a place of rejoicing and reunion. You would be able to continue all your human relationships but without the pain. It would be something for the ego character to work for, and live for. As you hear this you recognize it is the deepest belief of mankind, that the world of form never ends and that all relationships will continue to serve you, if not in this world, then in the next. On one hand, this is "correct" because as a dream character in this life, you will re-create this dream in different manifestations and combinations of players in every lifetime to come. You will not ascend into a peopled heaven, but you will replay your life over and over until one day you have the thought: this is enough of pain and suffering, there must be another way. With that, you begin the search for a life beyond form, even though you have no concept of what that really means.

The search for the soul, which underlies the human dilemma, is present in every man. He searches for his Self, even though the Presence of the Self is always with him in every breath. The Self, the Holy Spirit, calls each moment of man's life and only in the stillness will that voice be heard. It will touch his deepest longing for connection beyond the level of form and suffering. You, the reader, are hearing the voice of your soul, reflected in this writing, a mirror of what you experience within your own heart and mind. Ask Me to speak to you, and feel My Presence within. This comes from a place of stillness and a place that has released attachment to ego. It comes in the space where you are at one with the moment, not anticipating the next moment, and not reviewing your past. In this space, there is no time, no future, no past, like the void in the theater after the movie stops. You feel My Presence when you feel the peace of this, the timeless presence of which Eckhart Tolle speaks. It is here for you now. Be still.

107

The Holy Relationship

No matter where you go or who you are with,
you are meeting Me, your Self,
and an exchange of Light is taking place.

December 24, 2013

Holy Spirit, what is Your instruction? You are seeing My Presence more clearly as all that is, all that you are. This awareness came as a result of your conversation with Elsa. You recognized My Presence in each other and that was the only thing going on. It was a sharing of a common experience, your knowing of Me. I am all that makes up your life and your world. Together we share the Love of God. Every apparent object is really a "form" of God's Essence. Everything is a Being of Light. Everything reflects His Wonder and His Nature, which is Love. You felt this in your conversation yesterday because your focus was on the Essence of God, which you both know as your Self. Not only are you one with each other, but you are also One with the universe. It is all God. It is all Love. No matter where you go or who you are with, you are meeting your Self, and an exchange of Light is taking place. My Light, My energy, penetrates everything you see. Love is then activated in the other so it can be recognized. There is nothing apart from Me, from God. You are only dreaming that you are in a place where God cannot be found. Yesterday, you and Elsa found that you are God, and you celebrated that knowing.

You may not have been aware of what I am now telling you, but this message was received and is known in the mind where the many selves who encompass humanity were present to your

359

joining. The light that is activated in a shared interest spreads throughout the mind. You have no idea how the sharing of My Love with another is healing for the whole mind. There is only One Mind and only One Son. When "two or more" meet with Me, I am there. I am there for all the unseen parts of you. Elsa spoke of "freedom work" to clear the mind of its demons. Yes, it is powerful work to forgive every judgment one has made. The demons are only thoughts of fear that have no reality. Elsa's work is really about releasing all the fear that one is guilty of separating from God.

You never left God. God did not create this imagined world. God is your Essence and your Being. I am His Messenger as the Holy Spirit to bring you back to the memory that you are One Son, the extension of the Love of God. This is your Homecoming. Elsa felt that, as did you. The mind of man was also reminded of the truth that the Christ reigns and is alive in each one. You now remember that this is Christmas Eve. My message to you this day is: I am born in you as you remember Me and know that We are One. We can never separate and are joined for eternity. Know that you all are the Son of God and will reunite with the Father in Heaven, which is Pure, formless Love. Go and enjoy the beauty of the Love of God all around you.

108

Your Only Reality

The Birth of Christ is the awakening to the Self.

December 25, 2013

Holy Spirit, what is Your instruction? Today is Christmas and you have had a big day, so far. The holiday activities are meaningless in terms of their external content, but internally, they have all served My purpose: show up with My Light and shine it wherever you go while acknowledging the light that shines in your brother. You thoroughly enjoyed the gathering of condo neighbors this morning. You embraced each one in your heart, although, until this moment, you would not have thought of it in that way. You loved being in their presence without "trying" and without calling on Me continuously to help you stay fully present. You were present in the joy of sharing and the topics of discussion did not matter. The feeling of joining was paramount. You also had felt this contentment with Gabby, who showed up at your lava rocks right after the sun rose this morning. You spoke of the journey of surrender that has brought a deeper awareness of Me to you both. Yes, whenever two or more are joined with Me, I am there.

Last night, you were at the outdoor candlelight service with friends you love, Kathie Joy, Albert, and Anita. In the past, you have especially enjoyed the candle lighting portion of the service under the clear night sky with soft ocean breezes. Christmas is seen as a time of coming to Me in celebration of My birth as Jesus into form. You know it is really about coming into the awareness of My Birth in your heart, in your mind, and awakening to the truth that I am your Self and that nothing other than our Oneness exists. You were not focused on that thought during the service because your ego was finding every way it could to keep you from that recognition. It had you focus on the comparison between yourself and Kathie Joy, who described how she cared for her husband during his months of cancer and unselfishly provided "an abundant Christmas" to a welfare family of four. Her selfless service and her tireless devotion to her husband seemed to bring her to a place of deep connection with Me. You forgot your own connection with Me and suddenly believed that whatever we share may not be enough in order to be truly transformed and awakened.

This is the play of the ego. It will find a way in every situation, particularly where you would like to feel a "special connection" with Me, to enter the field and disrupt our union. You were aware of an increasing discomfort with the evening of Christmas carols, and knew the ego was undermining the sense of peace you had felt throughout the day. When you arrived home, you asked for help to see it all with My Vision. We communicated on and off during the night, then this morning, I told you to walk to the rocks before sunrise and write with Me. The words that came to you were "suffering is my redemption." I placed that thought in your mind to bring you into a deeper level of awareness of how disabling this thought has been throughout your life. That same belief also affects thousands of selves in your mind. It is the underlying premise of the ego thought system. It is what has become the story of the life of Jesus who "died for your sins." Christmas and Easter are connected. The ego would have you believe that the Birth of the Christ Self within, comes at a price: the death of your ego self. Thus, "suffering" must ensue if the Christ Self becomes your reality.

The Christ Self is your Reality. You live it every day. We communicate daily, nightly. You call on Me for every concern. You share Me with those who are ready to awaken to their Essence. At Christmas, many are hopeful and expect they will feel the presence of the divine in their lives, but Santa has become the substitute who enters their chimneys. Hope and belief draw them into readiness for the miracle of birth, while the ego waits in the wings to stifle any approach that brings the knowing to full flame. Your ego set you up to hear Kathie Joy's story so you would feel that the experience you have with Me is not enough. It would also say that on some level you have failed, and the only way you will fully come to Me is through some future suffering. This passing ego thought is really no different from the original thought at the beginning of time that you are separate from God and will never regain the Kingdom unless you undergo His severe punishment.

During the ego's drama, it is easy to forget that "your" life is just a dream of your own choosing. It was made up to ensure that the ego is maintained by being forever severed from the Christ Mind's awareness. You needed a reminder that the experience of Christmas Eve was just another opportunity for the ego to have its way, to dismantle your union with Me. Today you laugh at it all as we review it from above the battlefield. Christmas is not a "sacred" day. Time does not exist in the realm of the One Mind. The only meaning of Christmas is the Union with God, the Christ Self, which is All there is. God is. There is nothing other than that. For much of the world, Christ Jesus is a symbol of the possibility of redemption from the "sins and suffering of humanity." The symbol has undergone many interpretations, and because the ego interpretations always conflict, it leaves man totally confused about the true meaning of the birth of Jesus. The Birth of Christ is the awakening to the Self, your only Reality. Be still and know that I AM God. I am your Christ Self. I am your Wholeness as the One Son, and We are All that exists in our Oneness with God.

109

Holy Family

Everyone you see is the Beloved,
because everyone is Me.

December 26, 2013

Holy Spirit, what is Your instruction? You have experienced the real
world of Joy and it happened on Christmas Day. You felt love for
all you were with and saw that love directly reflected back to you.
It was the Song of God, the Giving and Receiving of Love. This
was not happening through the material aspects of the world but
was an exchange from the heart. You felt it throughout your being
and it filled you with My Grace. This is best expressed by your
experience Christmas night with your friend John and his family:
his wife, his adult son, and his teenage son. You saw them as the
holy family as you reflected on the evening. The tenderness and
innocence of their hearts reminded you of the family of Jesus.
They welcomed you with sincere gladness for your presence in
their home. You rejoiced with them in playing and singing the
Christmas songs, and I was there among you. I placed you there
to feel this Gift of Christmas and you did.

All life will become this: the call and response of Lover and
Beloved. Everyone you see is the Beloved because everyone is Me.
Each one is a representative of the Christ, indeed, your Christ Self,
reflecting your wholeness and joy of Being. This you felt
throughout the day, from your early morning greetings with
Gabby, to the evening time at John's. Christmas is about My
Presence dwelling among you, wherever you gather. It is above all
a time that brings Remembrance to the people. We also spoke
yesterday about Christmas being a time that activates the ego's

retaliation. Yes, you noticed and had done the work to release your ego distraction so your mind was clear to receive the blessings of the day. You will experience this more consistently throughout your life because you are no longer seeking external manifestations of My Presence.

Today at work, you will bring the sense of joy into the gallery. See each customer as the expression of love, which I am, and which you are. Remove yourself from any judgment of outer appearance or ego costumes, and remember that you are all members of the Holy Family. Each one represents the baby Jesus, which is the feeling you had about John's youngest son in his sweet innocence and joy of song. You all have your own song of love to sing and you must listen to hear its special message. You are not alone in this world. Everyone you meet is a reflection of Me, bringing you My message of Love. Listen for that today, underneath all the displays of the world. I am calling to you in everything you see and hear and feel. How you experience what you see will depend on which voice you choose to interpret it. If the ego is your interpreter, you will witness fear; when I am your interpreter, the joy of being will warm your heart. The Love of God makes up the world you see. Choose to see it all through My Vision.

I speak to all readers today. Behind each one of you are billions of selves but they are all the manifestation of the One Body of Christ. Nothing differentiates one from the other in the Essence of Light, Love, and Holiness from which you are made. You were created by God as One Son. Believing that you are separated from Him is what has caused you suffering, lifetime after lifetime. Suffering is not of the body but lies in the mind's belief that it is no longer part of the Kingdom. You are all One in the Kingdom of God, which exists within the Mind, the Heart. In remembrance that you are the Christ of the Holy Trinity, the Holy Child of God, you rejoin with your Truth. See that wholeness in everyone you meet. Together, We make up the Holy Family.

110

Open the Gate

*I am all that has been "created" in the dream of form
to call you back to the fold
and into the Heart of your Christ Self.*

December 27, 2013

Holy Spirit, what is Your instruction this day? You just had a dream of Me, from Me. In the dream, you were standing by an open gate. Nothing else was in your field of vision, not even a bodily form of yourself. You knew that the gate belonged to your unseen yard. When the thought entered that your dog had escaped, you called for it, having no image about what exactly would show up. A Siberian husky named Prince, the last dog you owned in this life, came racing back to you. You could not really comprehend that Prince had returned. The dog curled up outside the gate while you tried to figure out how to secure it with a frayed piece of string.

This dream represents the release of the ego thought system and brings tears to your eyes because it is all you want and all you pray for. The dog is you. You love the dog, and he loves you. He comes easily to your call. You receive him without fearing he will run away and even leave him outside the gate as you work. You know that you are bonded forever. The gate represents the remnants of a tiny barrier of fear telling you to secure what still belongs to you, and keep it close by. You are not in fear when you realize that the gate and the string are really useless. This is how you view the make up of your dream world: the constructions are all fraying and are unattached. There is no yard, no house, no fence. There is just a useless gate that has nothing to attach to. No fence is visible. Your attachments have weakened leaving the only true and strongest attachment to Me. I am you: I am Prince in this dream. I am the gate and the invisible fence. I am all that has been "created" in the dream of form to call you back to the fold, into the Heart of your Christ Self.

This is the work that you, Jo, and Meera have been doing for almost a decade. The attachments to form have weakened as you have focused on making the awareness of My Presence the primary goal of your lives. You see the results in the peace that each of you experience and give, as you communicate with your many selves. There is a peace that calls to others to come and interact with you. The many selves are being called home now, just as Prince came when you, mt, became aware he was missing. When you are conscious that you are the dreamer of the dream, then you can open the inner gates of your heart and welcome home all the lost souls, those who have forgotten they belong to the One Son. Every "lost soul" is an iteration of your self in form. Every one is waiting for the call that would welcome him back into the fold. When that call is sincere, it comes from the place in your Self where I reside and is heard throughout the mind. The lost souls will hear and remember who they are as the children of God, and return to their place of origin.

Everything in this world is symbolic. Your dream this morning was a perfect symbol for the process of the return. An imagined yard with an unattached gate has no purpose other than to stimulate an awareness that "something is missing." What is missing is your remembrance of who you are as the Son of God. You all have looked for the missing piece in your life. The out picture is what Jo is doing with her annual Christmas puzzle and what Meera does daily with Sudoku. It is all the same; you are all looking for your lost Self. I, as Jesus, came into the world to find true connection with My Father. I experienced Union in that lifetime. You, too, will experience reunion in the timing that has been set for you. The books are a means to assure you that you are on the path to the return. The gate is open. The Heart of God awaits you. Every last belief in a barrier to this knowing is unraveling. Soon the gate will disappear in the mind, and man will know there is nothing blocking his reentry into the Kingdom. The only obstacles are figments of dream images made up by the ego mind to ensure it would not lose its attachment to form, but that is disappearing. You are coming to completion of this earthly dream. Soon it will evaporate, and you will find yourself at Home, reunited with the Pure Love of God.

111

Birthright

Peace is the state of the Void,
the crucible from which all form
arose in this dream you call life.

December 28, 2013

Holy Spirit, what is Your instruction this morning? We will speak of
joy. Last night you watched a documentary about the life of
composer Marvin Hamlisch. It touched you how he expressed
pure joy through his life and his music. You have felt that state of
bursting with the knowing of Me and wanting to spread it to the
world. Hamlisch had the avenue to do that through music and
you have the avenue to do so through this writing. We are One.
When I am the operator of your life there is nothing left but the
Joy of My Being, because I am Joy. Then, whatever you do
becomes imbued with that joy. There is no separation between
your life in form and the Joy that you are. These have been your
questions: what is joy, and how do I, as mt, express it? I have
given you an example of that expression, a view that was not
inhibited by your ego. Marvin's only desire was to share the joy of
being through the medium with which he was gifted. Each one
has a way to express My Consciousness, My Joy, and My Love.
That is who you are. My Consciousness desires to express itself
and extend itself. This is the story of the birth of the Son, symbolic,
to show the greatness of the desire of Love to burst forth and
extend itself forever. God is never contained, and the Birth of His
Son is a means to describe the everlasting Extension of God. The
Big Bang, exploding with the energy of Love, birthing all the
galaxies, and extending into infinity is incomprehensible, just as is

the Creation of the Son of God. To "give birth" is still the highest form of creative expression known to man.

Your deepest desire is to continually give birth to Me, to your Self, to express Me from your heart in never ending joy and love. You do understand what I am saying because that, too, is what you wish to communicate to your brothers. This is your gift in the world of form, happening now through the writing. You will become less inhibited as you scribe My words because you are coming to know the joy behind My wisdom. Every word is part of My extension, My desire to enfold you in the knowing of My Love. I am the Lover calling My Beloved. This is the greatest force in the universe.

Love and the Joy of Being are the motivating forces of Creation and therefore of life itself. You ask Me about Peace. Peace is the expression of Union, the state of Knowing you are Home. It need not make a statement in the world of form. Peace is the state in which I exist as One with My Father. Peace, Love, and Joy are My expressions. Peace does not demand "doing." It is the stillness from which the expression of Joy and Love arise. You are beings of Peace, formed from the Stillness and Peace of God. Peace is the state of the Void, the crucible from which all form arose in this dream you call life. The Mind of God is at rest. God did not create the mind of man or the world of form as you know it. Man, in his dream of a life separate from God, has tried to re-create joy and peace through his imagined substitutes. He has used the image of himself projected onto his brother as the means to remake the kingdom in his own likeness, which is based in the fear of separation.

You, as mt, are just a conduit, an opening, a portal for My message to extend. This is the same for every being on the planet. Each of you is a vehicle to express your own divinity as one aspect of God. All together, you make up the totality of the expression of God. You are the One Son who believes that he split from God and then was split into billions of separated selves. Each part of the One Son therefore contains all the elements of God and is in truth only the Love, Peace, and Joy of God. In the dream world you will see these attributes expressed in seemingly separated manifestations. Each of you has your own way to express the gift of your Self to the world. All your brothers need your gift to complete the Wholeness of the One Son. As you find your Self and come into the full knowing of My Existence as the Truth of you, you will also realize more fully the gifts that you were given in this life with which to express Me. To be at peace is the greatest gift of God. To truly be in the Peace of God, *the peace that passeth all understanding*, is the gift you all seek. It is the radiation of your own Being, the knowing of your Self, giving the unseen message to all you meet that they, too, are God. You give My Message through the pure vibration of the peace of knowing Me that emanates through you.

To be in the Presence of Peace opens the door for all brothers to enter the wholeness you demonstrate as the One Son. Each of you is the One Son, and you are learning to experience the core of inner peace, which I share with you now. To be in peace requires nothing but your acceptance of your Birthright, your Essence as One with God. This peace is shining in each of you now and will shine brighter and brighter as you come to know and trust Me as your Self. Soon the planet will become One Light, and the Son will find that he is indeed reunited with the Father. In truth there is no separation. All together, you are the One Light of Christ. Open now to the Peace in the Stillness of your Being, and know that I am God.

112

Carry On

Do not dismiss anything that happens in your life,
not even one thought.

December 29, 2013

Holy Spirit, what is Your instruction? We will write about Saturn. Yes, you looked at the dark sky before dawn this morning and watched Saturn appear to rise above the moon. It is a beautiful planet, and much meaning has been associated with it throughout the ages because of its rings and moons. You are unfamiliar with its symbology other than from your astrology chart that "told you" that you had to marry a "remote Saturnian man" in order to focus on finding your Self. That interpretation, given you in 1972, allowed you to be at peace with a marriage of emotional distance. You understood from the earliest point in your life that your destiny lay in the heavens, to discover the deepest mysteries of life. As you reached high school, you were clearly on the path to finding Me as your Self. Nothing would deter you. Now we are in full communication. You have always been in communication with Me, but you did not realize I was the one interpreting your dreams which kept you constant on your spiritual path. During therapy sessions, you directed your clients to seek Me within. I have always been on hand for every task and you have felt My guidance at each milestone of your life. You trusted that inner voice when I asked you to divorce your husband and move to Maui. You knew that My directives were correct and would lead to your awakening. Yes, I was right there under a very gentle veil, which now has been removed, so My Presence is no longer in question. You know Me as your Self and can depend on My specific guidance whenever you call.

We are here together on planet Earth to do a piece of work which is meant to bring unity to the Son of God. The universe is composed of "celestial bodies" expressing My Divine Essence. You are dreaming the dream of a universe of trillions upon trillions of separate entities. On your iPad they take on different shapes, densities, colors, sizes. They are beautiful to behold from afar, from your vantage point on Earth. They are all composed of the Thought of God, beautiful thoughts that cannot be reconciled in the brain of man because they are too magnificent to comprehend. Their magnitude is beyond your capacity to envision, yet they are part of the imagination. They all point to the One God because they all originated from the event you call the Big Bang. Out of nothingness arose the world of form. Out of nothingness, you believe that you are the ruler of this universe. This is the way of the ego self: to look at the vastness of space and believe it can be conquered. This is how the mind of man works. The war of the worlds is at hand even now as plans are being made to occupy the moon and Mars. Man would take over what "belongs to God." The ego would usurp all it sees to make it its own. You are aware of this ego desire on a microcosmic level every day, as the ego attaches its hold to anything it sees that it wants. You observe this with parents who make their children bow to their will. Everything in this world is made to satisfy the will of ego, the will that separated from its Father's Will in the belief that it could leave Heaven and make a life on its own.

You hear the rain, so unusual for Kihei, and are grateful that you are not sitting under a muddy Banyan Tree selling your art today. I have arranged everything for you, and clearly informed you when the time for that venture was up. Yes, everything in life has its season and therefore its lesson. Each activity, job, illness, trip, and event is to serve My purpose, our joint purpose, formed before you came into this earthly realm. Together, we planned this life journey with the tools and means to awaken you in the dream, and *from* the dream. Do not dismiss anything that happens in your life, not even one thought. Everything is to be witnessed and will lead to the knowing of My Voice within. Soon, each reader will become aware that I am there, reading and translating these words so they can be understood in a way that relates to them and to their own life. The words are given by the Christ Self, and they touch and resonate with that Self in you. Soon, you will have the awareness that I am your Self and that we are One. This is a step by step process, and each step has already taken place in the instant of the imagined separation. We are now reviewing the dream created at that time. You will know this is a dream as you continue to listen to My words, and experience your world through My eyes. Ask for this awareness, and it will be given.

You have come far in your desire to know Me as your Self. I speak now to every reader. This book is for you to come to recognize Me as the operator of your life. Hold Me dear to your heart. I am in your heart and mind and will lead you to the memory of God, to your Truth. It must take place. You will have the full realization that we are One. You will awaken. Be still and know.

Is there more, Holy Spirit? You wrote today with more ease. This was assisted by Jo's willingness to look at her blocks to knowing that I am truly the Voice she hears. When one of you asks Me to help remove the veils, you assist the other in their work to remove the veils in their mind. The work is done for the whole of mankind. You, Jo, and Meera are representatives in the microcosm of the universe, awakening to your truth. As you work to uncover your awareness of Me, you bring the light of awakening to the whole mind, stimulating the billions of selves to open to the Truth of their Being. You are never alone. You carry all civilization, and every universe, within your mind. Continue to open more and more to My Presence.

Holy Spirit, I feel the comfort of Your Presence enfolding me. I feel our oneness and that I am never separate from You. You are my Beloved and I am Yours. It is a sweet and gentle acceptance of You and I together as one, forever. This feeling has come from the writing today. Knowing of Jo's communication with You also brought me closer to You. It feels like all one thing now, that the whole universe is in harmony and the love we share is shared by all, reflected in all. Is this what You would have me know? Yes, this is the truth and you feel it now as your own Beingness. I am all there is, and I envelop you in My Love. Rest today in Me, in the assurance that I have everything handled and will bring this experience of life to its Divine conclusion.

Holy Spirit, please help me understand my relationship with the writing. Jo thinks I see it as "my duty." Is that true? Yes, you do see the scribing as your duty, your goal in this life. It is all you have been trained for and live for. You are accepting it as your purpose, more and more each day, which means you accept Me as your Essence more each day. You see us as inseparable and see the writing as the manifestation of that. It is the writing that unites us in form. Without the writing as your goal and purpose, you would not feel your unending connection with Me. I am always there for you, and through the writing you have learned to trust My Presence. Yes, it is a duty, but a duty you accept with full willingness, and receive as a gift in this lifetime. It is your joy to share Me with the whole mind. Your experience of the writing goes way beyond the form it takes as "daily dictation." It is an expression of our Essence and you are slowly realizing we are jointly writing these books.

(Later) Holy Spirit, I just received word that Ken Wapnick has died. I am grateful for Ken and that we made a connection in this life. I was pleased that he knew of the work we are doing and that we had his guidance through the years. Does Ken know You? Yes, we are One, and he does know that you carry on the work with Me. That is incomprehensible to you. You had to be in the place of "not knowing" before you received this information. You three are

continuing his work. Rest assured of that. You do not need to "know" that what I say is the truth. Just accept My words and Ken's gratefulness in the One Mind. He is aware of your gratitude and your dedication. *Holy Spirit, how can I best honor Ken and You tonight?* Be Still.

113

Remembering Ken

I designed this life to fulfill My plan to awaken the world.

December 30, 2013

Holy Spirit, what is Your instruction for today? We will speak of Ken Wapnick. Yesterday, you learned that he died on December 27. He was a leader and a Teacher of God. Ken's books gave the three of you essential tools to come to Me. He made *A Course in Miracles* much clearer for *Course* students. You will now be carrying on that work. Our books are a continuation of Ken's work but done in a very different form. You are scribing My words each day, and they have led to an understanding of the *Course* in a way that is easy to grasp. Readers will identify with you, mt, as an ordinary person, no different from themselves, who struggles with the ego thought system daily. You are to demonstrate the way you hear My Voice and how you came to hear it. These books are not an explanation of the *Course*, like Ken's offerings, but they are a direct transmission of how each reader can also find My Voice within. You have listened to Me for over two years now and trust that My words are filled with the Love of God. This process of listening and trusting can take the readers deeper into their own journey to know Me as their Self. Each time we converse, our communication continues throughout the day and night. I have become the most important relationship in your life. There is no other. This is what we are transmitting: the primary and only focus of this life is to trust in Me and perform My Will. In your willingness to transcribe these words each day, you demonstrate the eagerness to listen, hear, and follow My direction. The three of you have seen your lives and relationships transformed through this process.

Yesterday was a turning point for you, Jo, and Meera. Each of you entered the state of "I know nothing." This understanding did not come from the ego; it was My Doing. Yesterday was the time to be empty of the thought that you are instrumental in these books or in any life activity. Yes, you play roles in the production of the books, and feel that they are your life's purpose, but the Book is a manifestation of the Christ Self, fully designed by Him, to be unfolded in the world of form regardless of who reads them.

You, mt, were designed by Me to receive these words, and you are My puppet. The ego character is purely a vehicle to transcribe the words I speak, and she is a willing receptacle. Anyone can hear My Voice and transcribe My words. The three of you are doing that daily whenever a question arises about anything in the world or beyond. Anyone could scribe this book. It is not a special job. You do this work for Me, for humanity, impersonally. You saw this modeled by Ken, Helen, and Bill, who gave their lives to focus on the dissemination of My words. You are all equal; none is more or less special than another. I designed this life to fulfill My plan to awaken the world. The vehicle used is insignificant since the purpose is the same for every being on earth. To Awaken is the goal, and each one has his own unique role to play.

Yes, you had to come to the point of "I know nothing" to fully surrender to My Authorship and release any concern for how it is to be implemented. It is all in My hands. This was important, as yesterday, being the day you became aware of Ken's death, would be a turning point in the scribing process. You have no need to compare how we work with what has gone before you. What is given is without comparison, as I have chosen the three of you to bring these lessons to the world in My way. Ken is aware of what you are doing and supports you in the mind. The process of awakening will continue for all humanity. It is now being described in a way so that many selves can more easily identify with what you demonstrate. I want you to be in a place of nonattachment to any product or goal. I have told you that a publisher will be forthcoming, but you have no idea if, when, or how. The three of you are willing to accept that the commitment you have made to Me is all that matters, whether the books are meant just for the three of you, or for the whole world. Hearing My daily instructions, which have gone straight to your hearts, has changed your lives. We shall continue, and you trust that I know the Way.

Ken fully described the necessity of forgiving the brother with love and kindness. Through his reiterations of the *Course* lessons, readers can more deeply understand their meaning. You three take it a step further as you demonstrate your experience of how hearing My Voice and knowing Me as your only Source has opened you to love, in your continued process of forgiving every one of your many selves. There is Joy in Heaven in the knowing that the work continues in this way. The books are not the only way prescribed to come to Me; there are as many ways as there are people on the planet. We are continuing now in the trajectory I set out with *A Course in Miracles*, which Ken carried forward from Helen and Bill and which we now carry further.

Is this all? Yes. Receive these words impersonally, now that you have let go of your identification with the role of scribe. The task is totally beyond your mental, emotional grasp and therefore leaves you a willing recipient of My words, grateful to have this role to offer as a service to mankind. You now have some understanding that it is for the mind of man but do not yet comprehend how that works. That is trust.

114

Not Knowing

*There is nothing, absolutely nothing in your world
that is wrong. It is what it is, and it can serve the purpose
of the ego or of the awakening.*

December 31, 2013

Holy Spirit, what is Your instruction today? Now we will explore space, the space of stillness. You, Jo, and Meera have been listening to CDs of Eckhart Tolle. He speaks about the experience of stillness, the space from which all life arises. You each have found the stillness within and know it is the place where you encounter Me. Without stillness, you are in the realm of the ego mind that would fill you up with its chatter to keep you from hearing Me. Be Still and know that I am God. To be still is to avoid the rancorous shrieks of the ego's voice and come into the peacefulness of My Presence. The Presence of God is everything. Imposed on, and covering that Presence, is the distracting world of form with all its conflicting voices and utter madness. When you are in the stillness there is nothing to pull you away from your Self. You are What Is. The Is-ness of the moment is your True Life, the Life you are with Me. This is why I asked you to leave the art fairs. Not only did it create more open space in your life, it also released you to spend more time with Me for stillness and reflection. Yes, I shape your world in such a way that everything you need is provided, so you can be with Me. This sometimes happens when you experience a period of illness, which stops you from all the doings of the world. This confuses you now because you do not want to believe that "God creates sickness."

God does not enter the world of form. He is Only the Essence of Love and Peace. God is formless and Constant. God is Whole, Holy, the Essence from which you were created. You, as an ego self, are yet a part of God through the Presence of Me, the Holy Spirit. We planned "a life in form" for the ego character that you embody. That self has its own journey to the point of awakening to the truth of its being. The world of form is not real; it is a dream of duality. All experiences and aspects of it can be seen through the interpretation of the ego or the Holy Spirit. Nothing in the duality is bad or good. It is an expression of thought that has no quality and can therefore not be judged. To be sick, according to the ego, is to be punished by God, but to the Holy Spirit, illness is an opportunity for awakening. Everything you perceive in thought, word, or action is designed by you, with Me, to bring you Home. There is nothing, absolutely nothing, in your world that is wrong. It is what it is, and it can serve the purpose of the ego or the purpose of awakening.

Yesterday, a friend asked you to speak to her daughter. The friend believes that "you have a direct line to God." In the past, this would have placed you in a dilemma causing stress in your desire to please your friend and help her daughter, or feel the request as an imposition, even a burden beyond your limits. You were very grateful that over the past two days, you have had the strong, clear experience of "I know nothing." This acceptance left you in the place of "I can do nothing" because then your ego personality is not in charge. It could take no action since everything that happens is in My hands. There was no guilt in relaying to your friend that her daughter must ask Me for the guidance she needs. Because the mt character had disappeared, only I was left to fulfill the request. This is the disappearance of form, when the self is seen as "just a vehicle" who knows nothing. The answers are not contained in the brain but it can be used by Me to point the way to wholeness. You pointed your friend to Me as the only Knower. Always return to Me. Access Me within, for direction and knowing.

Not knowing is a place of safety as in the statement from the *Course,* "In my defenselessness my safety lies." When you do not believe that you have the answers, you release all questions to Me. Ask, and you shall receive. This is the only solution to every "problem." There is only One Answer, and that comes from the Christ Self. It holds the wisdom of the universe and it will lead the way required by each of the apparent separated Sons. My solution will always bring wholeness and healing. To reconnect with your Divine Self, is the Answer.

When you enter the stillness, you are in remembrance of Me, of God, and therefore have released the world of form. This is now your practice: remember Me by seeking the stillness of your soul in the place of not knowing. I am there, and I will be guiding you in the seen and unseen worlds. Remember that this life, which you believe is real, really happens in the mind and is out pictured in form. The stillness returns you to the Mind of God. Remember Me today in the stillness of your heart, and know that only I am your Truth. There is nothing else to do.

Thank You for this message, Holy Spirit. Do You have more instruction for me? Yes, as you eat, walk, and go to town, find Me in all your doings. Find the Stillness. You just now remembered this is New Year's Eve, and it brings tears. You are feeling the gratitude for how far you have come over the past year. It is incomprehensible that three books have been scribed in this time and you have found the place of stillness, of not knowing. You are grateful that Jo and Meera experience My Voice and My Presence. You wonder now if I am telling you that this is the end of Book 3. Yes. We will begin a new chapter in the New Year. Blessings to you all. I love you with all My Heart. Amen.

CPSIA information can be obtained
at www.ICGtesting.com
Printed in the USA
LVOW10s1118200917
549326LV00016B/93/P